# THE McDONALDIZATION
# OF HIGHER EDUCATION

# THE McDONALDIZATION
# OF HIGHER EDUCATION

Edited by
*Dennis Hayes & Robin Wynyard*

**Bergin & Garvey**
Westport, Connecticut • London

**Library of Congress Cataloging-in-Publication Data**

The McDonaldization of higher education / edited by Dennis Hayes and Robin Wynyard.
    p. cm.
    Includes bibliographical references and index.
    ISBN 0-89789-856-7 (alk. paper)
    1. Education, Higher—Economic aspects. 2. Universities and colleges—Sociological aspects. 3. Universities and colleges—Administration. 4. Postmodernism and higher education. I. Hayes, Dennis, 1950– II. Wynyard, Robin.
  LC67.6.M395   2002
  378—dc21         2001058318

British Library Cataloguing in Publication Data is available.

Copyright © 2002 by Dennis Hayes and Robin Wynyard

Library of Congress Catalog Card Number: 2001058318
ISBN: 0-89789-856-7

First published in 2002

Bergin & Garvey, 88 Post Road West, Westport, CT 06881
An imprint of Greenwood Publishing Group, Inc.
www.greenwood.com

Printed in the United States of America

The paper used in this book complies with the
Permanent Paper Standard issued by the National
Information Standards Organization (Z39.48-1984).

10 9 8 7 6 5 4 3 2

# Contents

# Preface

Since its opening, McDonald's Hamburger University has produced over 70,000 graduates of *hamburgerology* who return after graduation to the shop floor of almost 29,000 retail outlets in 120 countries. This is a success story. But why does the name arouse particular opprobrium when linked to university education? George Ritzer, who coined the word *McDonaldization*, said, "I should make it clear that I do *not* expect tomorrow's university to look exactly like a shopping mall or a chain of fast-food restaurants. However, I do expect it to integrate applicable elements of these and other new means of consumption (and tourism) into the existing structure of the university" (Ritzer 1998: 161).

This book, with contributions from established academics in three countries, undertakes the first major examination of the McDonaldization of higher education. It addresses key questions such as: What is the McUniversity? Has the drive to open up access to the academy made it a reality? What are the forces behind it? Can its development be challenged? What role do human resource management techniques, quality initiatives, inspections, and new forms of lecturer training play in bringing the McUniversity into being? Will the McUniversity be as global a phenomenon as the Big Mac?

## REFERENCE

Ritzer, G. (1998). *The McDonaldization Thesis: Explorations and Extensions.* London & Thousand Oaks, CA: Sage.

# Abbreviations and Acronyms

| | |
|---|---|
| AAHE | American Association of Higher Education |
| ABS | Australian Bureau of Statistics |
| AUT | Association of University Teachers |
| BERA | British Educational Research Association |
| CIPD | Chartered Institute of Personnel Development |
| CVPC | Committe of Vice Chancellors and Principals |
| DfEE | Department for Education and Employment |
| EU | European Union |
| GEEMA | Group to Encourage Ethnic Minority Applications (Cambridge) |
| HEFC | Higher Education Funding Council |
| HEFCE | Higher Education Funding Council for England |
| HU | Hamburger University |
| ILT | Institute for Learning and Teaching |
| ILTPG | Institute for Learning and Teaching Planning Group |
| IMS | Instructional Managements System |
| MIT | Massachusetts Institute of Technology |
| MTC | Management Training Centre |
| Natfhe | National Association of Teachers in Further and Higher Education |
| NCPI | National Center for Postsecondary Improvement |
| NERCHE | New England Resource Center for Higher Education |
| NHS | National Health Service |
| NUS | National Union of Students |
| OKI | Open Knowledge Initiative |
| OU | Open University |

PIs          performance indicators
QAA          Quality Assurance Agency
RAE          Research Assessment Exercise
SPARC        Scholarly Publishing & Academic Resources Coalition
SRHE         Society for Research into Higher Education
STL          Standard Template Library
TA           teaching assistant
TQA          Teaching Quality Assessment
TQM          Total Quality Management
UNESCO       United Nations Economic, Social, and Commercial Organization
UOC          Open University of Catalonia
XML          eXtensible Mark-up Language

# Introduction

*Dennis Hayes and Robin Wynyard*

Talking about the university, Ritzer says, "I . . . expect the university to borrow liberally from many other sectors of society as well as to retain many of its traditional components" (Ritzer 1998: 161). He goes on to state that he does not want it to look like a "shopping mall" or "fast-food restaurant." But, all the same, he implies that it is inevitable that the university in the twenty-first century will borrow from many sectors of society, including the shopping mall and the fast-food restaurant.

Although the university is not excluded generally from his arguments concerning the globalizing features of McDonaldization (Ritzer 1998: 2000), our concern in this book is to disentangle the university from Ritzer's overview. While there is no intention on our part to ignore wider societal linkages between the university and wider society, our brief in this book is to keep the university in the central frame regarding Ritzer's arguments concerning the McDonaldization thesis. McDonaldization outlined by Ritzer is a valuable tool for providing a theoretical and practical debate concerning novel and defining features of our contemporary world. Of this contemporary world, the book argues throughout that, for good or ill, the university is a key component of it.

Whether they agree or disagree with the various arguments Ritzer puts forward about McDonaldization, the contributors to this book sense that he has *roused a sleeping dragon* as far as higher education is concerned. Their responses address their vivid reflections, both optimistic and pessimistic, regarding higher education. All of the contributors, even if they have not spent their entire working life within the confines of higher education, have spent long years as teachers or administrators, thus qualifying them to speak with authority of the predicted role of the university in the new century. If Ritzer wanted his ideas concerning the *McUniversity* to start a "dialogue" (1998: 161), then he has certainly succeeded.

The introduction to the book falls into two parts: The first examines the theoretical basis on which Ritzer draws in order to locate his McDonaldization thesis. The second part looks at how this theoretical underpinning has been used by Ritzer to expound his notion of the McUniversity in the "postmodern consumer society" (1998: 151–162).

## WEBER: RITZER'S SOLE THEORIST?

The sole theorist used by Ritzer in expounding the theory of McDonaldization is the German sociologist Max Weber, who died in 1930: "McDonaldization is an amplification and extension of Weber's theory of rationalization" (2000: 23). For Ritzer, McDonaldization as an almost inexorable process permeates most of the modern world, [including higher education] to varying degrees. Such permeation into higher education concerns all of the contributors to this volume. As Ritzer says, "There are degrees of McDonaldization. Fast-food restaurants, for example, have been heavily McDonaldized, universities moderately McDonaldized" (2000: 19). The purpose of this part of the introduction is to examine how valid the work of Max Weber is in examining issues of modernity and postmodernity, of which the nascent or full-blown McUniversity is a part.

Without doubt, Weber's thought is difficult and often not easy to follow. He might be seen as providing some kind of theoretical framework for Ritzer in *The McDonaldization of Society*. This, however, is something needing further work by the reader. A brief introduction to a few facets of his thought can only suffice to whet the reader's appetite for further study. If Weber were alive today, what would he have thought of the concept of McDonaldization? With what parts of Ritzer's argument would he have agreed or disagreed? Would Weber have given a more subtle consideration of workers' and customers' perceptions of the meaning of their McDonald's experience in analyzing McDonaldization?

There is a sense in which Weber would not disagree with McDonaldization at all—that is, in treating it as a neologism invented by Ritzer as a possible tool for further analysis and explanation. Any book with concepts such as this has to be judged on its merits. Weber, being totally unaware of brand-name burgers, could not, of course, comment. We suspect that he would be annoyed at the rather simple transposition of his thought by Ritzer. Weber was nothing if not meticulous in his work, closely examining empirical detail at all times. One of his major faults was that he overreached himself in terms of empirical observation, setting himself observable goals that could not be concluded by the time of his death. Thus, the somewhat cavalier way important explanatory concepts are transposed in Ritzer's book would have grated with him. One of Weber's key concepts, *rationalization*, is given very short shrift. It is this that Ritzer turns into McDonaldization, simply explaining the transformation from rationalization into the "more timely labelled McDonaldization" (Ritzer 1993: xiii).

Likewise, Weber would have been very interested in those pages where his name is used in conjunction with the McDonaldization thesis: *"iron cage of rationality"* (1993: xi, 18, 24, 147, 160, 162, 188), *rationalization* (1993: xi, xiii, 18, 20, 23, 147), *rationality* (1993: xi, 19, 22, 23, 121), *bureaucracy* (1993: 20, 21, 22, 24).

He would have been in broad agreement with the way Ritzer attempts to link concepts into some explanatory format—for example, rationality→ bureaucracy→ irrationality→ iron cage. On the other hand, he would have disagreed with how his thought is cannibalized in order to make a rather simplistic point about bureaucracy in general, and how this comes to vindicate the McDonaldization thesis.

There would seem to be little disagreement between Weber and Ritzer concerning the salient points of bureaucracy as an ideal typical form of organization—in this case, the use of *efficiency, calculability, predictability*, and *control* (Ritzer 2000: chs. 3–6). Perhaps his strongest disagreement would be reserved for the mechanical way Ritzer attributes rationalization (as a formal process) as the cause of his own "iron cage of rationality." Weber would cite partiality in terms of the attempted explanation, for Ritzer's use of McDonaldization totally ignores Weber's substantive rather than formal sociology: that is, the meanings that individuals give to their actions, which would at all times have to be checked with objective fact. This acknowledges that individuals utilize what passes for accepted societal concepts and how broadly they agree on accepted definitions of such concepts. It is perhaps easier to agree to *rationalization* as part of an abstract bureaucratic process than to agree to McDonaldization as a worldwide material practice.

Just taking one of Ritzer's basic dimensions of McDonaldization, the one of *control* (Ritzer 2000: ch. 6): Common sense says that control is not all bad, certainly not in the sense implied in this chapter. A concept is neither good nor bad—it can be either, or even both at the same time. School pupils will, more often than not, concede to teachers control over them in the interests of learning. Weber could see that what appeared as irrational behavior could indeed be highly rational. This exercise of control on the part of the pupil extends to teachers, significant others, schools as organizations, and increased use of technology on their part. Control can, of course, also be "bad": Ritzer uses this in the sense of the McDonaldization thesis, where individuals are turned into "zombies" by nonhuman technology (1993: 120). People often do become zombies when dealing with highly routinized processes, but how and why they do is open to much debate and scrutiny and is often far from obvious to the observer. Although this is hinted at (Ritzer 2000: 122–145), Weber would want a great deal more in terms of empirical observation to substantiate each individual example.

MacRae catches well this point behind Weber's substantive sociology when he says: "society is problematic because we cannot foreknow all the consequences—nor for that matter all the determinants of our acts. . . . No one intends to establish a market economy: such a state of affairs comes into being through the individual bargaining arrangements of people exchanging goods and services to maximise their advantages or minimise their deprivations" (1974: 73).

McDonaldization depends for academic respectability entirely on the theory of Weber. Ritzer tells us that Weber "fretted" (1993: 19) and became "animated" (1993: 22) by what Weber called the "iron cage of rationality." We are also told that Weber was "particularly upset" (1993: 19) by the irrationality of rationality. Such concepts as these are used by Ritzer in vindication of the McDonaldization thesis and get readily applied to fast-food restaurants. It might be helpful here to deal briefly with those ideas of Weber's that are particularly pertinent in the understanding of Ritzer's arguments.

Weber saw *rationalization* as a process as a continuation of secularization and disenchantment of the Western world. When the inevitable "benefits" of capitalism caught up, religious practices and other nonmaterialist ideologies in parts of the world like India and China would also in time succumb to the rationalization process. For Weber, though, in the West such a process was inevitable and did not depend on a particular ideology, so although socialism might succeed capitalism and the market mechanism in the allocation of goods and services, rationalization was still an inevitability (Weber 1968: 225).

Above all, Weber saw the rationalization process as economic, in the West helped by the "push" of technology and the "pull" of a developed monetary system. The kind of consumer goods produced by new technologies, such as cars, could not help but engender a new rationalized and "modern" way of life. For Weber, rationalization was a process by which magic and religion gave way to knowledge based not on superstition and tradition, but on empirically sound scientific knowledge. The components comprising this process were rational individuals of a new sort, who were engaged in the matching of means via logical reasoning to ends, which, because they were calculable, were also achievable. This is methodological individualism, but also constrained by the structure inherent in the rationalization process. Everyone could work hard to gain the money to purchase the goods they needed, but the understanding was that because as individuals they were not equally endowed with skills, they would all earn different amounts.

The reward and payment of individuals in the West was helped by the development of coined money. With such an invention, economic rationality could instantly be based on a common calculability. If we know the cost of something and know the means at our disposal, both can be reconciled in our paying or not paying the going price. Nation states were not slow to grasp the importance of money in the system of things. They made sure that they exercised control over the expansion and contraction of the money supply (Weber 1968: 167, 168).

Once money was established as the medium of exchange, there could be no going back to imprecise systems of exchange, like barter. The new system founded on money quickly became professionally and scientifically organized.

More specifically, a rational capitalistic establishment is one with capital accounting—that is, an establishment that determines its income-yielding power by calculation according to the methods of modern bookkeeping and the striking of a balance (Weber 1927: 275). Via accountants and bankers, individuality becomes enmeshed in "rational commerce," which is "the field in which quantitative reckoning first appeared, to become dominant finally over the whole extent of economic life" (1927: 223). Once this becomes established as regular practice, it is a short step to the legitimation of inventor and process—for example, the "first rational patent law of 1623" (1927: 312). Formulation of the rationalization process helped, not hindered, the individual, as the process was both predictable and calculable, making it much easier to understand. It also moved action away from the random movements of individuals to action by individuals on the grand scale: "But if a person acts subjectively rational, his expectations in relation to the behaviour of others may also be based on the assumption that he can expect a subjectively meaningful behaviour on their part" (Weber 1968: 1376). The development of Western science not only put new knowledge in the hands of people, it also removed partiality. Fever was no longer managed and controlled by the most powerful magician, as now all qualified medical practitioners could agree on the drugs needed to effect a cure. In this case, technique in the development and application of pharmacy joined hands with an economic organization of doctors. Included in this system was the training, professional organization, and payment of the doctors: "Now this process of rationalization in the field of technique and economic organization undoubtedly determines an important part of the ideals of life of modern bourgeois society" (Weber 1930: 75).

This was the basis of Weber's "formal sociology," on which Ritzer relies. But, this was not the end of the story as far as Weber was concerned. He wanted to draw a distinction between formal elements of rationality and substantive elements. Modern organization, technology, and cost accountancy may indeed produce a cheap-to-buy, cost-effective burger, but the elements of who eats McDonald's burgers and why they eat them is not explained. Often the formal and the substantive do coincide—for example, the production of tobacco and its purchase by the poor as a cheap narcotic. This is, however, not true for McDonald's, whose burgers are eaten by all social groups worldwide.

Weber further developed his ideas of rationalization into his concept of *bureaucracy*. This he saw as the inevitable consequence of Western capitalistic and technological development. Bureaucracy was impersonal, guided by written rules and regulations, resting on state-of-the-art knowledge of the production process. For Weber, bureaucracy was the pinnacle of efficiency.

According to Weber, such an organization is technically superior to all other forms of administration, much as machine production is superior to nonmechanical methods. In precision, speed, lack of equivocation, knowledge of the documentary

record, continuity, sense of direction, uniformity of operation, system of subordination, and reduction of frictions, bureaucracy surpasses honorific and avocational
forms of administration. This is a long list of advantages, but they are relative.
[Bendix 1966: 426]

Individuality poses a problem for the smooth running of bureaucracy. Commands and the authority connected to these must be depersonalized. If rules and
the consequences of rule breaking are knowable in advance, then the individual
cannot shout "foul" if he or she is fired for an infringement of the rules.

Weber equated discipline with rationalization and bureaucracy. If someone
willingly joins the army, that person would expect to be turned into an efficient
fighting machine and, with identically trained others, be part of an irresistible
force. In this sense the individual is part of what are termed the "armed forces."
As Weber said: "What is decisive for discipline is that the obedience of a
plurality of men is rationally uniform" (Weber 1968: 1149). It might not square
with Ritzer's view of the rationalization of the McDonaldization process, but
who would want the armed forces too different? Contained within this, though,
are seeds of irrationality: that is, in order to join the army, much of a person's
individuality—such as dress, appearance, speech, and so on— is willingly given
up. Without submission to this, the goal of joining the army cannot be achieved.

Although with Western rationalization bureaucracy was an inevitability and
Weber certainly felt gloomy over this prospect, he acknowledged that it could
still be an improvement over the tradition and mindless behavior of old: "Discipline puts drill for the sake of habitual routinized skill in place of heroic ecstasy,
loyalty, spirited enthusiasm for a leader and personal devotion to him" (Weber
1968: 1149).

## THE IRON CAGE

Sharing what he sees to be Weber's pessimism, Ritzer takes great interest in
what Weber has to say about the "iron cage of rationality." Weber makes reference to it in his book *The Protestant Ethic and the Spirit of Capitalism*, which
contains the nub of his rationality argument. Here Weber is clearly aware of
changes in the world around him. Material changes advancing rapidly in countries like the United States, Germany, and Great Britain had to be explained, as
they were not happening in the rest of the world.

Weber generally argued that technology, like everything else in culture, would
be subsumed under a growing "cloak" of rationality. Following his rationality
argument through, the public were becoming more and more dependent on the
products of advanced economies (see wa Mwachofi, chapter 14, this volume). In
suggesting that technologically induced economies were becoming supply-side-
led, Weber at the end of this particular book introduces the "iron cage of rationality." In doing so he dismisses the idea that we are purveyors of our own free

will, as the demand for external possessions cannot be cast off like a "light cloak" where "fate decreed that the cloak should become an iron cage" (Weber 1930: 181).

With some justification, Weber asserts that material goods had gained such a hold over men and women as has never been known before. In this context, not unreasonably, Weber saw the growing quantity of material possessions and the grip-like hold they had over people as an "inexorable power" (1930: 181). Older historical aestheticism "has escaped from the cage," as "wealth stripped of its religious and ethical meaning, tends to become associated with purely mundane passion." Weber finally concludes: "No one knows who will live in this cage in the future, or whether at the end of this tremendous development entirely new prophets will arise" (1930: 182). So, really, it all depends on where you stand, as the "iron cage" can be seen from different points of view; rationality can be a double-edged weapon, and as such neither good nor bad. As Zygmunt Bauman puts it: "To the strong, bold and determined, the patronage state feels like a most sinister rendition of the Weberian 'iron cage'; yet to many weak, shy and lacking in will it may also feel like a shelter" (1992: 163).

Ritzer and Weber share a similar pessimistic platform. For Weber, however, the cage door is at least slightly ajar, where for Ritzer it is firmly shut.

## FATALISM

What Bauman does not consider is the possibility of a destructive contemporary state wishing to render its citizens weak, shy, and lacking in will, thus encouraging a dependent personality. This might be an explanation of why the new ideologues of the British government have given preeminence to the concept of lifelong learning. Thinking of ourselves as lifelong learners places us in the psychological condition of the dependent learner. The view that we are all learners assigns an essentially dependent role to the university lecturer as well as the student (see Furedi, chapter 2, and Hayes, chapter 10, this volume).

Weber's concept of rationality as adapted initially by Ritzer is of an impersonal mechanistic force that is just taken as a given feature of contemporary capitalist society. From this objectivist position, McDonaldization is just happening. Rationalization leads to bureaucracy, which, in turn, leads to dehumanization. This comes out clearly in Ritzer's references to the consequences of rationality, which he also takes from Bauman's work. This is the view that "rationality" leads to the gas chamber and the systematic factory-like genocide of a people. The existence of McDonaldization should alert us to the fact that "something like the Holocaust could happen again" (Ritzer 2000: 28). The leading British writer on the contemporary state of higher education, Ronald Barnett, argues in exactly this way about the search for knowledge: "Knowledge and control are not, thankfully, available. (That belief partly led to Auschwitz.) What is both necessary and possible—just—is an enlightened societal self-monitoring" (Barnett 2000: 68)—self-monitoring to ensure that we make no more attempts at gaining knowledge and hence control of nature and our lives. This is a depressing and negative view of the potential of human beings to bring about progress. Behind Ritzer's initial analysis of McDonaldization, therefore, lies a fatalism that assumes that the process cannot be challenged, that rationalization as a feature of contemporary capitalism was inevitable and we can do no more than condemn it morally or throw a spanner or two in the works (Ritzer 1998: 182–188). There is a purely individualized conception of resistance here that Ritzer took from Weber. Many critics pointed out the fatalism in Ritzer's thinking (Parker 1998: 14; Rinehart 1998: 24; Wood 1998: 95; Wynyard 1998: 172), and Ritzer himself contributed to a collection of essays on *Resisting McDonaldization* (Smart 1999).

## RESISTANCE: MANURING McDONALD'S

Resistance can be individual or collective. Jane A. Rinehart, in her critique of Ritzer's fatalism, went beyond an individualistic approach and took heart from the possibility of a broader movement against rationalization. Although she had "not heard of any collective resistance to McDonaldization per se," she thought it was "already occurring in many group efforts to resist efficiency, predictability, calculability and control" (1998: 35). The forms of "resistance" with which we are familiar are symbolic actions to ensure media coverage of a motley assortment of young people breaking McDonald's windows from Seattle to Genoa. These remain isolated gestures of dislike that have no long-term importance. In a general climate that is anticollectivist and when unions are in decline, only individual action of this sort that attempts to make consumers suspicious about certain companies might be all that seems possible. The recent furore in Britain about McDonald's sponsorship of a dinner at the Labour Party conference reveals just how strong the suspicion and dislike is among some social groups.[1] This public relations disaster has led to the party being nicknamed McLabour. Journalist Polly Toynbee, commenting on the sponsorship deal, calls McDonald's "the hate-brand of all time" (2001), but she recognizes that there are worse places to eat. Despite this hatred and the predictable consequences on the streets of Britain, this will be nothing but an exercise in anger release. The only practical result will be that middle-class people who have never eaten in McDonald's will continue not to do so.

Equally dramatic media portrayals of French farmers dumping tons of manure at a McDonald's near them are nothing more than examples of local protectionism. Resistance of a more substantial nature might come from trade unions, but there is little to take heart from. Even spontaneous attempts to establish "McUnions" are fiercely resisted, apparently to the point of withdrawing franchises and closing restaurants (Klein 2000: 240–245). General, or popular, resistance to McDonaldization does not seem likely—so are we committed to some form of fatalism?[2]

## IMPERIAL OVERSTRETCH OR THE IMPLOSION
## OF McDONALDIZATION

Ritzer, in all his works, says very little about people, and less about notions such as class. His fatalism about humanity seems to be deep-rooted. But has he moved in his more recent writing to a postmodern position consistent with, but providing what seems an alternative to, his neglect, or is it his despair of people themselves opposing rationalization? He still holds to an inevitability thesis because: "It is difficult to anticipate anything other than the continued growth of consumption" (1999: 215). This is clearly a Western post-1945 perspective, which he shares with a range of writers from Galbraith and Marcuse to Beck and Giddens. But from his new perspective this very expansion may result in what he calls "implosion," an idea he takes from Baudrillard (Ritzer 1999: 132–134). "Implosion" is not something that is the result of any conscious critique or attack on rationalization, it just happens. As consumption moves from the mall to the home, this overstretch may bring about the collapse of the latter 'cathedrals of consumption' or consumer demand could in some unspecified way bring about "unsupportable expansion or a level of indebtedness that could help to bring the economy down" (1999: 217). What Ritzer labels "implosion" is a form of imperial overstretch by McDonaldized and McDonaldizing monopolies.

Although he now declares himself "wary of grand narratives," it is hard not to draw the conclusion that Ritzer is also wary of the possibility of "implosion." At one point he considers and rejects escape into the family and a private world uncontaminated as far as possible with consumerism. But his fatalism outs at the end. He concludes that we must learn to live with McDonaldization: "the most immediate issue is how to live a more meaningful life within a society increasingly defined by consumption" (1999: 217).


## PRODUCTION AND CONSUMPTION

Ritzer's analysis is restricted to the sphere of consumption. This is a natural way of looking at the world as we meet in the realm of exchange, in shops and pubs. The grubby world of production is hidden, and Ritzer's turn toward Baudrillard can only make his analysis more restricted as Baudrillard was skeptical of the very existence of the production process (Heartfield 1998: 38). The notion that we live in a world made up entirely of consumers, isolated from the increasingly unimportant sphere of production, is a result of a long retreat of the left from involvement in what they increasing saw as conservative industrial struggles. But it also has a partial and seemingly paradoxical explanation in economic downturn. Capitalists are increasingly timid about putting their surplus back into investment in production and are turning to consumption in the cultural realm, where profits—for example, on the sale of paintings—are more immediate (see Heartfield 1998: 44–49). There is, therefore, a real basis for the current obsession with the realm of consumption, but it is one based ultimately on the demise of production. This focus on consumption is mirrored throughout society and reflected back by sociologists such as Ritzer. Even from a capitalist point of view such a state of affairs must be short-term. Capitalists cannot cease acting as capitalists for long, or they will cease to be.

Ritzer approaches his few comments on production through Braverman, whom he connects closely with Marx. Braverman, however, had a distorted understanding of Marx, concentrating on how capitalists control their workers (Ritzer 1998: 63–65), but it is the concept of exploitation—getting more surplus value out of the labor power purchased by capitalists that is central to capitalism—that is the issue, rather than the issue of control. Ritzer sees the wage labor relationship as a swindle. The employer just cheats employees out of money, paying them "less than the value they produce" (1998: 65). Even a superficial reading of Marx would show that the commodity labor power exchanges at its value, the socially relative labor time necessary to reproduce the laborer. Ritzer's complete misunderstanding of surplus value production is shown by the fact that he considers that customers at McDonald's create value by putting litter in bins and so on. He considers customers to be more exploited than workers because they get paid nothing at all. But there is no exploitation here. Such work is done for free and is "valuable" to the restaurant, because it helps cut costs and realize profits, but it produces no surplus value.

Ritzer's fatalism about human activity stems from this focus on consumption. This is understandable because of two factors: The first is the constant increase in, and hence wider availability of, cheaper commodities as a result of the attempts by companies to overcome problems of profitability by increasing production. The cheapness and wide availability of the mobile phone is the best contemporary example of this phenomenon. The second and most important factor behind this general focus on consumer activity is that we are living in a period in which capitalists lack confidence in the risky and long-term process of investment in production and are going instead for the quick buck. Ritzer's discussion of the McDonaldization of higher education conceals rather than reveals how a lack of confidence in this other long-term investment has a base in production (see Poynter, chapter 4, and Hudson, chapter 7, this volume). Fatalism is not the consequence, however, as the seeming inevitability of the McUniversity is due to political rather than economic factors.

## WHIMPERING INTO THE GOOD NIGHT: RESISTING McUNIVERSITY

In 1993 Ritzer saw McDonaldization as an exemplar of *modernism* and not just a modern phenomenon. It is worth comparing the 1993 and Millennium editions of his seminal book and his later works to track the changes in his approach as they imply different futures for the university.

In *The McDonaldization of Society* Ritzer says very little about the university. It is seen straightforwardly as another rationalized institution. The analysis here is a simple Weberian one. Ritzer's description of the university could come out of F. W. Taylor's work or from any manual for the application of Fordist techniques. The university is the worst sort of factory. He depicts it as a savage place where staff and students are not just dehumanized but butchered:

The modern university has, in various ways, become a highly irrational place. Many students and faculty members are put off by its factory-like atmosphere. They may feel like automatons processed by the bureaucracy and computers or feel like cattle run through a meat processing plant. In other words, education in such settings can be a dehumanising experience. [Ritzer 1993: 143]

There is no recognition here of notions of students as consumers. They are simply there to be "burgered." This is the back door to McDonald's. There were no golden arches for students in 1993. The university is in the hands of Moloch, and staff and students are subject to control by nonhuman technologies. Why would you go? Would tenure—a job for life—keep you there? What future generations of middle-class employees would such a factory produce?

The techniques for avoiding the dehumanizing consequences of the university are of the sort known to any subversive (or is it successful?) consumer: shop elsewhere; choose small classes; get to know the assistants (professors); and, if you are sent unsolicited goods or marketing questionnaires, send them back (without a stamp!); damage the exam papers (so they cannot be marked by computer!). In the early analysis there is little said about challenging McDonald-ization.

The growing literature on McDonaldization shows the power of the term to describe the extension of industrial rationalization (commodification) to wider society. It "nicely points to the exemplary role of one of the most successful contemporary practitioners of Weberian rationalization" (Kumar 1995: 189). It is often used by educationalists in this descriptive way (Lomas 2001; see also Smart, chapter 3, Poynter, chapter 4, and Persell, chapter 5, this volume).

This descriptive analysis usually consists of a simple application of Ritzer's four features of McDonaldization: *efficiency, calculability, predictability*, and *control* of the higher-education sector. We can summarize the basic idea here, and readers can add examples from their own experience. Higher education is said be becoming more *efficient* because it is processing more students by introducing multiple-choice examinations (United States) or by removing examinations altogether (United Kingdom) and replacing them by forms of continuous assessment. This leads to grade inflation, and more students pass. It is easier to get something called a degree—and a "good" degree at that. League tables of universities are now produced grading research and teaching, as well as increased access by nonparticipating groups (ethnic minorities, working-class students). These make the system subject to quantitative, rather than the previous qualitative evaluations and therefore clearly *calculable* (see Parker, chapter 8, this volume).[3] Higher education is also becoming *predictable* as content is standardized in terms of uniform units of delivery (modularization) with agreed learning outcomes. *Control* over what happens in the universities is established through the introduction first of appraisal systems for academics, and then through the introduction of initial teacher training qualifications and systems of continuing professional development. The sort of control that is implied here is, of course, based on self-regulation. All these systems have been introduced in the interest of maintaining standards and supporting students. This leads many lay people to ask: Is McDonaldization a good thing or a bad thing? The failure to answer this, or even discuss it, is a major reason for addressing the issues in this book. Up to now the striking response to all these initiatives by academics has been "passivity" (Smith & Webster 1997: 4).

Several early commentators (Hartley 1995; Parker & Jary 1995) noted that Ritzer was writing within a modernist perspective and suggested that post-modernism offered a better way of approaching McDonaldization, one that allowed much more scope for contesting the bureaucratic rationality that was afflicting universities:

the culture of postmodernism is said to be dismantling the very disciplinary structures of the age of modernity. Systems thinking and grand over-arching structures cannot easily cope with a world that is in flux, a world where moral codes and scientific canons no longer command compliance, a world where relativism rears its head. Given all this, a number of questions suggest themselves. Is the systematisation of education a doomed endeavour, one bound to disintegrate in the centrifugal forces of post-modern culture? Are we witnessing the last stand of the grand, bureaucratic system—the "structure," as it is called? [Hartley 1995: 419]

Hartley believes that "increasing bureaucratisation does have an egalitarian effect, for it increases (though does not necessarily widen) access to higher education" (1995: 420; compare Fox, chapter 9, this volume). He sees two forces at work: "a centrifugal force, allowing choice, flexibility and diversity; and a centripetal force towards central control" (1995: 421). Tensions will be created because of the "emerging disorder of post-modern culture" (1995: 410), staff and students will come to see the "falsity of the fraternisation" involved, and the government will be forced to "resort to strong bureaucratic control over the dissenting academics" (1995: 421).

What Hartley never considers is that there need be no tension here and that what appear to be forces in contraposition are in fact complementary. It takes only a little reflection to see how notions like "empowerment" and, in Britain, "inclusion" have been appropriated by policymakers.

Ritzer simply changed his mind after reviewing the comments of his post-modern critics. In a footnote in *The McDonaldization Thesis* he claims that borrowing liberally from consumer society "will make the university of the near future even more postmodern than it is today" (1998: 151). In a footnote, he adds: "Thus, I disagree with Bloland's contention that the university is necessarily the quintessential modern institution" (Ritzer 1998: 161). But he is still ambiguous in his attitude to the McUniversity:

I should make it clear that I do *not* expect tomorrow's university to look exactly like a shopping mall or a chain of fast food restaurants. However, I do expect it to integrate applicable elements of these and other new means of consumption (and tourism) into the existing structure of the university. I also expect the university to borrow liberally from many other sectors of society as well as to retain many of its traditional components. I emphasize the new means of consumption . . . in part because, counterintuitively, I think they will be an important model for future universities. [Ritzer 1998: 161]

Yet within a few pages he is envisioning the end of the McDonaldized university. Citing Baudrillard and echoing *The Waste Land,* he declares:

"we are no longer in the age of grandiose collapses and resurrections, of games of death and eternity, but of little factual events, smooth annihilations and gradual slides." Thus, for example, McUniversity will not be destroyed with a bang, but in a series of whimpers. [Ritzer 1998: 171]

At the end of the 1990s Ritzer was ambiguous in his attitude to the McUniversity. This follows from his adopting the theory of implosion: that it might be doomed, whatever value it has, but this will not be the result of any collective or group action.

In his writing for this volume, Ritzer (chapter 1) is set clearly against the McUniversity: "everyday educational activity is one of those areas (another is the doctor–patient relationship) that has been overly and inappropriately McDonaldized. What a spectacle it would be if the quotidian activities of the university were truly deMcDonaldized! And just imagine how much better the educational process itself would function!" He concludes that the university cannot compete with Las Vegas; instead, the university must "focus on making more spectacular the quotidian activities that go to the heart of its educational functioning. While everything around it is growing increasingly McDonaldized, the route open to the university is to create spectacle by deMcDonaldizing its quotidian activities. Inefficient, unpredictable, incalculable education employing human technologies will seem quite spectacular to students, especially in contrast to the numbing McDonaldization that is increasingly found almost everywhere else. The spectacle of the deMcDonaldization of the university's everyday activities will not only be spectacular and attract students, but it will also serve to enhance dramatically the quality of the educational process" (Ritzer, chapter 1, this volume).

One element of the traditional university that is clearly close to Ritzer's heart is the academic tutorial (see chapter 1). One way of making this quotidian activity spectacular would be to offer it to all students on a massive scale, although this would be impossibly expensive. We would need thousands of new academic staff. But it would be an example of (de)McDonaldization par excellence! Instead, he envisages a digital alternative, where new technology creates this relationship within a lecture theater. He sees technology as possibly liberating rather than as dehumanizing (This is a question discussed at length by Persell, chapter 5, and Woudhuysen, chapter 6, this volume). Ritzer does not seem to recognize that this would be nothing more than a complex form of scripted communication, familiar to us all from McDonald's training manuals and exemplified in the modern call center. What Ritzer's emphasis on the tutorial shows is that ultimately he believes in the traditional liberal university. This university cannot be McDonalidized. The university in this society is the place that pursues knowledge—a creative activity that is uncertain in its outcomes. So why is the McUniversity inevitable?

## McJOBS AND THE McUNIVERSITY

If we look at the expansion of student number in the 1960s and in the 1990s, there is a clear difference. In the 1960s (see Hudson, chapter 7, this volume) young people were being trained for work. The difference now is that the huge expansion of student numbers in Britain and the United States (see Hayes, chapter 10, this volume; Ryan 1999) has one consequence that is of enormous benefit to capitalism: it delays entry into the labor market for up to five years— two years doing preparatory study (A Levels or Vocational Qualifications in Britain) and three at university. A 17-year-old can, on average, expect to receive 2.3 years of full-time tertiary education, with more than one year of full-time equivalent education between the ages of 25 and 64. The transition to work continues to fall later in life. Between the ages of 15 and 29, young people spend 6.5 years in a job, 1 year unemployed, and 1.5 years neither studying nor seeking work. The other 5 years are spent in education (source: OECD 2000). The youth labor market as we knew it has disappeared, and young people now seek full-time employment in their early twenties rather than at 16, as in the 1960s. This is of great benefit for an economy, as it does away with a potentially volatile group of unemployed or underemployed. While "consuming" education, this group also comes to accept the usual ascetic and impoverished experience of student life and the need to do McWork. It is also worth remembering that in Britain this new student group leave with £12,000 ($18,000) of debt after paying for their consumption. The earlier generation of students had state funding that covered everything, including books, and there was even some money left over to buy albums!

This expansion of educational consumption is held to be something of value in itself. The British target is for 50% of all young people to attend university. But it is far from obvious that 50% of any generation would want a liberal education. And, even if they do, we shall see in the next section that this is not what is intended (see also Furedi, chapter 2, Fox, chapter 9, and Evans, chapter 11, this volume).

## SOME RELISH WITH THAT DEGREE?

Claire Fox, in her contribution to this volume (chapter 9), reminds us of a distinction made between two sorts of knowledge—knowledges 1 and 2—and argues that the sort of knowing peddled in the contemporary university is no longer "knowledge 1" or academic, subject-based knowledge. Rather, it is "knowledge 2," or everyday knowledge—an idea that flatters students when they discover how much they already know! It would be tempting to make a distinction between university 1 and university 2, where "university 2" is the McUniversity, with its "commodified" knowledge and modularized courses, delivered by teachers who do no research and are in no sense scholars. This would comfort the supporters of the Ivy League or Russell groups of universities and destroy morale elsewhere. This distinction would be wrong because all universities are subject to McDonaldizing tendencies, not just those processing huge numbers.

To explore this, let us return to the idea that McDonaldization exists in a situation of tension or opposition between ideas that are modern and postmodern (Hartley 1995; Wynyard, chapter 15, this volume). It is more profitable to see these elements as complementary. As Kumar puts it: "To eat at McDonald's is not necessarily to be McDonalized" (1995: 194). This simple phrase helps pose what Kumar calls a central, if not the central, question of contemporary social theory, the relationship of capitalism to postmodernism. One example, a discussion of competence, will show that such an opposition is an illusion. Statements of competence are the form in which training schemes at all levels are expressed. The notion of "competence" is what Fox refers to as "everyday knowledge," Hudson as "cultural capital," and others as "learning objectives." It is the general form of the new higher education, first supplementing then replacing subject knowledge. Usher and Edwards point out that the notion of competence is "cast in behavioural terms but the discourse is itself not behaviourist. It is precisely because it is not, but rather interwoven with liberal humanist discourse that it is powerful" (1994: 110). They add that "In its liberal humanist form, competence is more a form of 'seduction' than of oppression" (1994: 111).

What this indicates is that what is said to be "oppositional" can be used to support rather than oppose McDonaldizing tendencies. The idea of oppositional postmodernism neglects the way in which the state appropriates cultural concepts such as those associated with postmodernism and uses them as a means of legitimization (this might also be true of feminist ideas—see Rinehart, chapter 12, this volume). This is because postmodern discourse largely ignores the state. But the idea that the state has become postmodern is clearly unsustainable. A more convincing argument is that the state takes elements of what appear to be unorthodox or oppositional cultural ideas to replace older modes of justification in relation to traditional moral codes.

James L. Nolan has argued that the central cultural trend influencing the state is the therapeutic ethos. This ethos centers on building up individual self-esteem. In the face of rationalization, it helps people cope to with the effects on their private lives. It helps every person subject to racial, sexual, or other discrimination to come to cope with their "victimhood." Moreover, it accommodates religious and cultural pluralism by offering "a religion-like system of collective meaning" devoid of divisive sectarianism (Nolan 1998: 19). Like postmodernism, the therapeutic ethos is seen as oppositional:

Though sometimes portrayed as a reaction against utilitarian capitalism, the therapeutic cultural impulse does not directly challenge or threaten the utilitarian orientation of the capitalistic order. To the contrary, the therapeutic ethic appears to complement the utilitarian ethic. It offers to soften the harshness of life in the machine without removing the machine. In fact, it is often defended as a viable source of action because of its purported efficacy. Though these two dispositions seem intuitively disparate, they may actually be complementary. [Nolan 1998: 20]

More succinctly, he argues:

The therapeutic orientation provides a personalized remedy to a highly impersonal, rationalized, bureaucratic system, but without fundamentally altering the system. [1998: 20]

Nolan seems to weaken his analysis when he reverses what has just been argued here and suggests that at heart the "therapeutic ethos" rejects the orthodox concepts of reason and revelation in favor of subjective meanings, which: "may well signify a shift towards a distinctly postmodern cultural system" (1998: 289).

But we do not have to go with him down a line of argument already rejected. The consequences for the McUniversity are that students will be given courses not in how to pursue knowledge for its own sake (see Finkelstein, chapter 13, this volume), a demanding and self-denying activity, but courses that are effectively exercises in building self-esteem. As graduates of what Dennis Hayes (chapter 10, this volume) has called the *therapeutic university*, they will be impoverished human beings taught to seek not dangerous things like knowledge and truth, but more experiences that build up their self-esteem and that of others. This has already impacted on many training and business conferences and everyday meetings, where being "positive" is the cardinal value and criticism is seen as negative and confrontational.

The therapeutic university is the McUniversity of the near future. Aspects of the therapeutic ethos of the university are discussed in several of the contributions to this volume. In his closing chapter (chapter 15), Robin Wynyard points out that, whether or not academics bemoan the coming of McUniversity, students will still value the experience. If that is so, it will be a triumph for the therapeutic approach in building their self-esteem. They will feel positive about what they have achieved. They will lack self-doubt. But their confidence will be fragile and constantly require more therapeutic attention. Never before has such a therapeutic focus been part of a university education.

The discussions in this book are about the future of higher education—if, indeed, it has a future! The theme of all the contributions in this book is an ancient one: to argue that the unexamined life, the life built around improving people's self-esteem, is not worth living.

## NOTES

1. Even characterizing the process in this way or by referring to concepts such to managerialism, marketization, consumerism, commercialism, or bureaucratization, may seem to reenforce individual passivity as these terms are not seen as descriptions of political action by powerful people but forces with which we have to deal. This is shown by the fact that opposition is never to these concepts per se but to the way in which managerial, market, consumer, or commercial ideas are being implemented. Our opposition to McDonaldization is total.

2. See the discussion which began in the British newspaper *The Guardian* in August 2001: K. Maguire, "New Labour: Out with the red rose and in with the Big Mac" (30 August 2001); P. Toynbee, "McLabour is so naff" (31 August 2001); G. Monbiot, "Sleeping with the enemy" (4 September 2001); and C. Hitchens, "The sour taste of McLabour" (5 September 2001).

3. Martin Parker's critique in chapter 8, this volume, was timely, as the chief executive of the Quality Assurance Agency for Higher Education (QAA) resigned in August 2001 initiating a national debate about the future of that organization. See P. Baty, "Randall's exit imperils light touch regime," *THES*, (24 August 2001) and other articles in that journal. A contributor to this volume engaged in a debate with the former chief executive: see F. Furedi, "Why the QAA should RIP" and J. Randall, "A Question of Quality," *Guardian Education* (30 August 2001).

## REFERENCES

Barnett, R. (2000). *Realizing the University in an Age of Supercomplexity.* Buckingham, U.K.: Society for Research into Higher Education & Open University Press.

Bauman, Z. (1992). *Intimations of Postmodernity.* London & New York: Routledge.

Bendix, R. (1966). *Max Weber. An Intellectual Portrait.* London: Methuen.

Hartley, D. (1995). The "McDonaldization" of higher education: Food for thought? *Oxford Review of Education, 21* (4): 409–423.

Heartfield, J. (1998). *Need and Desire in the Post-Material Economy.* Sheffield, U.K.: Sheffield Hallam University.

Klein, N. (2000). *No Logo.* London: Flamingo.

Kumar, K. (1995). *From Post-Industrial to Post-Modern Society: New Theories of the Contemporary World.* Oxford: Blackwell.

Lomas, L. (2001). Does the development of mass education mean the end of quality? Paper presented to the SRHE Conference, Birmingham, U.K., 25–26 May.

MacRae, D. G. (1974). *Weber.* Glasgow, U.K.: Fontana.

Nolan, J. L. (1998). *The Therapeutic State: Justifying Government at Century's End.* New York: New York University Press.

OECD (2000). *Education at a Glance 2000.* Paris: OECD. <http:\\www.oecd.org// els/education/ei/eag2000/hl.htm>.

Parker, M. (1998). Nostalgia and mass culture: McDonaldization and cultural elitism. In M. Alfino, J. S. Caputo, & R. Wynyard (Eds.), *McDonaldization Revisited: Critical Essays on Consumer Culture.* Westport, CT, & London: Praeger (1–18).

Parker, M., & Jary, D. (1995). The McUniversity: Organisation, management and academic subjectivity. *Organisation,* 2: 1–20.

Rinehart, J. A. (1998). It may be a polar night of icy darkness, but feminists are building a fire. In M. Alfino, J. S. Caputo, & R. Wynyard (Eds.), *McDonaldization Revisited: Critical Essays on Consumer Culture.* Westport, CT, & London: Praeger (19–38).

Ritzer, G. (1993). *The McDonaldization of Society,* 1st ed. Thousand Oaks, CA: Pine Forge Press.

Ritzer, G. (1998). *The McDonaldization Thesis: Explorations and Extensions.* Thousand Oaks, CA: Pine Forge Press.

Ritzer, G. (1999). *Enchanting a Disenchanted World: Revolutionizing the Means of Consumption.* Thousand Oaks, CA: Pine Forge Press.

Ritzer, G. (2000). *The McDonaldization of Society: New Century Edition.* Thousand Oaks, CA: Pine Forge Press.

Ryan, A. (1999). *Liberal Anxieties and Liberal Education.* London: Profile Books.

Smart, B. (Ed.) (1999). *Resisting McDonaldization.* London & Thousand Oaks, CA: Sage.

Smith, A., & Webster. F. (1997). *The Postmodern University?* Buckingham, U.K.: Society for Research into Higher Education & Open University Press.

Toynbee, P. (2001). McLabour is so naff. *The Guardian,* 31 August.

Weber, M. (1927). *General Economic History.* New Brunswick, NJ, & London: Transaction Books, 1981.

Weber, M. (1930). *The Protestant Ethic and the Spirit of Capitalism.* New York: Charles Scribner's Sons; London: Allen & Unwin.

Weber, M. (1968). *Economy and Society,* 3 volumes. New York: Bedminster Press.

Wood, R. C. (1998). Old wine in new bottles: Critical limitations of the McDonaldization thesis—The case of hospitality services. In M. Alfino, J. S. Caputo, & R. Wynyard (Eds.), *McDonaldization Revisited: Critical Essays on Consumer Culture.* Westport, CT, & London: Praeger (85–104).

Wynyard R. (1998). The bunless burger. In M. Alfino, J. S. Caputo, & R. Wynyard (Eds.), *McDonaldization Revisited: Critical Essays on Consumer Culture.* Westport, CT, & London: Praeger (159–174).

Usher, R., & Edwards, R. (1994). *Postmodernism and Education.* London & New York: Routledge.

# 1

# Enchanting McUniversity: Toward a Spectacularly Irrational University Quotidian

*George Ritzer*

The McDonaldization of the university—the creation of McUniversity (Ritzer 1998)—is not only a reality, but the process continues to expand and accelerate—that is, the university operates in an increasingly efficient manner, its operations are more and more predictable, it relies more than ever before on quantifiable measures (often to the detriment of quality), and it utilizes an increasing number of nonhuman technologies that control and even replace professors. Furthermore, the acceleration of these processes, as well as of McDonaldization in general, brings with it a series of irrationalities of rationality, especially a decline in the quality of education.

Given the ever-increasing reality of McUniversity, the purpose of this chapter is to discuss what can be done about problems caused by excessive rationalization. The analysis follows the logic not only of *The McDonaldization of Society* (Ritzer, 2000), but also of *Enchanting a Disenchanted World: Revolutionizing the Means of Consumption* (Ritzer 1999). While the rationale for relying on *McDonaldization* is obvious, the utilization of the approach derived from the latter work is based on the assumption that the university is a means of consumption—that is, it is a setting that makes it possible for customers (in this case, students and their parents) to consume education. This, of course, presumes that there has been a change in the relationship between students (and their parents) and the university. They increasingly see themselves as consumers of education in much the same way as they are consumers of what the mall (including the cybermall) and Disney World have to offer. This, in turn, has altered the way in which the university and its staff relate to them. Instead of viewing them as reliable, long-term clients, the university must now treat students as fickle customers who may be difficult to attract and retain.

This leads to many different kinds of changes in the university, but those focused on here are the changes in the university as a setting of consumption. It is the setting that has been McDonaldized to, among other things, deliver education efficiently and at a reasonable cost. The McDonaldization of the university's setting is attractive to consumers, especially because in a McDonaldized society they come to expect things like efficiency and low cost (e.g. the McDonald's value meal picked up at the drive-through window). However, there are limits to the attractiveness of a McDonaldized setting, especially in the university. Students are unlikely to be attracted to, and to remain long at, a bare-bones university that resembles and operates like a factory in an enterprise zone in Thailand or a no-frills warehouse store. As consumers, students have become accustomed to far more elaborate means of consumption that combine McDonaldization with spectacle[1] (in some cases McDonaldization itself can be spectacular). Thus, contemporary indoor shopping malls (and megamalls like Mall of America in Minneapolis), Las Vegas casino–hotels, cruise-ships, and theme parks (like Disney World) are clearly McDonaldized, but much of the rationalized workings of these systems is concealed beneath a spectacular surface. Masses of consumers are drawn by the spectacles and are well served by the McDonaldized operations. Students want the same things from the university and while the university has been delivering increasingly McDonaldized processes, it has not been notably successful in creating spectacles. The university needs to be *both* McDonaldized *and* spectacular.

Because they are both McDonaldized and spectacular, I have also called the new means of consumption "cathedrals of consumption." The challenge to the university is to become a cathedral for the consumption of education. Cathedrals of consumption are rationalized, but this brings with it disenchantment. To attract their clientele, cathedrals cannot remain disenchanted, and they seek to reenchant themselves by becoming more spectacular. Spectacles give cathedrals an aura of magic, of enchantment. The world's great religious cathedrals have long sought to become spectacular through their great size, high vaulted ceilings, huge stained-glass windows, and so on. However, we must remember that great rationality is required to build and operate religious cathedrals, and this exists side-by-side with the enchantment produced by spectacles. Today's great cathedrals of consumption have followed a similar course, albeit to a much greater degree than religious cathedrals—that is, they are both more rationalized and more spectacular than religious cathedrals. Consider Disney World or the Bellagio casino–hotel and the degree of rationalization required to operate these settings and to accommodate the hordes of people that pass through them each day, as well as the enormous spectacle produced by them.

As with the modern cathedrals of consumption, today's universities cannot simply McDonaldize—they must also utilize spectacles in order to make themselves seem enchanted to their consumer base. What can the modern university "learn from Las Vegas"? Are the spectacles produced by the modern cathedrals of consumption in Las Vegas (and elsewhere) of relevance to the university? Can they be used by the university to overcome the liabilities associated with a heavy reliance on McDonaldization and become a source of enchantment that allows the university to attract and keep students? Perhaps more importantly, can they be used to *improve* the quality of education? To begin to answer these questions, we must first examine, at least briefly, the ways in which the cathedrals of consumption make themselves more spectacular and enchanted.

## CREATING SPECTACLES

There are at least three broad mechanisms used by the cathedrals of consumption to create spectacles. The first is development and use of *simulations,* or elaborate fakes, designed to amaze and delight consumers. This focus on simulations is motivated by the fact that the real, the authentic, is difficult to work with, is often not in the right place, and is difficult or impossible to manipulate in ways that could make it even more spectacular. Thus, from the point of view of Las Vegas entrepreneurs, the "real" Venice in Italy is in the wrong place (it is not in Las Vegas and cannot be transported there), it is difficult to work with (those pesky Venetians might object to major changes in their city), and it is hard, to say the least, to make it more spectacular. Thus, the entrepreneurs built a simulated Venice in Las Vegas: the Venetian casino–hotel (and shopping mall). Las Vegas is increasingly defined by such simulations (e.g., New York, New York; Bellagio; Mandalay Bay), and simulations mark many other cathedrals of consumption. For example, Disney World is a world of innumerable simulations (e.g. the fake Main Street by which one enters and leaves); a new park has recently opened adjacent to Disneyland in Anaheim that is a simulation of California (in, no less, the "real" state of California). Such simulations are spectacular and magical, and they serve to enchant the settings in which they are found.

A second mechanism for the production of spectacle and enchantment is *implosion.* If explosion (often associated with modernity) involves the creation of innumerable new phenomena, implosion (usually associated with postmodernity) involves the elimination of boundaries between extant phenomena so that they collapse in on one another. The existence of two or more phenomena—once deemed as necessarily distinct—in the same setting creates a sense of spectacle and magic for consumers. Thus, malls and theme parks were at one time seen as distinct settings that were each spectacular in their own way. However, with the arrival of the Edmonton Mall and the Mall of America, the boundaries collapsed, and malls and theme parks came to exist under one roof.

A third technique for enchanting the new means of consumption is the manipulation of time and space. The manipulation of the latter can take the form of time compression: things that formerly took days or weeks can now be done in hours, minutes, or even nanoseconds. The spectacle associated with the fast-food restaurant, especially in its early years, was the fact that food was available in seconds or minutes. Today, the time needed to purchase stock on line has been reduced to virtually nothing. One of the ways in which space is made spectacular is to encompass enormous areas under one roof or in one setting. The modern cruise ship, sometimes as long as three football fields, encompasses a "hotel" for 3–4,000 people, a casino, a spa, restaurants, swimming pools, and so on. Universities have already made many efforts to manipulate time and space in order seem more spectacular. For example, classes taught by closed-circuit television or online make it possible for students across the country to take courses at a given university. These courses can be taken at very different times in the several time zones, or they can be taken at any time, at the leisure of the student. And universities pour funds into building immense facilities such as stadiums and athletic centers with the intention of attracting students.

## TOWARD A SPECTACULARLY IRRATIONAL UNIVERSITY QUOTIDIAN

Since it is a means of consumption, the university *could* follow the lead of the major cathedrals of consumption and seek to reenchant itself through the creation of spectacles using mechanisms like simulation, implosion, and the manipulation of time and space. However, while the university has, in various ways, taken this course of action, there are severe limitations in this regard. It simply cannot afford to grow too, to become much like a Las Vegas casino–hotel or Disney World. If it did, it would delegitimize itself and lose far more than it would gain. Furthermore, creating a spectacular physical plant and superstructure would attract students, but it would do nothing about improving the quality of education. Thus, the issue is: are there any lessons to be gained from the cathedrals of consumption that the university can use in its effort to attract and retain students *and* to improve the quality of their educational experience?

I think the answer is yes, but the university must adapt the ideas of enchantment and spectacle to its own particular characteristics and realities. (In fact, all means of consumption must do this.) What this means is that, unlike the Las Vegas casino, the university cannot focus exclusively on massive external structures (the size of its football stadium, the impressiveness and beauty of its grounds), but must, rather, devote most of its attention to the quite unspectacular day-to-day operations, the most fundamental everyday realities, that make a university a university. This is far from an astounding conclusion, but the focus of this essay on spectacle and enchantment does lead us to a somewhat counter-intuitive conclusion: what the university needs to do is to seek in various ways to *make the seemingly unspectacular spectacular!* What it needs to do is to focus on its quotidian activities and to find ways to make them spectacular and enchanting. What are those unspectacular activities? And how can they be made more spectacular, more enchanted, *and* more beneficial from an educational point of view?

Of course, the irreducible minimum of the university involves professors teaching and students learning (and, to some degree, vice versa). Perhaps the most spectacular and enchanted thing the university could do would involve a return to personal, direct, intensive contact between professor and student. Imagine what a sensation a university would make by announcing that henceforth all undergraduate (and graduate) education would involve only one-on-one tutorials and seminars involving a maximum of ten students. The news would ricochet around the world, and students would flock to that university. The spectacular reenchanted university would have done its job and attracted the clientele it needs to survive. Furthermore, that clientele would probably involve better students who are willing, and maybe even able, to pay for such an education, which, undoubtedly, would be of higher quality than that which is currently generally available in McUniversity.

There are several problems with this scenario (e.g., where are all these new professors to come from?), but the crucial stumbling block is the astronomical costs involved. A massive influx of new (and costly) faculty would be required to create such a university. The university, and especially the governmental agencies that back most universities, would need to come up with billions, perhaps trillions, of dollars to fund such a university, and/or the tuition for paying students would have to multiply manyfold. If the latter were the case, the newly enchanted university would be counterproductive and many able students attracted by the "spectacular unspectacular" would be put off by the high cost. And, if the government were asked to foot the bill, it would undoubtedly refuse. In an era in the United States of "no new taxes," and even gigantic tax cuts, there would be virtually no support for such a massive infusion of funds into higher education. This is especially likely to be the reaction since the bulk of the new money would go into hiring and paying staff. We live in an era in which the emphasis is on cutting back on personnel costs, not increasing them on a massive scale. This is especially true of hiring new faculty members, as there is already a widespread suspicion that there are now too many of them and too much money is spent on them.

So it comes as no surprise that we are *not* returning to an academia characterized by tutorials and small seminars. How, then, do we make the quotidian activities of the university more enchanting and spectacular? In answering this question, we must look forward rather than backward, although we can take our lead from the historic activities of the university. Thus, one of the things that is needed is to speculate about the use of advanced technologies, some of which may not yet be in existence, that can give the university of the future a flavor of the past. In the following section I will sketch out a few ideas that are somewhere between contemporary realities, easily envisioned technological advances, and science fiction. They all involve making the unspectacular activities of the university more spectacular. They are also based on the assumption that high-tech solutions, even though they may be costly, are far cheaper than the low-tech solution of hiring hordes of new faculty members. However, in contrast to increasing McDonaldization, these solutions involve the use of nonhuman technologies to *enhance* human technology.

The reader will no doubt notice that this involves a complete inversion of one of the basic characteristics of McDonaldization: instead of replacing human with nonhuman technology, the focus here is on the use of nonhuman technology to enhance human technology. This is of crucial importance because it leads to the broader argument that informs the rest of this chapter—in order to make its quotidian activities more spectacular and better educationally, the university must *deMcDonaldize* (Ritzer 1998) them—that is, those activities must be reconceptualized and reorganized so that they involve the obverse of each of the basic principles of McDonaldization. To put it another way, those activities must be made *spectacularly irrational.*

## NONHUMAN TECHNOLOGY THAT *ENHANCES* HUMAN TECHNOLOGY

The idea of a high-tech, wired lecture hall is nothing new—indeed, many are already in existence[2] and as they currently exist, they do create something of a spectacle that is attractive to students. However, the high-tech classrooms with which I am familiar do not deal with the quotidian issues of concern here. In fact, if anything, they exacerbate the problem of a lack of personalized contact between teacher and student. If the idea is to recreate something like the personal contact that existed between students and professors, how can that be accomplished in the high-tech lecture hall? I envision something like the following: A lecture hall seating 500, even 1,000, students is fully wired; computer screens are found on each student's desk and at the podium. Students, professors, and teaching assistants bring their personal disks to class and insert them into their disk drives. Each disk has the name and some personal information on each of the participants. With a tap on the keyboard, a professor can bring up the name of any student anywhere in the class and call on that student *by name.* Or, when students want to ask questions of the professor, their names, locations in the classroom, and bits of personal information about them (e.g. major, interests, grade point average, grades in the class, attendance records, etc.) are highlighted on the professor's computer screen. (Much more personal information can even be added if the professor wishes.) Such information permits the professor to have a *more personal interaction* with each student, perhaps tailoring questions and answers to the student's interests, major, and even personality. This clearly involves the use of nonhuman technology to enhance, not control or replace, the interaction between professor and student.

As the lecture unfolds, students enter additional questions that come to mind (and that may not require class time to answer) into their computers, and these are transmitted directly to the computers of teaching assistants (TAs). The assistants can answer such questions as they come in, thereby giving students *instantaneous and personalized feedback.* Especially important questions, or those that are of general interest, can be transmitted by TAs to the professor's computer, along with the identity of the student raising the questions. The professor takes occasional (and welcome) breaks from the lecture to bring up a screen with the questions that have come in since the previous break for questions. The professor (or a designated TA) selects the best questions and/or those that are of most general interest and responds *directly and personally to the student* who asked each question.

Also during the lecture, students offer continual feedback, noting when a particular example is unclear, the point of a given slide is obscure, and so on. TAs can clarify immediately (it would be impossible for the lecturer to deal with all of these issues during the lecture), or bring up the issue with the professor later. TAs can then give students the needed clarifications via computer. In addition, assistants and professors are given the feedback they need in order to come up with better examples, clearer slides, and so forth, for the next time the lecture is given or the course is taught.

At the end of each class period, students give instant evaluations of the lecture (and the professor can offer similar evaluations of student performance during class). All involved can reassess what transpired on the basis of these instantaneous evaluations.

Of course, this kind of relationship would not stop with the end of class. Students can transmit all sorts of questions to TAs from their dorm rooms, apartments, or even the library. TAs can filter these questions, answering most and passing some on to the professor, perhaps to be dealt with in the next class.

Online chats between students, assistants, and professors are already common. An integral part of the course could be an online chat of an hour or two with the professor. Assistants could be available for longer periods of time for such chats with students.

One could go on with this, spinning out all sorts of variations on this theme. Much will emerge as the technology becomes available and all involved learn how to use it better. However, the essential point is that advanced nonhuman technology would be used in spectacular new ways to enhance the most essential of the day-to-day educational activities involving interaction between students, professors, and assistants. Of course, this would not be of the kind of interaction that takes place in one-on-one tutorials or miniseminars. However, given the fact that we are not returning to such an educational world, it is the best we can do, and it may, in some ways, even be superior to older methods. For example, students can raise questions via the computer, and they can be answered immediately by TAs, even as the lecture proceeds. In the "old days" professors had to interrupt their lectures to answer such questions. Many questions that might have gone unraised or unanswered are now more likely to be asked and answered.

However, what immediately comes to mind about this set of suggestions, and others to be discussed below, is: does this not all involve a further McDonaldization of education? And does it not bring with it a further disenchantment, not reenchantment, of education? Yes, this does involve a further McDonaldization of education. Of course, McDonaldization itself can be spectacular in various ways, but it also brings with it disenchantment. More specifically, we are here discussing one element of McDonaldization: increasing control through the substitution of nonhuman for human technology. However, it all depends on how the technology is being used. In the preceding scenario nonhuman technology is *not* being used to control humans, but, rather, to enhance their ability to interact with one another within the context of a large lecture. Furthermore, the nonhuman technology is not being used to replace human beings—as students, assistants, or professors—but to enhance their ability to function as human beings, at least in the context of the given of a large lecture. The latter may not be the ideal educational method, but given the fact that large lectures are likely to grow increasingly ubiquitous, technology can be used to allow it to function in a more human (i.e., personalized) way.

The real danger lies in using such technology to control instructors and their assistants (and students) or to replace them completely with nonhuman technologies.[3] For example, we already have classes consisting wholly of videotaped lectures by professors that can be accessed at home or in the library, or classes employing elaborate computer programs that answer student questions rather than having answers provided by TAs or professors. This is the worst of the McDonaldization of education, involving its complete dehumanization. The objective, instead, should be to use nonhuman technology to humanize education as much as possible given the realities (e.g. large lectures) of today's (and tomorrow's) university.

Technology could be used in many other ways to enhance the relationship between students and professors. For example, students could use their computers to access their professor's works in progress. Students could be given access to grant proposals under consideration, raw data sets, and articles and books in process. In terms of the latter, students could follow their professor's work as it evolves, even on a page-by-page basis. Much of the material would be beyond most students, but they would get a glimpse of the creative process. This access to the emergence of scholarly works, especially by their own teachers, would seem (and be) quite spectacular to most students, and it would certainly be beneficial from an educational point of view. Of course, it would work best when the works in question are textbooks aimed at students. Students would understand what they are reading, and they could even be allowed to make comments on the text and suggestions for improvement. The greatest spectacle from a students' point of view would be to see their own ideas integrated into the emerging text (and, hopefully, being thanked in print for them).

The reverse process would also be possible: professors—more probably, teaching assistants—could access student papers in process and even comment as they are being written. Problems could be picked up as papers are being written rather than at the end of the process, when nothing can be done about them. The best students would certainly find this quite spectacular, and the result would be better papers. Those who do their papers at the last minute or purchase term papers over the web or from other students might not be so thrilled by this possibility. Of course, students (and professors) would be free to block access to some or all of their work.

All of the ideas discussed in this section rely on the use of advanced technology, but in the following sections we focus on more human ways of making the unspectacular aspects of education more spectacular and better educationally through the inversion of the basic principles of McDonaldization.

## THE UNPREDICTABLE UNIVERSITY QUOTIDIAN

The university is currently characterized by a highly predictable round of lectures, discussions, reading assignments in textbooks, exams (often in the quite routine multiple-choice format), and grades or marks at the end of the process. It would be quite a spectacle if the university sought to inject as much unpredictability as possible into the day-to-day life of the university. This builds, in part, on ideas like "mass customization" and "sneakerization"—that is, one can create considerable diversity without totally surrendering the advantages of McDonaldization. What universities need to do is to find ways of teaching large numbers of students in more customized or at least "sneakerized" ways. In the latter, they need to follow the lessons of the athletic shoe industry and its discovery that it could produce hundreds of different varieties of shoes without sacrificing the McDonaldization of production and distribution. If the university were to find ways to "mass customize" or "sneakerize" its educational system, it would inject much more unpredictability into the process, and that unpredictability would be quite spectacular to students accustomed to an educational system where they have relatively few options. And any kind of greater customization, be it through sneakerization or mass customization, is likely to improve educational quality.

In fact, advanced technologies can be used to help to accomplish these goals. The kinds of lectures discussed in the previous section permit some degree of customization by allowing students to ask questions electronically and permitting professors to respond in a more personal way, even one that is tailored to students. However, rather than exploring the possibilities offered by technology in this realm (and there are many), I prefer to focus on what universities, departments, and professors could do to inject more unpredictability into the educational process.

Once again, let us focus on the introductory course, because it is subject to the greatest pressure to undergo McDonaldization. While many universities make use of large lectures, others use multiple sections involving, say, fifty students each. There is often much commonality in these sections; in fact, departments often impose a common textbook and curriculum. What I envision, in contrast, is a series of sections each of which is designed to be different from all the others. Each section would be clearly labeled and defined, so that its distinctive focus and its differences from all other sections would be clear to students, who would be free to choose the one that best fits their needs and interests. Below I outline a number of hypothetical "sneakerized" sections for an imagined course in introductory sociology that implements such an approach:

Introduction to sociology

1. using a basic textbook, a lecture format, and multiple-choice questions;
2. using only original works of classic and contemporary sociologists, lecture format, essay exams;
3. through the novel, discussion format, outline for a proposed novel required;
4. through motion pictures (or television programs), discussion format, story board for a proposed movie (or TV program) required;
5. through the newspaper, subscription to the *New York Times* required, discussion format, students required to write several newspaper-style articles;
6. through the Internet, all basic topics in sociology covered through visits to a wide range of websites, construction of an original website required;
7. taught by nonacademics (e.g. businesspeople, social workers, government administrators) with degrees in sociology; the focus would be on applied issues, and reading assignments would utilize applied materials; grades would be based on an internship in the "real" world;
8. for those who plan on majoring in sociology and doing sociological research, focus is on methods and statistics, lecture and discussion, a research article required.

Clearly such a list is nearly endless, but such an array of available sections gets away from the numbing sameness of introductory sociology and offers some level of sneakerization.

While the above leads to diversity, it does not deal satisfactorily with the issue of unpredictability. That is best handled by (human) instructors and their assistants. What can be done to inject unpredictability into today's university?

1. Avoid textbooks! Instead, use a great many diverse reading assignments from many different types of sources. Better yet, have instructors create their own textual material.
2. Avoid doing the same thing from class to class. A lecture in one class period followed by a discussion in the next and then viewing a movie/videotape, some sort of field trip, and so on.
3. Consciously try to inject unpredictability into each class. Lecture for a time, invite questions, get students to speak on the issue, invite graduate assistants to add their perspective, and so on. Try to efficiently cover a given topic in one period, ramble off on a series of tangents in another, and totally refuse to stay on topic in the next one.
4. Bring in unannounced guest speakers as discussion leaders at various points during the semester.

5. Give impromptu writing assignments in class. Pop quizzes would also inject some (unwelcome to students) unpredictability.

6. Give only subjective evaluations of exams, papers, quizzes during the semester. Put off giving a letter or number grade until as late as possible.

Clearly, these suggestions do little more than scratch the surface. Each instructor is in a position to create all sorts of unpredictable events during a class and a semester. Given the great predictability of virtually everything else they encounter in the university (and in the larger society), many students will find unpredictable classes truly spectacular and educationally beneficial.

However, bear in mind that it is very possible to McDonaldize unpredictability and thereby to eliminate the very spectacle and educational advance we are trying to create. I have previously written about two imaginary chains (Ritzer 1998), "Miss Haps" and "Miss Steaks," based on the routinization of a series of mishaps and mistakes. Thus, for example, the activities of waitpersons would be choreographed so that they would occasionally engage in pratfalls or "accidentally" spill a plate of (plastic) french fries. In these and other ways, the unpredictable would be McDonaldized. In much the same way, the university could McDonaldize the unpredictable events discussed above. This might create a spectacle, but it would not be the kind of spectacle the university needs. Such a spectacle requires more genuine unpredictability and not the kind of simulated unpredictability one might experience were Miss Haps and Miss Steaks real restaurant chains.

## QUALITY, *NOT* QUANTITY

Another inversion of the principles of McDonaldization—an emphasis on quality not quantity—would also help to make the day-to-day activities of the university more spectacular. Too often, the demands of mass education cause the quality of education, particularly what goes on in the classroom, to suffer. Much of what has been said in this part of this essay has to do with improving the quality of education. Beyond the things discussed thus far, I would suggest the truly radical idea of having the very best people in the university teach the most and have the greatest amount of contact with students. While this is often accorded lipservice, the fact is that in the main the university's best-known and most important professors are usually rewarded with *reduced* teaching loads, especially at the undergraduate level. Instead of concentrating on their research, graduate seminars, and international academic jetsetting, let us have our very best professors teach undergraduates, especially in lower-level, even introductory, courses. Just having some of the university's "stars" walking into such a classroom would cause a stir, if not a spectacle. Spectacle would certainly be created if they were able to integrate their own work and ideas with the traditional material taught in lower-level courses and do it all in an interesting and accessible manner.

Not all, or even most, will be able to do that, at least initially. To deal with that problem there is another revolutionary idea: let us devote considerable time, energy, and resources to teaching professors how to teach. This would involve everything from required courses in graduate school on teaching, periodic refresher courses for professors, and special tutelage for the "stars" who are to be brought into the basic courses. Improving the quality of teacher training will lead to improvements in the quality of their teaching.

## INEFFICIENCY

There is much to be said in favor of making education as inefficient as possible. Again, the clients (students), who are accustomed to efficiency in all areas of their lives, would find an inefficient educational process spectacular and often to their advantage educationally. Ordinarily, the emphasis is on efficiently covering a wide range of topics. How about courses that strive to be inefficient? Courses that pause to devote as much time as necessary to issues that catch students' attention and that elicit intense interest from them. Does it really matter whether all fifteen predesignated topics are covered in a semester? If it does, do they all have to be covered in class? Could not whatever topics are not covered in class be left to the students to cover on their own? (My most memorable college course was one in which the professor *refused* to *ever* cover *any* topic in the course. He referred us to the text and ancillary readings on each topic but devoted every class to whatever the class wanted to discuss. It was a highly stimulating class, and I learned a lot in it: it was a spectacle to me and others in the class—although still others found it frustrating and misguided. Whatever I learned about the subject—clinical psychology, as I recall—I got from readings done outside class-time.)

My thinking on spectacular inefficiency is guided by the following example from the education of small children requiring you to imagine "a cluster of excited children examining a turtle with enormous fascination and intensity. Now children, put away the turtle, the teacher insists. We're going to have our science lesson. The lesson is on crabs" (Silberman 1970: 125). While it may be efficient to move from subject to subject (from turtles to crabs) according to a preset schedule, it would be better educationally to stay with one subject (turtles) until the interest in it is exhausted. It may be inefficient to spend so much time on turtles (the lesson on crabs may be delayed, shortened, or even eliminated), but the educational advantages may be enormous.

## THE RATIONALITY OF IRRATIONALITY

Ultimately it is quite rational—or, more accurately, reasonable—for the university to organize its quotidian activities in a highly irrational manner. The quality of education would, I believe, improve with an increase in the irrationality of education. The McDonaldization of the university's everyday educational activities produces a number of irrationalities, especially a decline in the quality of education. It behooves the university to deMcDonaldize its everyday educational activities—to increase their degree of *in*efficiency, *un*predictability, *in*calculability, and use of *human* technology—in order to improve their quality. Furthermore, such a deMcDonaldized education will seem quite spectacular to students. Thus, there is a double advantage to deMcDonaldized education: it both works better and will attract and keep larger numbers of students.

I am not suggesting that the university as a whole needs to deMcDonaldize in order to deliver deMcDonaldized education. In fact, it could be argued that a highly McDonaldized university structure and system is required to deliver such an education. Record-keeping in a deMcDonaldized educational system, for example, might be more difficult because of differentiation in educational programs. If we had more differentiated introductory sociology courses, for instance, then the university would need to keep track of which classes are prerequisites for what academic and career directions. More advisers would be needed to explain the much more complicated educational systems to prospective students, employers, and admissions directors of graduate programs at other universities. One of the ironic consequences of deMcDonaldizing the quotidian activities of the university is the further McDonaldization of the structure of the university.

Yet in a way this makes perfect sense. The problem is not McDonaldization per se, but *excessive McDonaldization* (Ritzer & Ovadia, 2000) and the *inappropriate extension of McDonaldization* to domains that ought not to be McDonaldized to any great extent. As Weber pointed out long ago, there are good reasons for large-scale organizations to be bureaucratized—that is, rationalized. And there might be good reasons to McDonaldize a factory, an army, and so on.[4] However, that does not mean that everything should be McDonaldized; and that everything gains from increases in McDonaldization. Clearly, everyday educational activity is one of those areas (another is the doctor–patient relationship) that have been overly and inappropriately McDonaldized. What a spectacle it would be if the quotidian activities of the university were truly deMcDonaldized! And just imagine how much better the educational process itself would function!

## CONCLUSION

To survive as a means of consumption, the university must learn from the highly successful cathedrals of consumption and find ways of becoming more spectacular. However, while the cathedrals of consumption focus on grand, colossal, and superficial spectacles, the university cannot take this direction. It must, instead, focus on making more spectacular the quotidian activities that go to the heart of its educational functioning. While everything around it is growing increasingly McDonaldized, the route open to the university is to create spectacle by deMcDonaldizing its quotidian activities. Inefficient, unpredictable, incalculable education employing human technologies will seem quite spectacular to students, especially in contrast to the numbing McDonaldization that is increasingly found almost everywhere else. The spectacle of the deMcDonaldization of the university's everyday activities will not only be spectacular and attract students, but it will also serve to enhance dramatically the quality of the educational process.

## NOTES

1. I am using the concept of the spectacle throughout this analysis. While it is drawn from Debord (1968) and the Situationists (Ritzer & Stillman, 2001), it is used differently here. I am simply using the idea to refer to anything that is attention-grabbing, exciting, and interesting.

2. While I will focus on large lectures, it is clearly possible (as Caroline Persell reminds me) that such technology can also be used to enhance collaborative and cooperative learning.

3. As Caroline Persell has pointed out to me, much of my discussion implies that faculty would control the introduction of new technologies and use them to enhance day-to-day education. However, the political economy of the university makes it clear that there are other powerful forces that might be inclined to adopt and deploy such technologies for very different, even antithetical, purposes.

4. If not, there are at least sound reasons to McDonaldize aspects or levels of these structures.

## REFERENCES

Debord, G. (1968). *The Society of the Spectacle*. London: Verso, 1994.

Ritzer, G. (1998). *The McDonaldization Thesis: Explorations and Extensions*. London & Thousand Oaks, CA: Sage.

Ritzer, G. (1999). *Enchanting a Disenchanted World: Revolutionizing the Means of Consumption*. Thousand Oaks, CA: Pine Forge Press.

Ritzer, G. (2000). *The McDonaldization of Society: New Century Edition*. Thousand Oaks, CA: Pine Forge Press.

Ritzer, G., & Ovadia, S. (2000). The process of McDonaldization is not uniform, nor are its settings, consumers, or the consumption of its goods and services. In M. Gottdiener (Ed.), *New Forms of Consumption: Consumers, Culture and Commodification*. Lanham, MD: Rowman and Littlefield (33–49).

Ritzer, G., & Stillman, T. (2001). The new means of consumption and the situationist perspective. In G. Ritzer (Ed.), *Explorations in the Sociology of Consumption: Fast Food, Credit Cards and Casinos*. London & Thousand Oaks, CA: Sage (181–202).

Silberman, C. E. (1970). *Crisis in the Classroom: The Remaking of American Education*. New York: Random House.

# 2

# The Bureaucratization
# of the British University

*Frank Furedi*

Outwardly, the British university system appears to confirm the trend toward the McDonaldization of higher education. However, on closer inspection it is evident that the British system lacks the flexibility and efficiency that is sometimes claimed on behalf of the McDonaldization of the U.S. University. In the case of Britain, the transformation of higher education can be most appropriately characterized as one of bureaucratization rather than one of McDonaldization. What we have is a highly centralized system of higher education run by an interventionist bureaucracy. The impact of government policy on British higher education is unusually direct and pervasive. This centrally directed bureaucratic form of governance weakens institutional diversity and autonomy. It has led to the homogenization of institutional practices, leading to the erosion of organizational flexibility.

The expansion of a centralized system of auditing and bureaucratic control in the higher-education sector was justified on the ground that the university needed to be made more efficient and enterprising. In the 1980s, successive governments have encouraged the marketization of education and promoted the ethos of treating students as consumers or customers. As a result, a new managerial ideology of "quality, efficiency, and enterprise" has shaped British higher education. The justification for subjecting the university sector to this culture of auditing was that academics tended to hide behind their professional authority and refused to yield to acceptable forms of public accountability. No doubt, like any professional body, academics were quite capable of being motivated by their self-interest. Unfortunately, the introduction of hard managerialism has not solved this problem. The university sector has not become more open, flexible, or creative. It has merely been forced to become more accountable to the formal criteria designated by external auditing agencies. Managerial colonization has led to the erosion of the professional autonomy of academic life, but it has not succeeded in introducing a genuine system of public accountability. Worse still, the bureaucratic pressures placed on university life have diverted academics toward an endless round of meaningless paperwork in order to meet the demands of different auditing agencies. Academics are compelled to adopt practices that are consistent with the demands of bureaucratic institutions that audit their teaching and research, regardless of what they believe is in the best interest of their students or of university life, and, sadly, these externally imposed demands have encouraged practices that lead to formulaic teaching and superficial research.

The imposition of a managerial ethos on university life has inevitably encouraged docility and conformity. Dissident voices are routinely accused of being out of touch or trying to cling on to discredited elitist practices. The policing of the academy by outside agencies—most controversially by the Quality Assurance Agency (QAA)—has created a situation where British academic life has become more scrutinized than at any time in its previous history. This has not made the British university a more transparent institution. Rather, it has forced the academic community to neglect its traditional responsibilities toward research and teaching in favor of producing red tape for the central auditing machine.

However, making sense of the transformation of university life is no simple task. It would be foolish to suggest that successive governments or members of the higher-education bureaucracy actually set out to undermine standards in British universities. It is worth noting that many leading figures in the higher-education establishment genuinely take the view that their policies have led to an improvement of standards in British universities. Advocates of the ideology of managerialism fervently believed that they were embarking on a program of reform. But, as often happens, reforms from above turn into counterreforms. The motives that inspire a program of reform are never straightforward and often express a variety of competing interests. In this case, from the outset, issues that pertain to the quality of higher education were confused with quite separate concerns about finance and the exigencies of managerial control. In retrospect, it is evident that pressures that were external to problems specific to higher education were the impulse behind the changes. But to this day, it is often difficult to distinguish rhetoric from policy objectives. For example, is the project rooted in a commitment to widening access, or is the government primarily concerned with university education on the cheap?

## THE FALSE PROMISE OF THE MARKET

Successive British education ministers have come to regard the university sector as a commercial enterprise that ought to be run along straightforward business lines. According to this perspective, universities exist not simply to educate, but also to sell education in a competitive market to customers who, in the past, were wrongly thought of as just scholars. Academics and their institutions are continually encouraged to compete against one another and to market their courses as if they were selling just another consumer good.

In reality, the provision of academic teaching does not easily fit into the paradigm of consumption. University education is not a thing that can be bought and sold—it is the outcome of a relationship. Knowledge about a discipline cannot be passively consumed. Its provision and acquisition requires a creative tension between teaching and learning. In particular, research-based teaching presupposes an interactive relationship with students. Such teaching does not rely merely on imparting information, but on the transmission of the kind of knowledge that could stimulate students to work out their own ideas. Such research-based knowledge cannot be standardized and transformed into a pre-packaged consumer good. It is interactive and subjective, and it relies on provoking interest in the subject matter.

The very attempt to reorient education toward the dictates of consumption turns into something other than a relationship. In reality, what consumer-oriented teaching provides is not knowledge, but a form of education that is equated with information or a skill. The shift from knowledge to skill is one of the defining outcomes of the attempt to marketize higher education. This shift is by no means an accidental outcome of the process. A skills-based system of higher education was robustly advocated by Lord Dearing in his 1997 report, *Higher Education in the Learning Society*. The Dearing Report, which has come to dominate government policy on higher education, advocates a form of university teaching that can be readily consumed by the customer. The report sought to formalize the trend toward separating teaching from research. It proposed a style of teaching that could be treated as a technical skill—one that was readily quantifiable and easily audited and assessed on the bases of predictable outcomes. From the Dearing perspective teaching becomes less the communication of subject-based knowledge than the imparting of skills. Although the report pays lip service to the objective of "world-class higher-education teaching," the objective of Dearing is the commodification of university life. It was this report that proposed the mandatory training of university teachers. It demanded the accreditation of university teachers through the Institute for Learning and Teaching in Higher Education (ILT). The assembly-line teacher training of a new generation of university lecturers aims to create a new breed of academic, one that has been socialized into accepting the worldview of the ILT.

The orientation toward the customer has not improved the quality of university life. What it has done is to force academics to become subservient to philistine bureaucrats. The auditor runs the system, but it is far from clear just what is being audited. The attempt to reduce the qualitative process of intellectual engagement to a series of figures makes little sense. There is simply no way of measuring quality when it comes to intellectual exploration and the imparting of knowledge. Policymakers and their bureaucrats understand this dilemma and periodically try to find artificial ways of introducing forms of control that resemble the pressure of market forces. It was in this vein that Baroness Blackstone, the former minister in charge of university education, floated the idea of using student feedback as the basis on which lecturers' promotion and salary enhancement would be based. In February 2001, she told the Commons Education Select Committee that taking the evidence from students—who, according to Blackstone, "should know best"—was an excellent way of making decisions about lecturers' salaries.

The idea that the customer/student knows best fundamentally alters the relationship between the university teacher and the student. A relationship based on collaboration and cooperation is swiftly transformed into one that is characterized by a basic conflict of interest. Unfortunately by transferring the relationship of conflict that characterizes the marketplace into the classroom, bureaucrats threaten to erode further the collaboration and trust between teacher and student that is the prerequisite of higher education. The shift toward the customer forces lecturers to adopt practices that they think students will want. And if what students want conflicts with what they need to acquire knowledge of a discipline, many lecturers now feel that they need to give way to customer demand. In this way, the very attempt to sell education devalues its content. Lecturers who know that their position is closely linked to the approval they receive from their students will learn to avoid teaching practices that might undermine their popularity. As a result many university courses have already dropped theoretical themes and other "difficult" bits from their program.

The market may work efficiently in the sphere of economic life. But it is difficult to reconcile the provision of knowledge, intellectual experimentation, and academic endeavor with economic calculation and the search for profit. Academic work requires long-term commitment to a specific subject. It often has little direct relevance to the demands of economic life, and its importance cannot be calculated in the language of hard cash. Sometimes, difficult and unpopular ideas generated in one era all of a sudden acquire significance in another a long time after their authors have died. The benefits of such work cannot be judged in the here and now. Furthermore, the merits of academic work may well be realized through the contribution of another researcher working in another society. The imposition of a short-termist regime of calculation fosters a climate where academics have little incentive to work creatively. In the domain of university life, the market neither stimulates efficiency nor provides an incentive for creativity. It merely offers a short-term, quick-fix approach to intellectual life.

Of course, academics like to earn high salaries and are no less interested in money than are other professionals. However, high-quality academic work is not primarily defined by economic calculation. World-class research requires an interest in a subject for its own sake. Such work is driven by an ambition for rewards that are not directly calculable in monetary terms. Many of the important things that academics do make no economic sense. Individuals who spend years researching an obscure topic and then spend half a decade writing up their findings are unlikely to be responsive to market fluctuations. Nevertheless, what they do constitutes an important aspect of academic life. The marketization of education has negated this spirit of intellectual enterprise. As we shall see, it has also altered the way that the British university works.

## THE CULTURE OF AUDITING

Despite the attempt to subordinate the academy to the dictates of economic calculation, it is not market forces but a centralized system of bureaucratic auditing that dominates university life. The relentless expansion of red tape is the clearest manifestation of this development. It seems that every post-Dearing initiative begets more administration and paperwork. The recently established Institute for Learning and Teaching in Higher Education has provided yet another opportunity to test the skills of academics in the art of filling in forms. Some universities now devote precious resources to training their staff to fill in application forms for joining the ILT. Academics are now encouraged to take part in a two-hour course designed to introduce them to the mysteries of this highly complex enterprise. The time devoted to learning how to get around the red tape pales into insignificance in light of the effort that individual academics spend on their paperwork, most of which has little purpose other than to provide the data necessary to placate quality assurance inspectors.

Although there is widespread awareness—even resentment—of the high cost of living under the regime of the quality assurance industry, its long-term consequences for teaching are seldom explored. Many proponents of quality assurance auditing genuinely believe that the pain inflicted on the university sector is temporary and soon the Quality Assurance Agency will deliver a "lighter touch." Others contend that the system has "worked" and that soon academics will be able to reallocate the time they now spend on filling in forms toward applying themselves to teaching and research. Sadly, the bureaucratization of teaching is unlikely to be a temporary episode, and this will have regrettable consequences for teaching quality. The regime of quality assurance auditing does not merely lead to an increase in the volume of paperwork. The pressure of red tape distracts teachers from a creative engagement with their subject matter and leads to the diminishing of the quality of university education. Red tape also eats into the time teachers have to spend with their students. Externally imposed auditing diverts teaching away from pedagogic issues and toward a quantifiable territory. The main objective of quality assurance is the inspection of how departments go about doing their job. This stress on process is oriented toward assuring systems of management rather than the quality of teaching. The ethos of auditing puts pressure on teachers to elaborate procedures, which can be compared and standardized throughout the university system. As a result, the university sector has become so obsessed with procedures that little creative energy is devoted to the content of what is being taught. In any case, the description of process says little about the quality of teaching. Reports from colleagues suggest that quality assurance inspectors have little interest in the content of teaching or pedagogic issues that pertain to specific academic disciplines. Their preoccupation is not so much with the quality of teaching but with the formal procedures that departments deploy. Unfortunately, the elaboration of formal processes of delivery does not necessarily secure the outcome desired. The obsession with paper trails inexorably leads to the demand for more paper.

The auditing ethos does not leave the prevailing culture of teaching untouched. It encourages teachers to become more concerned with how they are seen to be doing their job rather than what they actually do. From the perspective of the quality assurance industry, the content of teaching is actually subservient to its form. This centralized machinery, which is driven by the mission of imposing a common framework on diverse institutions, is committed to a style of teaching that can be quantified and audited. Unfortunately, once teaching becomes an auditable object, it has little in common with the subtle, ambitious, critical, and open-ended phenomenon that once went by the name of a good university education.

## THE OUTCOME OF BUREAUCRATIZATION

In a very short period of time, the British university system has adopted practices unrecognizable to students who studied a generation ago. The most important developments of this process of bureaucratization are outlined below.

### The Loss of Institutional Flexibility

In global terms, the loss of institutional flexibility is one of the most striking developments to afflict the British university. In most industrial societies it is expected that different institutions of higher education do different things. In the United States, there are distinct institutional cultures that inform pedagogic practices. Elite institutions, such as Ivy League universities, are not expected to compete with community colleges. In Britain, a highly centralized system of auditing subjects all higher-education institutions to the same system of regulation. As a result, the effect of government policy is to encourage a dreary atmosphere of uniformity, which actually prevents institutions from playing to their strengths.

Even in its own terms, we now have an irrational system devoted to meeting formal targets imposed from above. Anyone familiar with organizational theory knows that centrally set targets and the demands of the market contradict one another. In this case the university's relations with its ostensible consumers is mediated through a central bureaucracy. As a result, the British university is responding not so much to the demands of real customers than to the way the educational establishment interprets these demands. There is considerable evidence that the bureaucratization of the university actually puts off many "customers." *The Student Living Report*, a survey published by MORI in January 2001, indicated that something like four out of ten students found that their courses did not stretch them intellectually.

### The Transformation of the Student–Teacher Relationship

Managerial pressure toward the standardization of lecturing has undermined the idea that the student–teacher relationship is a collaborative one. University administrators now force lecturers to treat their relationship with students as if it were a formal transaction. The relatively informal student–teacher relationship has been turned into a contractual one. A course outline and reading list is increasingly regarded as a contract that obliges the academic to deliver clearly outlined objectives. This contractual approach directly violates the idea of openended learning. By guaranteeing in advance that a course will deliver such and such outcomes, a teacher actually short-circuits the process of learning.

The normalization of the student–teacher relationship into a transaction creates the potential for a permanent, silent conflict of interest between two parties that have every reason to act in a calculating way toward one another. Gone is the idea that a student is there to be inspired and challenged by his or her academic mentor. Lecturers who are concerned with avoiding unpopularity, hassle, complaints, and litigation have little energy to provide a high standard of education.

Lecturers are increasingly more interested in communicating what they think students want to hear than what undergraduates need in order to master a subject. Many lecturers are reluctant to take actions that might offend their students. Yet many important aspects of creative teaching, such as criticizing poor work and putting pressure on undergraduates, are likely to be experienced as offensive by some. Worse still, the pressure of a contractual obligation forces teachers to adopt a formulaic style that treats everyone the same. The normalization of the student–teacher relationship encourages a disregard for the needs of the individual. It limits the room available for flexible and spontaneous interaction. Why? Because the contract comes in between teacher and student. Even with the best will, academics are likely to risk their position if they deviate from the contract in order to do what is right for the individual student.

The transformation of the student–teacher relationship into a commercial one does not simply have a regrettable impact on what happens in seminars and lecture halls. It bears on every aspect of university life. The change it brings to assessment and examination is a good example of this. Academics who are forced to court student approval know that what concerns their customers above all is the mark they receive for their essays and exams. According to the new ethos, what defines a good course is that it holds out the promise of good grades.

### The Deskilling of Academics into Learners

Auditing agencies like the QAA and the ILT actively promote a teaching style that devalues the transformative component of pedagogy. Teachers are encouraged to speak to a script. They are offered advice and guidance about what constitutes a discipline and what kinds of outcomes are expected of their courses. This bureaucratic pressure reconstructs teaching as a predictable skill. The construction of an informal curriculum, a system of benchmarking or of quality assurance, deprives academics of the autonomy to explore their subject in accordance with their intellectual interest and research.

The deskilling of academics is taken further and strikingly affirmed through eliding the distinction between teacher and learner. This pseudodemocratic innovation expresses the conviction that the academic can make no special claim to intellectual authority. The academic who is a learner plays the role of a facilitator rather than that of a generator of knowledge. This is a pseudodemocratic masquerade that obscures the fact that the university is systematically lowering the expectations it has of it students.

### Rendering Research Banal

The culture of auditing has also helped to render British academic research banal. Bureaucratic pressure mediated through the Research Assessment Exercise (RAE) forces academics to produce a certain number of publications by a particular date. Predictably, the emphasis is on quantity rather than content. Academics are producing far more publications than ever before, and most of these publications help to stimulate the British paper industry rather than intellectual development. When academics are forced to research and write on demand, the creative spirit behind intellectual endeavor becomes exhausted.

One of the most unfortunate outcomes of the bureaucratization of the university has been the imposition of a policy agenda on funding for research. Increasingly, public and charitable foundations invite academics to apply for funding for projects that these bodies consider important. As a result, independent academic research is compromised by the dictates of outside policy consideration. Many academics have little choice but to sign up for such projects.

### The Rationalization of Knowledge

The standardization of teaching has fostered a climate where knowledge has become rationalized and turned into easily digestible products. This process is most clearly symbolized by the ascendancy of the "handout culture." Teachers are expected to provide students with "information" or skills that are useful in the world of work. The training of the mind is no longer the central role for academics, who are now in the business of ensuring that their teaching has a vocational ethos.

### The Infantilization of Education

Probably the most objectionable consequence of the bureaucratization of the university is the infantilization of education. Patronizing students has become institutionalized. Students are treated as if they were an endangered species, or at least as if they were pupils in a primary school. The contract demands that everything is spelled out and little is left to chance. Student-centered teaching has become a euphemism for accommodating the customer. Academics are there to "support" rather than transform the vulnerable population of students. The trend toward treating students as if they were children is clearly reflected in the way the university is increasingly assuming a familial role. The growing therapeutic function of the university—guidance, counseling, formal support systems—highlights the minimalist expectation that the academy has of its undergraduates.

It is difficult for academics to disagree with the customer—for the customer is always right. Consequently, academics are expected to adopt a "Have a Good Day!" attitude toward students. The university is not merely selling courses—it also needs to throw marking and assessment into the deal. As a result, the infantilized university systematically practices "positive marking." The pressure to fulfill the bureaucracy's targets forces lecturers and their departments to adopt customer-friendly forms of assessment, resulting in the demise of the examination and its replacement by a diffuse pattern of assessment. In most universities, lecturers and departments are almost never reprimanded for grade inflation and other customer-friendly practices. There are, however, numerous instances where departments have been warned that they are failing too many students or that they are not giving enough 2.1 or first-class degrees (in Britain, 1 or 2.1 shows that students have achieved very high marks).

The infantilization of education is also promoted through pedagogic styles that are designed to flatter the students. Students are no longer expected to study but to learn, and since complex ideas are not learned but studied, the intellectual horizon of the learner is restricted to the assimilation of information and the acquisition of skills. The bureaucracy's advocacy of the idea that we are all "learners" affirms its intense anti-intellectual ethos.

The pedagogy peddled by the ILT is primarily designed to keep students keen and interested. In principle, every teaching technique is worth a try. But the manner in which the ILT promotes its techniques indicates that it has a distinct objective of keeping students engaged and happy. For example, group work is used in a way similar to the use of "circle time" in primary education. While this technique makes sense when used with 5-year-olds, in the university it serves to distract students from gaining knowledge through intellectual struggle and hard work. As teaching acquires a greater therapeutic function, the idea that university students are mature, intelligent individuals capable of intellectual independence becomes further devalued.

## CONCLUSION

Since the 1990s, the bureaucratization of the university has been justified on the grounds that these changes are necessary for expanding access to higher education. Advocates of the new university contend that it is not possible to retain the ideals that were once associated with academic education. Worse still, apologists for the present system are more than happy to accept the idea that in this brave new world quality can and sometimes must be compromised. Sadly, quality education is often stigmatized as elitist for excluding those who cannot take advantage of it. Implicitly, the educational bureaucracy takes the view that access to the university must mean access to an inferior product. It is, however, reluctant to acknowledge that although there is greater access, it is to something other than a university.

Paradoxically, the transformation of the British university is sometimes promoted as part of a program of reform. The idea that the university has undergone a program of reform is a very strange one. Reforms in other spheres of life do not proceed on the assumption that the institution they are about to tackle will be inferior to the one that preceded it. So in the postwar period, universal access to health care was not promoted on the premise that this was away of providing a quality of service inferior to what had existed previously. The establishment of the National Health Service (NHS) did not mean that the hospital was turned into a first-aid station in the way that the university has been reinvented as a college of further education.

It is important to note that the forward march of bureaucracy has rarely been tested and even less rarely resisted. Bureaucracy has succeeded in gaining the acquiescence and sometimes the collusion of a significant section of the academic community. One reason why it has been so spectacularly successful is because it has created an atmosphere where academics have forgotten what the university should be about. It is not too late to do a bit of remembering.

# 3

# Accounting for Anxiety: Economic and Cultural Imperatives Transforming University Life

*Barry Smart*

## INTRODUCTION: THE UNIVERSITY IN AN AGE OF "PERMANENT TRANSITION"

Although the university as an institution is longstanding, having been around since the Middle Ages, it has lost its relatively protected status and become increasingly exposed to processes of economic and cultural transformation. The university has been identified as a key source of innovative technological information as an increasingly informational, flexible, and globally extensive neoliberal capitalism has developed. Through its increasingly close articulation with the new informational mode of capitalist economic development, the institution of the university has become subject to a process of permanent transition (Castells 1989; Delanty 2001). The adoption of neoliberal economic policies has precipitated a wide-ranging promotion of market forces and has contributed to a process of transformation, and in some respects an erosion, of public services, particularly in the areas of education, health, and welfare (Bourdieu 1998). In the case of the university, a process of "marketization" has had a considerable impact not only on how the institution operates, but also more broadly on the status and value of knowledge (Delanty 2001; Lyotard 1984). The promotion and adoption of entrepreneurial values and commercial practices within higher education, and the increasing tendency to regard students as consumers and knowledge as a commodity, has led a number of analysts to speculate on the emergence of a significantly transformed system of higher education (Delanty 2001; Parker & Jary 1995; Plater 1995; Prichard & Willmott 1997; Ritzer 1996; 1998; Ryan 1998).

The principle that secular learning had value independently of theology was established in the course of the twelfth century in Europe. From that time, university institutions, divided into four or five faculties (Theology, Arts or Philosophy, Law, Medicine, and Music), licensed by the Church, and "incorporated by charter and regulated by a self-governing academic body" (Davies 1997: 361), began to emerge across the length and breadth of the continent. Signs of a medieval monastic legacy remain in some of the forms of organization, ceremonial rituals, and cultural practices that continue to be a part of contemporary university life. Medieval monastic traces are evident in "the conferring of degrees and honours, the role of ceremony, the belief in an underlying principle of harmony and the notion of faculties of knowledge" (Delanty 2001: 29). But with the development of the modern university from the Enlightenment onwards, the legacy has been reduced in significance. The modern "rationalization of higher education," initiated and shaped by the nation state, effected a wide-ranging transformation of university life (Parker & Jary 1995; Ritzer 1996; 1998). Now the analogy frequently drawn between the institution of the university and that of the monastery (Eco 1987) is increasingly difficult to sustain. The rationalization of higher education has transformed the modern university into an institution that is increasingly embracing the values of the "corporate culture of industry" (Delanty 2001: 120), and as this has occurred, the institution has begun to resemble a knowledge-processing factory (Ritzer 1996: 139).

In a series of reflections on Europe and the United States during the closing decades of the twentieth century, Umberto Eco (1987) notes that contemporary social life is in "permanent transition" and is, in consequence, marked by insecurity, anxiety, and a sense of crisis. Aspects of contemporary social life that exemplify these features include, "the medievalization of the city" and the fragmentation of social life, environmental problems, risks associated with the consequences of economic and technological developments, the worry and discomfort—"adventurous insecurity"—that has become a frequent feature of both the local and the more extensive modern journey, and last, but by no means least, the signs of a "general crisis" affecting universities (1987: 75–79). Insofar as our age is one of permanent transition, new ways of coping with the consequences and making the most of any disorganization and disorder are required. Acknowledging the emergence of a new "culture of constant readjustment," Eco remarks that this is "how medieval man invented the university," but then he adds in a more critical vein, "with the same carefree attitude that the vagabond clerks today assume in transforming and perhaps destroying it" (1987: 84). The identity of Eco's "vagabond clerks" is not clear, but analyses of the processes of permanent transformation to which the university and higher education have become subject effectively illustrate the respects in which the values of commercialism, a managerial and marketing ethos, and the imposition of an audit culture are steadily transforming, if not compromising, the standards, values, and practices of intellectual life (Klein 2000; Parker and Jary 1995; Ritzer 1998; Ryan 1998).

Notwithstanding its medieval roots, the institution of the university has changed significantly, and it continues to be transformed by neoliberal economic policies, innovations in information technology, and the cultural values of a consumer society (Delanty 2001). While no longer subject to the sacred authority of the Church, universities remain subject to the secular authority of the State, and, in turn, they have been increasingly exposed to the vagaries of the capitalist marketplace with the imposition of "free-market" economic policies and the growth of a culture of consumption. Learning undoubtedly still has value, but *what* is (to be) learned and the *value* accorded to learning has changed considerably, as has the institution within which higher learning is promoted and practiced.

## REFLECTIONS ON THE TRANSFORMATION OF UNIVERSITY LIFE

There are two key questions that need to be addressed: (1) "What is happening to universities and to higher education?" and (2) "How are we to account for the changes that are taking place?" University life has been subject to transformation throughout the modern era, and concern has been expressed by different generations of social scientists about the direction in which the institution of the university has been moving under the impact of processes of "rationalization."

In a lecture on "science as a vocation" presented in 1918 in Munich, Max Weber reflected on the changing conditions of university life in Germany. Weber argued that German universities were beginning to resemble their U.S. counterparts and were becoming "state capitalist" enterprises as increased operating costs meant that they required "considerable funds." Elaborating on the implications for those working within higher education Weber noted their loss of autonomy and their increasingly "quasi-proletarian existence," and he remarked that an "extraordinarily wide gulf . . . exists between the chief of these large, capitalist, university enterprises and the usual full professor of the old style" (1970: 131). Driven by an interest in maximizing fee income, German universities became "engaged in a most ridiculous competition for enrolments" (1970: 133). In consequence, it became increasingly necessary for new recruits to be effective not only as "scholars" but also as "teachers," even though it was recognized that the two do not necessarily coincide, and enrollment levels on courses began to be regarded as a key indicator of the quality of teaching. In response to these developments Weber commented that he had a "deep distrust" of crowd-pleasing courses and that academic life had become a "mad hazard" (1970: 134).

Although writing half a century later, Theodore Roszak surveys a period of transformation in U.S. university life that overlaps to some extent the historical moment addressed by Weber. Roszak describes U.S. universities as accommodating to the interests of the agencies of church, state, and corporate wealth responsible for funding higher education. Outlining the development of two traditions—those of "service" and "scholarship"—associated with U.S. higher learning, Roszak notes that "service came to mean the indiscriminate adaptation of the university to every demand that moneyed interests and the general public could imagine making" (1969: 15). The emphasis in this tradition was placed upon catering to the community and its needs and developing the university as an "emporium of marketable skills" (1969: 15). The other tradition of learning, "scholarship," derived from the German university system and the experiences of those who went there to work and study after the Civil War. Roszak argues that the two traditions have remained in unresolved conflict, with the "service station" ideal being expressed in indiscriminate "collaboration between the universities, the corporate world and the government" and the ideal of "scholarship" degenerating into the production of "barnloads of dissertations, monographs, learned journals, . . . new interpretations, revised interpretations and revised revisions of interpretations," which have rendered it increasingly socially irrelevant (1969: 16–19). Roszak laments both the "lack of moral discrimination" in the work of the service technician and the "lack of moral responsiveness" on the part of the academic scholar. In a manner that bears comparison with our own shortcomings, Roszak notes a reticence to raise fundamental questions of "purpose, direction and value," to ask: "What is to be learnt and why?"

The academic world described by Roszak is one in which the tradition of service increasingly predominates, for it delivers the goods—"the money, the students, and the prestige that are rapidly making higher education one of the country's largest industries" (1969: 25). Roszak's conclusion is that the relative generosity of the "world-as-it-is" toward higher education is reciprocated by higher education's unquestioning preparation of new recruits equipped and ready to assume their places in the "skilled ranks of an increasingly cybernated society: the corporation, the military, the government bureaucracy" (1969: 25). The cultural and economic imperatives shaping the modern university depicted by Roszak derive from the close articulation between the needs and interests of a Fordist industrial capitalism and those of the Federal government, particularly in relation to military and defense requirements. What is implicated here is the influential impact of the "military–industrial complex" on the shaping of academic life (Rosen 1969). In the current neoliberal, postindustrial, and globalized context, the influence of government and industry on higher education and university life has grown significantly. Increasingly, higher education is required to accommodate, if not submit to, the market, as well as service the technological needs of a rapidly developing informational economy.

In the aftermath of protests on campuses across France associated with the events of "May '68," Jean-François Lyotard made a number of critical observations on the question of what was happening to universities. In a manner that has close parallels with the views of Roszak, Lyotard notes how the university is increasingly required to adapt to the requirements of modern capitalism. Specifically, Lyotard argues that whereas the institution of the university was formerly sheltered from the requirement to contribute to the increased reproduction of capital, now higher-education and teaching functions constitute moments in the circuit of capital reproduction. Elaborating on the way in which the university is being transformed under the domination of capital, Lyotard notes that the "'contents' of culture and the pedagogical relation" are being increasingly subordinated to the "operative categories of capital: production and consumption" (1993: 48). Lyotard describes the despair and anxiety of students and teachers in the face of a system that "ends up by devouring everything that is outside it," and he emphasizes the inappropriateness of "ancient university practices" to the process of expansion required to enhance the circulation of capital (1993: 48: 51). The university has become a vital component of the capitalist and bureaucratic system, and this is exemplified for Lyotard by the function of the university teacher, which has become, "to consume cultural contents in order to produce cultural contents that can be consumed by the students: to produce saleable students (consumable labour force) . . . the only value that governs the real functioning of the teaching establishments is the same that operates openly at the surface of society: produce and consume no matter what, in ever-increasing quantity" (1993: 57). Implied here is a new condition of knowledge, one subsequently identified as "postmodern."

## THE "POSTMODERN" CONDITIONING
## OF UNIVERSITY LIFE

Where knowledge is deemed to be of intrinsic value (as in the case of nineteenth-century Germany), the function of the university is represented as being the opening up of the whole body of learning and the elaboration of the principles and foundations of knowledge. Here we are on the terrain of the disinterested pursuit of learning, a position that has an affinity with the tradition of "scholarship" discussed by Roszak. In contrast to this form of self-legitimation of knowledge, Lyotard (1984) identifies a second form of legitimation that invokes a different criterion, one of "usefulness." The role of knowledge in this instance is to inform about reality, to enhance the understanding of what might be possible for the potentially autonomous or self-managing subject. Here, Lyotard notes, "the relation of knowledge to society and the State . . . is in principle a relation of the means to the end" (1984: 36). However, in contrast to the "service" tradition identified by Roszak, Lyotard argues that a critical function remains implicit in this second form of knowledge legitimation, in two related senses: (1) Scholarly cooperation may be withdrawn where the state is recognized to be unjust or to be badly representing the interests of civil society. (2) Authority and expertise can be deployed to reveal the extent to which autonomy remains a project that has yet to be realized. Both of these forms of legitimation have been prominent in university life, but as the status of knowledge has been transformed, they have become far less significant.

A combination of factors is identified by Lyotard as having transformed the condition of knowledge and as having rendered earlier ways of legitimating the pursuit of knowledge is irrelevant, if not meaningless. Prominent among these are post-Second-World-War developments in computer technologies, a neo-liberal renewal of capitalist accumulation, and the emergence of new forms of capital circulation in the form of "multinational corporations," and the cultivation of a culture of consumption.

With the development of information-processing technology, important aspects of learning (acquisition, classification, availability, and exploitation) have been transformed. In this context, knowledge, and the manner in which knowledge is legitimated, cannot remain the same. Increasingly, what counts as knowledge is determined by the potential for translatability into "bits" of information, into computer language and the simultaneous possibility of the realization of commodity value in the marketplace. In short, what is emerging, in Lyotard's view, is a "mercantilization of knowledge." The relationship that exists between those involved in the activity of knowledge production and use and what is regarded as "knowledge" increasingly assumes the form of a commodity relation. Knowledge, as Lyotard observes, is "produced in order to be sold . . . and consumed in order to be valorized in a new production: in both cases the goal is exchange" (1984: 5). As Marx (1973) anticipated, knowledge has become *the* force of production and with growing recognition of its commercial value, what is demanded of knowledge by students, the state and institutions of higher education is not "truth" or "wisdom" but the salability of "performance-oriented skills" (Lyotard 1984: 51; see also Ryan 1998).

Increasingly it is "performativity," the technical capacity to augment power— or what in this case amounts to the same thing, to produce context control—that legitimates education and learning. Modern technology is promoted as promising mastery or control and the prospect of enhancing the performance of the system within which it is deployed, although not, as we now increasingly realize, without risk (Beck 1992). In so far as performativity now constitutes the criterion for the legitimation of knowledge, research funds are allocated accordingly, and those "sectors that are unable to argue that they contribute even indirectly to the optimization of the system's performance are doomed to senescence" (Lyotard 1984: 47).

The consequences of these developments for the university are far-reaching. Higher education has become subject to the demand that it should become far more "functional." What this generally means is that universities should increasingly tailor their activities to meet the demands for forms of knowledge and skill deemed necessary to enhance the performance of the existing institutions of economic and social life. Within higher education, this has led to increasing significance being accorded to the requirement to be more responsive to the needs of the economy. The upshot has been that universities are under pressure to meet the training requirements of the growing numbers of "professionals employed by corporations to invent, maintain, and innovate with regard to sophisticated technologies and products" (Slaughter & Leslie 1997: 27). As well as professional and technical training components in degree programs, there are now more vocationally related courses and an increased emphasis on careers, job retraining, and continuing education.

As the impact of neoliberal economic policies on the funding of higher education further accelerates the "mercantilization of knowledge," so knowledge is increasingly rendered into a commodity and the learning process into a commercial exchange between the producer–teacher and the consumer–student. Furthermore, the deployment of labor-saving new technologies is transforming the communication or delivery of knowledge, making it possible for teachers to be replaced by "memory banks" (Lyotard 1984: 50). This fits in well with the neoliberal equation of greater economic "efficiency" with relative reductions in levels of public expenditure (Gorz 1999). Just as the learning process is being transformed, so, in a comparable manner, the research process is increasingly vulnerable to becoming a commercial exchange between the producer–researcher and the consumer–corporation (Ahuja 2001). In turn, the research process has become increasingly distorted by the imposition of performance targets and associated auditing processes. Increasingly, research is being designed to meet the demands of the research auditing exercise, an exemplification of what has been described as "the irrationality of rationality" (Ritzer 1996: 139; see also O'Leary 2001).

An influential attempt to account for these wide-ranging changes taking place in the field of higher education has been offered by George Ritzer (1996: 1998), who has drawn parallels between the commercial processes of rationalization that have transformed the fast-food industry and those to which modern universities have become increasingly subject.

## "McUNIVERSITY" AND THE PROCESSING OF HIGHER EDUCATION

The broad argument outlined by Ritzer is that the attributes of instrumental rationality associated with modern bureaucracy by Max Weber (1970) have been extended and enhanced within the fast-food business developed by McDonald's. Subsequently the principles governing McDonald's business practices have been adopted by organizations in other sectors of the economy. In a discussion of this wide-ranging social process of "McDonaldization," the key features of which include the pursuit of increasing efficiency, calculability, predictability, and control, Ritzer argues that few, if any, organizations have remained unaffected. The impact on institutions of higher education is evident, Ritzer argues, in the proliferation of computer-graded assessments and the adoption of textbooks and accompanying multichoice questions (*efficiency*); the increasing preoccupation with quantification exemplified by the emphasis on numbers enrolled, grades achieved, rankings of universities in terms of teaching quality scores and research output grades, which are assumed to correspond to differences in quality of performance (*calculability*); the growth of standardized courses with comparable syllabuses, employing textbooks and multichoice modes of examination (*predictability*); and the regulation of teaching, learning, and assessment through the introduction of centralized timetable, appraisal, and evaluation and grading procedures (*control*) (Ritzer 1996: 42–43, 64–68, 86–87, 106–107).

Ritzer argues that these features of a wide-ranging process of rationalization have had the paradoxical effect of turning the modern university into a "highly irrational place" (1996: 139) where student–consumers are processed through an environment that is increasingly adopting the organizational practices of commercial enterprises engaged in commodity production (Klein 2001). Increasing numbers of students passing through higher-education institutions without an appropriate increase in the level of funding has meant more large lectures, fewer opportunities for face-to-face contact with teachers, and an increase in bureaucracy and administration, effectively turning the higher-education experience into an assembly-line process. Factor in proliferating forms of auditing associated with teaching quality and research assessment exercises, along with the additional demands placed on university staff by the Higher Education Funding Council's transparency review, and it is not difficult to understand Ritzer's conclusion that modern universities have become irrational places where increasingly scarce resources of staff time and funds are being redeployed to prepare an account of teaching and research activity for the purposes of external audit. These developments have been described as manifestations of the increased power of management, marketing, and business philosophy within higher education and the significantly diminished autonomy of teachers and researchers (Parker & Jary 1995). But what lies behind such changes?

In a time of permanent transition, where change has become a routine feature of everyday life, social, cultural, and economic institutions must of necessity continually readjust to the changing world around them.

Elaborating on the ways in which the modern university has been changing with the development of a society increasingly shaped by a culture of consumerism, Ritzer remarks that the university is becoming "a means of educational consumption" (1998: 151) and the student a consumer. Noting the rising cost of higher education, Ritzer adds that students and their parents will be inclined to bring a consumer mentality to the process of higher learning. The implication is of a significant process of transformation affecting higher learning—choices of institution, fields of study, what it is to be a student, what counts as worth knowing, and what value is accorded to knowledge. In the McUniversity the answer given by the student–consumer to Robert Lynd's (1939) challenging question: "Knowledge for *what*," is likely to be "a good (2.1) degree" or "a good job," and within the political establishment the answer given by the "new public management" (Ryan 1998) is likely to be "economic growth" or "economic competitiveness." The reality of university life, as Ritzer depicts it, is that students want their institutions to "operate like their banks and fast-food restaurants" (1998: 152); they want their consumer expectations met, and universities have little choice but to respond positively to the demands of their "customers."

In the words of one report, following the introduction of tuition fees at British universities, "fees will let students wield customer clout" (Wild 1998). It is in the new means of consumption that it is suggested universities may find an answer to their predicament, of how to maintain and perhaps increase enrollment levels while coping with reduced levels of funding and the cost-cutting that is a corollary. Automatic cash machines, the fast-food industry, megamalls, and home shopping networks are identified as exemplars of the reduced-cost but increased consumer satisfaction scenario that Ritzer considers universities have to emulate.

The consequences of a consumerist orientation in higher education are already becoming apparent. The question of compromised academic standards and grade-inflation refuses to go away (Yorke & Alderman 1999; Furedi 2001). Consumer–students do not expect to have to put up with "substandard goods" (something less than a 2.1 degree?) or "substandard service." (A poor mark must reflect a course poorly taught if the customer is always right?) Certainly Ritzer believes that the consumer-sensitive McUniversity will be inclined to limit poor grades, reduce the drop-out rate, and do all it can to ensure that students benefit and, more importantly, feel they have benefited from the educational services provided (1998: 156). And in this context "benefit" is generally equated with obtaining a decent job rather than finding courses that are intellectually challenging (Furedi 2001). Should the satisfaction of the student–consumer be the primary objective of higher education? What is the point of higher education, of going to university? Is there any similarity with the consumer experience of going to a fast-food outlet or a shopping mall, as Ritzer implies? It might be argued that the central point of going to university is not to engage in another form of consumption but to become different—that the objective is, "to change the customer, and the process by which this is done, and the end results, may leave the customer very dissatisfied indeed: the high grades that were unreasonably expected and never achieved; the easy ride that was anticipated but never experienced; the cherished assumptions and ideas that were blown apart" (Alderman 2001).

In so far as cultivation of the intellect, helping to "make public opinion more self-critical and more circumspect" (Roszak 1969: 33), remains a part of university life worth preserving, the development of the university as a means of educational consumption is to be regarded with regret and alarm.

## NEOLIBERAL CAPITALISM AND THE CORPORATE SPONSORSHIP OF UNIVERSITY LIFE

The common denominator behind many of the forms of reorganization and restructuring to which higher-education institutions have been subjected in the past 25 years is the issue of inadequate levels of funding. As Ritzer briefly acknowledges in his discussion of the pressures on universities, economic factors are prominent, the "relative decline in the funding of higher education"

(1998: 154) has precipitated reductions in full-time tenured faculty staff, an increase in part-time, short-contract forms of employment (McJobs), and continuing poor levels of pay compared to other comparable professions. The various forms of audit that have been introduced in Britain in relation to teaching and research, frequently justified in terms of the need to ensure "accountability" and secure better value from public expenditure, have in practice merely served as blunt mechanisms for allocating inadequate levels of funding that have not kept pace with the increase in student numbers (Ryan 1998: 31).

The problem of funding in the public sector has long been recognized. In 1918 Joseph Schumpeter drew attention to limits on the fiscal capacity of the state and anticipated the future difficulty of raising sufficient tax revenue to meet demands for "higher and higher public expenditure" in a society within which the "driving force is individual interest" (1954: 24). In the 1960s, a period in which the pursuit of individual interest had become an even more significant driving force, J. K. Galbraith noted the "affluence in private goods" and lamented the "discrimination against . . . investment in the public domain" (Galbraith 1963: 249: 223) in general, and education in particular. Furthermore, where a claim tends to be made in favor of the value of education, Galbraith argues, the conventional wisdom is to talk in terms of the benefits of economic growth rather than "its independent and . . . higher justification" (1963: 226; see also Ryan 1998). In a broadly related manner, Daniel Bell wrote in the 1970s of the "real crises ahead for the public household" (1976: 236). The critical issue for Bell was the difficulty governments in the West were destined to face as they sought to reconcile an individualist ethos and a defense of the idea of personal liberty, the values of private consumption, and an antipathy toward personal taxation with rising demands for public services. In the absence of any "normative commitment to a public household" (Bell 1976: 249), how are self-interest and public interest to be reconciled? The economic dilemma Bell anticipated has been met with a neoliberal response, one that has sought to "undermine the public interest" and simultaneously eulogize and encourage private interest and the private sector (Bourdieu 1998: 3).

Reflecting on the development in Britain from 1979 onwards of a "free market society," Philo and Miller (2001) have drawn attention to the impact of a concerted policy of public-sector regulation. The representation of the public sector as "inefficient" has provided a politically effective rationale for the introduction of various mechanisms of accountability and the employment of strata of managers and accountants to ensure that those providing public services are formally required to give an account of the quality of their work. Philo and Miller argue that a key function of the new managerial strata has been "to impose 'efficiency savings'" (2001: 9), which has generally meant enforcing increased levels of production at a reduced level, in relative terms, of both resource and reward. In turn, the introduction of various measures of performance—in the case of the university sector the rounds of teaching quality assessment visits and research assessment exercises—has led to increased levels of bureaucracy and a redirection of scarce resources, which otherwise would have been devoted to teaching and research, to meet the requirements for accountability. The combination of cuts in funding and demands for increased levels and quality of output, coupled with the requirement to carry the cost of an expanding stratum of bureaucrats—managerial, accounting, and marketing staff—has, not surprisingly, led to an intensification of pressure on those engaged in teaching and research in universities and rising levels of occupational stress and illness (Philo & Miller 2001).

In 1918 Max Weber raised the question of the "conditions of science as a vocation" and the prospects awaiting a dedicated graduate student (1970: 129). Whether, given the imposition of various external mechanisms of accountability, other signs of the erosion of institutional autonomy, and wide-ranging transformations in the structure, organization, and employment conditions consistent with the emergence of the "McUniversity," there is any sense in which working in a university can still be considered a "calling" is highly debatable (Lyotard 1984; Ritzer 1996, 1998). The process of a growing articulation between the structure of higher education and the organization of university life on the one hand and the business and commercial requirements of corporate capitalism on the other, to which Weber briefly alluded, has become a far more prominent, if not dominant, feature (Ryan 1998). Increasingly, universities are "major agents of diffusion of social innovation," particularly in the field of computer-mediated communication, which is fundamental for the new informational mode of development "shaped by the restructuring of the capitalist mode of production towards the end of the twentieth century" (Castells 1996: 356). Also universities are becoming increasingly corporate-linked, as the evidence of corporate-endowed research chairs and other forms of corporate sponsorship indicates. Reflecting on the process of corporate intrusion into university life, Klein comments that "the more campuses act and look like malls, the more students behave like consumers," and the more research resources in universities are dependent on corporate funding, the more the "mandate of universities as sites for public-interest research" is placed in jeopardy (2001: 98–99; see also Smith 2001). What is being lost as universities embrace the corporate world, Klein argues, is "our culture's most tangible embodiment of public space and collective responsibility" (2001: 105).

## CONCLUSION: ANOTHER AGE OF ANXIETY?

In 1963—in many ways a very different era from our own—Ferdynand Zweig published an account of student life at the universities of Oxford and Manchester. In his investigation of the problems encountered by students, Zweig remarked on the "aridity of the affluent society" (1963: xv) and the new problems that he considered were beginning to emerge with the expansion of university education. In particular, Zweig was concerned about the new generation of students—"more harassed, more anxious and more worried"—and the "more harassed atmosphere" that expansion appeared to have brought to university life. The survey of student opinion conducted by Zweig was wide-ranging and dealt with most areas of public and private life. One of the issues that students were considered to feel strongly about was the "gross materialism" associated with "our affluent society," and this led Zweig to anticipate that a further expansion of universities was likely to produce a movement opposed to increasing commercialism (1963: 58–59).

The expansion of the university sector in Britain in the course of the 1960s coincided with an increase in student radicalism that, in some respects and in the short term, may be considered to constitute confirmation of Zweig's anticipation of a growing anticommercial mood among students. The events at Warwick University from 1968 onwards may serve as an appropriate example of the radicalism that Zweig anticipated. Political activism on the part of students at Warwick, including occupation of the Registry in 1970, have been described as particular manifestations of the problematic "relationship of our institutions of higher education to industrial capitalism" (Thompson 1970: 16). The problems that became apparent at *Warwick University Ltd* are considered by Thompson to be a consequence of "a particular kind of subordinate relationship with industrial [informational] capitalism—with an industrial capitalism, moreover, which exerts its influence not only directly in the councils of the University but also within the educational organs of the State, and which, from both directions, is demanding, for its better service, an approved educational product" (1970: 18).

The anticommercial mood identified by Zweig and the forms of radicalism documented by Thompson have almost entirely disappeared with the development of what has been called "academic capitalism" (Slaughter & Leslie 1997), the increasing "branding of learning" (Klein 2001: 87–105), and the associated transformation of universities into "means of educational consumption" and of students into consumers (Ritzer 1998: 151). In Britain, university life now appears to be even more harassed, and the anxiety Zweig identified seems to be even more pronounced as students are required to cope with the new burdens of paying fees and securing loans if they are to participate in "educational consumption" (Macleod and Major 1999; Williams 2000). Moreover, anxiety is no longer confined to the student body: academic staff are increasingly vulnerable to the economic and cultural imperatives that are transforming university life (Annan 1999; Macleod 2001; Ryan 1998; Smith 2001). Rising levels of stress and associated health problems are now an increasing feature of higher education (Cox 2001).

Thirty years or so ago, in a series of concluding personal comments on "the role of a university in a modern capitalist society," E. P. Thompson asked, "Is it inevitable that the university will be reduced to the function of providing, with increasingly authoritarian efficiency, prepackaged intellectual commodities which meet the requirements of management?" (1970: 165–166). Times may have changed, but the question has lost none of its relevance.

## REFERENCES

Ahuja, A. (2001). When corporate cash corrupts. *The Times, 2*, 7 May: 10–11.

Alderman, G. (2001). Opinion. *Guardian Education*, 6 March: 13.

Annan, N. (1999). *The Dons*. London: HarperCollins.

Beck, U. (1992). *Risk Society: Towards a New Modernity*. London & Thousand Oaks, CA: Sage.

Bell, D. (1976). *The Cultural Contradictions of Capitalism*. New York: Basic Books.

Bourdieu, P. (1998). *Acts of Resistance: Against the New Myths of Our Time*. Cambridge, U.K.: Polity.

Castells, M. (1989). *The Informational City*. Oxford: Blackwell.

Castells, M. (1996). *The Rise of the Network Society*. Oxford: Blackwell.

Cox, K. (2001). Vanishing calm. *Guardian Higher*, 12 June: 14.

Davies, N. (1997). *Europe: A History*. London: Pimlico.

Delanty, G. (2001). *Challenging Knowledge: The University in the Knowledge Society*. Buckingham, U.K.: Open University Press.

Eco, U. (1987). *Travels in Hyperreality*. London: Picador.

Furedi, F. (2001). What is university for now? *The Sunday Times*, 20 May: 15.

Galbraith, J. K. (1963). *The Affluent Society*. Harmondsworth, U.K.: Penguin.

Gorz, A. (1999). *Reclaiming Work—Beyond the Wage-Based Society*. Cambridge, U.K.: Polity.

Klein, N. (2000). *No Logo*. London: Flamingo.

Lynd, R. S. (1939). *Knowledge for What?* Princeton, NJ: Princeton University Press.

Lyotard, J.-F. (1984). *The Postmodern Condition. A Report on Knowledge*. Manchester, U.K.: Manchester University Press.

Lyotard, J.-F. (1993). *Political Writings*. London: UCL Press.

Macleod, D. (2001). Ride gets rougher. *Guardian Higher*, 15 May: 1.

Macleod, D., & Major, E. L. (1999). Sicker and sicker. *Guardian Higher*, 2 February: 1.

Marx, K. (1973). *Grundrisse*. Harmondsworth: Penguin.

O'Leary, J. (2001). £40m study "stifling research." *The Times*, 1 May: 2.

Parker, M., & Jary, D. (1995). The McUniversity: Organization, management and academic subjectivity. *Organization, 2* (2): 319–338.

Philo, G., Miller, D., et al. (2001). *Market Killing—What the Free Market Does and What Social Scientists Can Do About It*. London: Longman.

Plater, W. M. (1995). Faculty time in the 21st century. *Change, 27* (3): 22–33.

Prichard, C., & Willmott, H. (1997). Just how managed is the McUniversity? *Organization Studies, 18* (2): 287–316.

Ritzer, G. (1996). *The McDonaldization of Society*, 3d ed. Thousand Oaks, CA: Pine Forge Press.

Ritzer, G. (1998). *The McDonaldization Thesis: Explorations and Extensions*. London & Thousand Oaks, CA: Sage.

Rosen, S. M. (1969). Keynes without gadflies. In T. Roszak (Ed.), *The Dissenting Academy*. Harmondsworth, U.K.: Penguin.

Roszak, T. (1969). Academic delinquency. In T. Roszak (Ed.), *The Dissenting Academy*. Harmondsworth, U.K.: Penguin.

Ryan, D. (1998). The Thatcher government's attack on higher education. *New Left Review,* 227: 3–32.

Schumpeter, J. A. (1954). The crisis of the tax state. In A. T. Peacock et al. (Eds.), *International Economic Papers,* 4: 5–38. London: Macmillan.

Slaughter, S., & Leslie, L. (1997). Academic *Capitalism: Politics, Policies and the Entrepreneurial University.* Baltimore, MD: Johns Hopkins University Press.

Smith, R. (2001). A tainted university. *The Guardian,* 21 May: 19.

Thompson, E. P. (Ed.) (1970). *Warwick University Ltd.* Harmondsworth, U.K.: Penguin.

Weber, M. (1970). *From Max Weber: Essays in Sociology* (edited by H. H. Gerth & C. Wright Mills). London: Routledge.

Wild, R. (1998). Fees will let students wield customer clout. *The Sunday Times,* 8 November: 17.

Williams, E. (2000). Tears and fears. *Guardian Education,* 14 March: 10.

Yorke, M., & Alderman, G. (1999). "Money talks" mentality is taking its toll. *Guardian Higher,* 15 June: ii–iii.

Zweig, F. (1963). *The Student in the Age of Anxiety.* London: Heinemann.

# 4

# Modules and Markets: Education and Work in the "Information Age"

*Gavin Poynter*

Following the publication of the National Council of Inquiry into Higher Education's report on *Higher Education in the Learning Society* (DfEE 1997), the Higher Education Funding Council in the United Kingdom established a steering group to develop a series of performance indicators (PIs) for higher-education institutions. The first performance indicators covered recruitment, retention and progression, access and research and were published in December 1999. At the same time, the Chancellor of the Exchequer, Gordon Brown, called for the second set of PIs to include indicators to show employment outcomes for those graduating from higher-education institutions in the United Kingdom. The first survey covering employability was published for those graduating in 1999–2000 (HEFCE 2001).

The government's close interest in measuring the employability of graduates arose from its concern to ensure that the rapid expansion of higher education was accompanied by an increased capacity within the system to provide graduates who have a "firm grip on the world of work" (Kelly 2000: III). The U.K. government's preoccupation with the relationship between education, employability, and economic performance echoed the analysis provided by Robert Reich (1991) in the United States in the early days of the Clinton administration and the views of many business and academic writers who have written since, an important recent example being the U.S. Chamber of Commerce's 1999 report on *21st-Century Skills for 21st-Century Jobs*.

The underlying argument contained in such reports may be briefly summarized. Globalization, the rapid diffusion of information and communication technologies, and, in particular, the emergence of the Internet have given rise to a new world of work in which competition and market uncertainty prevail. The main determinant of the economic success of an economy under such conditions is the development of a flexible and highly skilled population that is capable of operating in new kinds of enterprises that allow labor the opportunity to use its knowledge in relatively autonomous and accountable ways (Brown & Lauder 2001: 118). Wealth creation rests upon knowledge, and universities should play a key role in providing the seed corn of intellectual capital for the new forms of enterprise and work organization associated with the emergence of the "information age."

This perspective contains an apparently compelling logic. It has a long pedigree in the writings of academics such as Becker (1964) and business writers like Peter Drucker (1993) and Thomas Stewart (1998). It has been firmly embraced by successive U.S. and British governments and is reflected in various reports and policy statements. This chapter focuses upon the implications of this perspective for understanding the relationship between work and education in the twenty-first century, particularly in the Anglo–U.S. context in which it has been most explicitly articulated. The argument developed here recognizes the historical and analytical complexity of the interactions between work, education, and economic performance and suggests that a new type of relationship is being created in the twenty-first century. The vocational role of education and the experience of learning at work are, of course, not new, but the current ideological and practical manifestations of their interaction are serving to undermine their specific roles and blur the distinctions between them. This process has been orchestrated in particular by an increase in the range and intensity of government intervention (Robins & Webster 1999: 194). In the United Kingdom, for example, successive governments since the early 1980s have used their role as the primary source of funds for higher education to dilute the independence of the academic professions and direct their activities toward more work-related and vocational forms of course provision. To this end, polytechnics were given the status of universities in 1992, and both old and new were encouraged to expand student numbers while also adapting and developing their provision to meet the needs of industry.

The massification of higher education was accompanied by an unprecedented intrusion by the state into areas of curriculum design and development. This process was broadly initiated by the Manpower Services Commission's document *Enterprise in Higher Education* published in 1987 and reached new levels of intensity under the Labour government following the publication of its *Higher Education and Employment Development Programme* published in its first year of office in 1997 (Robins & Webster 1999: 194). The expansion of state interference in higher-education provision culminated by the end of the 1990s with the achievement of a qualitative change in societal perceptions of the relationship between education and work. Those receiving education, arguably at all levels of compulsory and postcompulsory tuition, were encouraged to perceive their experience primarily through the prism of its instrumental function as a means to employment, and, in turn, many employers began to see their own enterprises as places of learning, even going so far as creating in several instances their own "virtual" corporate universities. As a result of these developments, promoted by state intervention and lent legitimacy by the apparently inexorable demands arising from the arrival of the "information age," the contemporary worlds of work and education, once conceptually distinctive areas of human creativity, have established a pattern of interdependence in which each is contributing to the degradation of the other.

The analysis developed in this chapter focuses upon three aspects of this trend. First, the concept of the information age is examined in relation to its role as legitimator of the changing relationships between work and employment. The ubiquitous character of the information and communication technology revolution provides an apparently compelling case for the development of new skills and occupations that operate in an economy in which knowledge appears to be the key variable in creating value. The argument developed below suggests that all is not what it seems. The new knowledge economy is more potential than reality, advanced industrial economies are experiencing changes in domestic and international divisions of labor, but the process of innovation and diffusion is relatively slow in comparison to previous "industrial revolutions." The changes occurring at the workplace are as likely to produce unskilled and routine forms of manual and white-collar employment as they are opportunities for creative work and self-expression (Poynter & de Miranda 2000). The primary purpose of the contemporary fixation with the information age is an ideological one, in which the prevailing consensus is around a rather simplistic understanding of change as an externally driven and technologically determined trajectory in which the role of human agency is much diminished.

Second, this determinist view of the emergence of an information age rests in a paradoxical relation to recent developments in the sphere of education itself. Here it is argued that the new emphasis in curriculum design and development is less concerned with the theoretical and intellectual knowledge and practice that underpins the information technology revolution and more concerned with the development of so-called "key skills" and "competencies." The new curricula of compulsory, and increasingly postcompulsory, education is far less about subject content and far more about the process of learning itself. Here the modularization of higher-education provision into discreet and bite-size modules symbolizes the triumph of process over content.

Finally, it is argued that the new relationship between education and work is not only transforming the domestic curricula of educational institutions, it is also having a profound impact upon the experience of work. At one level, the "educationalizing" of work diminishes the role of education, particularly higher education, as a sphere in which the primary purpose is reflection rather than action, conceptualization based upon the critical engagement with theoretical disciplines and distinctive spheres of knowledge rather than merely an opportunity to reflect upon practices arising from existing marketized forms of work relations. At another level the role and purpose of work itself is much diminished since the "transferable skills" associated with vocationalized forms of education tend to emphasize the "soft"—communications and interpersonal skills—at the expense of the "hard," developing the knowledge and skills that constitute the essential ingredients of being an effective contributor to the work process itself. In this context, and in conclusion, it is suggested that the recent increase in state intervention in the education sphere has primarily focused upon the socialization of the individual into values consistent with those required of a flexible and malleable labor force rather than being designed to contribute to the creation of the independent and autonomous knowledge worker.

## THE RISE OF THE "INFORMATION AGE"

Contemporary debate on work and education is typically set within the analysis of the emergence of a new information age. The origins of this new age lie in the underlying shift in economic activity and employment from production industries, which mainly relied on manual labor, to services that rely increasingly on nonmanual forms of employment, and particularly those engaged in the assembly, manipulation, and analysis of information. This shift is accompanied by a growing significance attached to knowledge as the most important factor of production and catalyst of economic growth (Burton-Jones 1999). In turn, the expansion of service industries and the growing importance of knowledge work and the knowledge worker are facilitated by the digital technologies that enable the reform of enterprises and organizational structures and foster the emergence of new ways of learning, working, and living. The shift to postindustrialism began in the 1970s and gathered momentum in the last half of the 1990s in countries like the United States and Britain with the emergence of the Internet as a virtual marketplace for the conduct of economic commerce. By the beginning of the twenty-first century, the information age had many subtitles—knowledge capitalism, the digital economy, and the e-society.

The enthusiasts of the new economy could typically be found in government reports and the futuristic writings of the business world. Several economists like Solow (1990; Pasinetti & Solow 1994) tended to be more skeptical about the transformative power of the new technologies. The skeptics pointed to evidence that suggested that while the new technologies could be found everywhere—in the high street, in cafés, and in millions of homes—they did not turn up in the productivity statistics. Even by the mid-1990s, U.S. productivity growth remained stubbornly low, at around 1.5% per annum. It was not until after 1995 that the skeptics began to change their views. When the rate of decline in computer chip prices suddenly doubled to 30%, their lower price sparked a buying boom. In the United States, the economy began to experience a growth rate that doubled to 3% per annum, and the dot.com revolution commenced around the exciting opportunities presented by the expansion of e-commerce via the Internet.

The change in the fortunes of the U.S. productivity performance was symbolized by Intel. In 1995, the semiconductor company reduced its production cycle from three years to two and announced that it could keep on producing faster and cheaper chips until at least 2008 (Emerson 2001a). The new network economy appeared to produce "virtuous circles" and "positive feedback loops" (Emerson 2001b: 20) arising from the capacity to produce faster and cheaper computers and to combine these with new innovations in telecommunications. Most significantly, according to theorists of the new economy, businesses that lay outside the IT sector itself began to experience the benefits of computerization, whether this took place in the back offices of insurance companies or on the shop floors of steel-making plants.

In Europe, over the same five-year period between 1995 and 2000, business writers began to identify the shoots of the new economy as blue-chip European multinationals like Siemens and Daimler Chrysler began to organize themselves around the Internet. In 1990 Europe had no semiconductor manufacturers in the global top ten, a decade later it had three—Philips of the Netherlands, Infineon of Germany, and Microelectronics of Switzerland (Miller 2001: 27). European expansion in the information sector was to be underpinned by new EU-wide regulatory frameworks aimed at promoting e-commerce agreed at the intergovernmental "dot.com" summit in Lisbon in 2000, and Europe was ahead of the United States in developing wireless technologies. While Europe was still behind the United States in investing in the new economy, optimists pointed to developments that could achieve a significant rise in the annual productivity growth rates that had languished at a 0.5% rise for the whole of the 1990s.

The optimism surrounding the performance of the U.S. economy, and the potential for Europe to play catch-up, did not last long. The investment boom in information technology that occurred during the latter part of the 1990s in the United States and Europe quickly evaporated. Before the end of 2000, the U.S. economy was in danger of dipping into recession, and by the spring of 2001, Charles Dallara, the managing director of the Institute of International Finance, warned the International Monetary Fund and the World Bank of "clouds appearing in many directions": "Perhaps we are facing the most challenging global economic environment that we have seen for many years. I would even say the most challenging since the 1970s" (quoted in Fidler 2001).

The pessimism arose from the slowdown of the U.S. economy in 2000, a slowdown prompted by the collapse in capital spending, in particular on information technologies, higher energy prices, a loss of consumer confidence, and the announcement by many high technology companies like Cisco, Intel, Hewlett Packard, Nortel, Lucent Technologies, and Motorola of significant job cuts. Concern over the U.S. economy was matched by alarm over Japan's continuing economic crisis and by the decline in private capital flows to developing countries. Net private flows of capital to the developing world had averaged $210 billion dollars per annum between 1996 and 2000. In 2001 the flows were likely to fall to less than $150 billion, leaving many developing economies prone to severe recession (Fidler 2001).

The sudden downturn in the fortunes of the U.S. economy and the weaknesses revealed in the international economy prompted in a few short months a sharp shift in business confidence from one based on optimism in the late 1990s to one that was deeply pessimistic by summer 2001. This sharp fluctuation in the confidence of the Western business elite requires an explanation.

First, the period between 1995 and 2000 produced an overoptimistic view of the performance of, in particular the U.S. economy (Brenner 2000: 29). The period of U.S. economic growth achieved in the 1990s was good in comparison to its performance in the post-1973 period, but it was hardly impressive compared to the growth rates achieved by its competitors in earlier phases of economic growth in the long post-1945 boom (Maddison 1991: 128–165). Second, much of the improvement in U.S. performance in production industries arose from the performance of the IT sector itself and not from the diffusion of its products to other industrial sectors (Bresnahem & Gordon 1997), and, finally, nonproduction industries, typically referred to as the service sector, tended to deploy new technologies in ways that achieved short-term cost cutting but did not achieve real improvements in white collar productivity of the kind that was transformative or that could be effectively measured (Poynter 2000). Announcements, whether by government or business writers, of the coming of the information age, of a long period of sustained economic growth based upon the widespread diffusion of information and communication technologies, proved elusive, futuristic, or, at the very least, premature.

The consequence of this "false dawn" has been significant for understanding the relationship between work and education. In the United States and the United Kingdom, the continuation of a lengthy period of economic restructuring has created conditions in which a significant proportion of the new jobs generated, particularly in the service sector, may have demanded greater labor flexibility and multitasking, but they have not generated a significant rise in the proportion of highly skilled, technically capable labor within the economy as a whole. An OECD Report (OECD 1994) on the U.S. economy revealed that over half the jobs created in the service sector in the early 1990s were low-skilled and required little or no training. This statistical evidence is supported by authors like Milkman (1997, 1998). From her detailed studies of the American workplace she concluded that "In short, the low wage, low trust, low skill 'low road' is the path most U.S. firms are following, despite overwhelming evidence that the 'high road' a few of them have forged would serve the long term interests of both corporations and workers far better" (Milkman 1998: 38).

Second, the consequence of the Anglo–U.S. approach to creating more flexible labor markets has been to sharpen the tendency toward the polarization between the minority in skilled and secure jobs and the majority in less secure and low-skilled occupations (Brown & Lauder 2001: 183; Sennett 1998).

Finally, the mismatch between the "hype" surrounding the apparent demand for the creation of the new knowledge workers of the information age and the "low road" that the United States and the United Kingdom have tended to follow has served to legitimate and underpin changes in educational provision that have contributed to the creation of a new generation of workers, whose development of "transferable skills" and competencies has created a new more malleable form of graduate labor. Aware that a degree is not a passport to a good career or job, students have willingly pursued studies that contain transferable skills as an important component of their educational programs, despite the fact that employers have tended to perceive these programs as an inferior form of "compensatory education." This paradox is eloquently explained by Robins and Webster in their examination of recent changes in higher education in the United Kingdom:

Time and again employers stress that they want recruits to have transferable skills— team working abilities, problem-solving skills, communicative and numerate capabilities, etc.—but time and again they appear to find these manifest, not in those students from new universities who have most often undergone programmes that have consciously nurtured them because of their sensitivity to the world of work, but in the products of the more elite—and preferably ancient universities, where the language of transferable skills has penetrated least. Indeed, employers regard those graduates from the ex-polytechnics who have undergone explicit training in transferable skills as deficient for that very reason: had they been any good in the first place such students would not have required this compensatory education. [Robins & Webster 1999: 207]

In summary, the assumption that society has entered a new phase—an information age—is reflected in countless government policies and reports and is contained in the influential writings of many business authors. This perspective has served to legitimize a significant increase in state intervention in reshaping the structure of compulsory and postcompulsory education and reforming course design and program planning. The logic underpinning these reforms has arisen from an uncritical view of the role played by technology in determining the pace and character of social and industrial change. A closer examination of this process of change reveals a significant gap between the "hype" and the reality. Western economies, particularly those in the Anglo–U.S. world, continue to experience an uneven process of restructuring and sharp fluctuations in patterns of economic growth, investment, and expansion. The resulting insecurity arising in business confidence and expectations tends to push enterprises to pursue short-term expediencies in cost cutting and rationalization and leads to uneven patterns of investment in the new technologies themselves. Rather than having already arrived, the new society of the information age remains merely a potential. The new forms of education and training provided adhere to the aspirations of the technological revolution while within an increasing number of institutions their content has become geared toward the creation of a workforce whose educational experience has already attuned them to a flexible labor market in which the "portfolio" career is the dominant expectation.

## MODULAR MINDS

George Ritzer has provided a compelling picture of the rise of the postmodern university—the McUniversity. He points to several trends evident in U.S. and British higher-education institutions. (1) Students increasingly perceive education as a commodity for consumption. The student as consumer seeks choice, "edutainment," and a diversity in the forms of educational delivery. As a result, academe is expected to adapt from a producer- to a consumer-driven approach to educational provision. Interdisciplinarity and modularity creates choices in the patterns of consumption, and as a consequence traditional and highly structured single disciplinary courses based upon the established disciplines begin to whither away. (2) Propelled by this changing balance between production and consumption, higher education enters into new market-oriented forms of relations with their student consumers and the business world. Arising from this marketization, universities begin to adopt the objectives and practices of the business world, working more closely with enterprises and adapting their practices to measure academe's performance and productivity. In the United Kingdom, for example, a raft of performance measures have been used to compare and evaluate the activities of institutions, leading to the creation of university league tables that potential students, and their parents, may use to make choices about their future place of study. In addition to measuring the overall performance of institutions, other business tools have been widely adopted to create mechanisms by which the daily process of teaching and learning may be evaluated against "quality criteria" derived from the total quality management approach of the business world. (3) The McUniversity has a leaner and meaner campus than was provided before. Academic staff find themselves delivering educational products in an increasing diversity of forms and often at a distance, using information and communication technologies. A small core of permanent staff, including "star" professors, manage an increasingly casualized form of intellectual labor—graduate assistants, part-time and hourly paid staff. The McUniversity implodes "into the locations of their satellites, the media (especially television), the computer, cyberspace, entertainment, consumption and so on" (Ritzer 1998: 159).

There is considerable evidence to support this analysis. In the United Kingdom, for example, the Labour government (1997–2001) replaced grants with loans to pay fees and maintenance. As a result the student debt burden has risen significantly over recent years, and students have become increasingly litigious when the education they pay to consume falls beneath their expectations. A growing proportion of students, in turn, have tended to work during term time in order to reduce the debt burden (Callender & Kempson 1996). Studying, as a consequence, has become only one of many pursuits that must be fitted into the student's life. Many higher-education institutions, particularly the new universities, have moved toward modular and credit-rated undergraduate and postgraduate degree schemes, with modes of delivery increasingly accommodating to the new patterns of engagement of the consumer with the educational institution. Paradoxically, the division of degree courses into credit-rated modules may have enhanced the transportability of credits between courses and institutions, but it has also served to homogenize the modes and methods of teaching, learning, and assessment. Arguably, the postmodern university has been driven toward greater flexibility in the mix of subjects offered but within an increasingly standardized or Fordist administrative framework of course provision.

Modularization has been accompanied by the development of new criteria for the validation and review of courses. Here, the dilution of subject-specific study, and with it the attenuation of student study of the components or building blocks of a specific sphere of knowledge, has coincided with the introduction of quality criteria aimed at nurturing transferable skills and competencies. In this context, the validation and review of courses in higher education becomes increasingly concerned with the process of learning and the development of soft skills rather than the rigor and integrity of knowledge development and academic content. As a "sovereign" consumer, the individual student has increased choice and discretion over her or his subjects of study but the discreet subject content that differentiates one academic program from another is much diluted.

The shift in the relationship between the "producers" and the "consumers" of education has significant consequences. The student takes greater responsibility for mapping out her or his course, but such freedom tends to transform the relationship between teacher and taught. The former becomes the "facilitator" of the latter's learning, and traditional patterns of authority within the relationship apparently disappear. As a result, the academic exercises power without authority, and students seek to prove themselves, but there is no one in authority to respond. The process of teaching and learning is enacted as part of a set of relativistic relations in which the knowledge and experience of the student is increasingly regarded as being as valuable as those of the teacher, whose capacity to challenge the limitations of "lived experience" with the rigors of critical and conceptual thought is much diminished. The egalitarian symbolism of the marketized relationship between student and teacher echoes that of the egalitarian symbolism of teamwork in the contemporary workplace. As Sennett has argued, such superficiality arising from the blurring or dilution of roles, power, and authority leads to the enactment of human relations as farce (Sennett 1998: 116).

Universities have also been subjected to the pressures arising from initiatives designed to pull together the business and academic worlds. The partial privatization of U.K. training provision through the activities of Learning and Skills Councils and their predecessors, the Training and Enterprise Councils, has created circumstances in which these semiautonomous state agencies have acted as "brokers" between business and education institutions, with the latter accrediting the training schemes of the former and universities and colleges increasingly providing accredited "tailor-made" courses for their business partners. More threateningly for some higher-education institutions in the United States and the United Kingdom, the development of corporate universities has acted as a further pressure to assimilate the values of the business world within the framework of course design and curriculum content. One U.S. estimate provided by Corporate University Xchange suggests that over the last fifteen years the number of corporate universities has expanded from around 400 to 2,000, with expansion set to rise to 3,700 by the end of the first decade of this century (FT Careerpoint 2001).

This assimilation of business values within the academic world has been powerfully examined by Robins and Webster in relation to their arguments concerning critical thinking. Critical thinking is one of the key distinctions between courses that educate and those that train. Most universities, the authors argue, claim to provide courses that encourage critical thinking:

We suspect that it is difficult to find any degree programme in the country that does not profess to develop critical thought. It is our view that the only way that such a potentially destabilising concept such as critical thinking can find inclusion in degrees on midwifery and business administration, estate management and tourism studies, is to denude it of real force by limiting it to pre-established (and incontestable) goals. In such a way critical thinking is operationalised as a practical competence which might allow the more effective delivery of babies (while the organisation of welfare services is out of bounds), or might reflect on how best to maximise corporate interests (but will not open wider questions about business behaviour). . . . [Robins & Webster 1998: 128]

Critical thought is established within predefined goals and assumptions that preclude a wider engagement with the values and ideas that underpin the subject of study. This preclusion is not confined to courses that are more vocational in their orientation; it has become an important component of even the more traditional disciplines in which the marketability of the graduate is apparently enhanced by an emphasis on transferable skills. Arising in part from such pressures, the curriculum is extensively remodeled to ensure its relevance to the world of work and the demands of the student consumer. As a consequence, for example, the study of literature is absorbed into media studies, sociology mutates into social policy and social work, and economics becomes part of the world of business or management studies. This narrowing of the educational curriculum or agenda within a predefined framework, with its thinly disguised underlying goals and assumptions, can only be reinforced by current moves within the funding council in the United Kingdom to support programs of "work-based training" and schemes designed to achieve the accreditation of prior learning. The shift toward a market-oriented and instrumental mode of education provision and the apparently inexorable movement toward the creation of the

McUniversity has another dimension that is the final theme of this chapter. The attenuation of critical thinking, the modularization of knowledge into bit-size chunks, and the reinvention of the student as consumer has played an increasingly significant role in assisting in the creation of a new kind of malleable workforce.

## MALLEABLE LABOR

Today the phrase "flexible capitalism" describes a system which is more than a permutation of an old theme. The emphasis is on flexibility. Rigid forms of bureaucracy are under attack, as are the evils of blind routine. Workers are asked to behave nimbly, to be open to change at short notice, to take risks continually, to become ever less dependent on regulations and formal procedures.

This emphasis on flexibility is changing the very meaning of work, and the words we use for it. . . . Flexible capitalism has blocked the straight roadway of a career, diverting employees suddenly from one kind of work into another. The word "job" in English of the fourteenth century meant a lump or piece of something that could be carted around. Flexibility today brings back this arcane sense of the job, as people do lumps of labour, pieces of work, over the course of a lifetime. [Sennett 1998: 9]

The increased malleability or flexibility of today's worker has several causes. The underlying structural changes associated with the rise of what Sennett describes as a new type of capitalism have been well documented over recent years. The increase in service sector employment, the growth in part-time work, the rise of outsourcing, and the relative decline of public sector employment have created a sense of greater job insecurity among nonmanual workers and facilitated important changes in the employment contract. Equally, and perhaps more importantly, these structural changes have been accompanied by reforms in management's approach to influencing the attitudes and values of labor. Enterprises have sought to develop a new culture within workplaces. Employees have been encouraged to adopt a service-orientation and to modify personal behavior in order to put the customer first. The pursuit of this attitudinal change has been at the core of many training and educational programs adopted by enterprises and public- and private-sector institutions over recent years (Blyton & Turnbull 1994: 66–67; Poynter 2000).

This focus on fostering a customer orientation has also had an important impact on relations between managers and staff. The distinctions between "them" and "us" have become blurred as all engaged within an enterprise have been encouraged to perceive themselves as the common providers of "services" to the consumer. In becoming service providers, the classic distinctions between those who do the work and those who supervise them have tended to break down. Old-style personnel management has been displaced by human resource management, the old work ethic that emphasized routine and functionality has been replaced by the ethics of creativity and "play" (Himanen 2001; Kane 2000), and, typically, staff have been reorganized into "teams." Teamwork has assumed the function of an "egalitarian symbol" (Sennett 1998: 112) that permeates the employment relation and obscures the underlying inequalities in authority, power, and responsibility that once were visible even in the clothes or uniforms worn by the different layers of the workplace hierarchy.

These changes in workplace relations have gone largely unchallenged. The diminished role of trade unions and craft-based organizations and the dilution in the prominence attached to independent as opposed to state-sponsored professional associations (Perkin 1989) has ensured that any countervailing attitudes or social values are much diminished or have disappeared. In these circumstances, enterprises have sought to create a new pattern of social relations, a new form of social connectedness at work. In this task, enterprises have been ably assisted by the values and attitudes generated from within the education sector. Vocationalism and employability have become key themes in higher education in terms of socializing students into this "new" world of work, and the pedagogic methods associated with "progressive" learner-centered forms of education practice have been appropriated to serve this socialization process. The emphasis on the production of graduates with adaptability and soft skills and the vaguely defined capacity for the "management of ideas" (Reich 1991) prepares them to absorb the kinds of values and attitudes that are consistent with the prevailing norms of the twenty-first-century workplace. As the distinction between education and work, learning and doing diminishes, so the space for reflection and critique is narrowed, and for many students the experience of study amounts to an immersion in the core values of the world of business. While an elite minority of students is educated in traditional disciplines and taught via traditional "Oxbridge-style" tutorials, with, ironically, many moving on into "high-flying" jobs, the majority receive a form of instrumental education whose prevailing ethics and values prepare them for entrance into the world of flexible capitalism and its "portfolio" careers.

## CONCLUSION

The changing relationship between education and work is a complex affair. The dynamic appears to be driven by the rapid changes associated with the emergence of an information age. Closer inspection reveals that the new global economy based upon the diffusion of information and communication technologies is more potential than reality. In practice, advanced industrial economies in North America and northern Europe are experiencing a protracted process of industrial restructuring in which economic growth and improved performance has not achieved a sustained momentum of the kind comparable to that in the years following the Second World War. In such uncertain times, business confidence is fragile, and the actions of the business and political elites are legitimized less by what they argue they can do and more by what they present as an externally driven technological necessity. Technology appears to propel social (and particularly educational) change rather than the reverse, and this shallow determinism is used to legitimize the actions of government and business alike.

In turn, the workplace has been characterized as the site for the creation of a form of flexible capitalism for which tomorrow's workers must be prepared. The vocationalizing of education, in particular higher education, has much to do with this process of socialization that diminishes the role of human agency and privileges the importance of the inanimate object. Technology is the subject and society its predicate. The vaguely defined skills and competencies associated with "employability" agendas facilitate the creation of a whole generation of 18–24-year-olds with values and attitudes that help to bridge the divide between school and work and, arguably, keeps them within the "system" and reduces the likelihood of that generation questioning the legitimacy of, for example, flexible working and the portfolio career. The use of the education system as a vehicle for sustaining social cohesion has assumed new dimensions in recent years as state intervention has reached unprecedented levels in terms of influencing curriculum design and development, course quality and standards, student numbers in higher and further education, and relations between education and the business world. The vocationalizing of education has simultaneously contributed to the degradation of the concept of the university and, for many, to the dilution of their aspirations toward the world of work.

## REFERENCES

Becker, G. (1964). *Human Capital*. New York: University of Columbia Press.

Blyton, P., & Turnbull, P. (1994). *The Dynamics of Employee Relations*. London: Macmillan.

Brenner, R. (2000). The boom and the bubble. *New Left Review* (November/December): 5–44.

Bresnahem, T., & Gordon, R. (Eds.) (1997). *Economics of New Goods*. Chicago, IL: University of Chicago.

Brown, P., & Lauder, H. (2001). *Capitalism and Social Progress. The Future of Society in a Global Economy*. Basingstoke & New York: Palgrave.

Burton-Jones, A. (1999). *Knowledge Capitalism*. Oxford, U.K.: Oxford University Press.

Callender, C., &. Kempson, E. (1996). *Student Finances: A Survey of Student Income and Expenditure*. London: Policy Studies Institute.

DfEE (1997). *Higher Education in the Learning Society*. London: Department for Education and Employment.

Drucker, P. (1993). *Post-Capitalist Society*. New York: HarperCollins.

Emerson, T. (2001a). The Intel economy? *Newsweek,* 29 January: 24.

Emerson, T. (2001b). Only the beginning. *Newsweek,* Special Report, 29 January: 19–24.

Fidler, S. (2001). World economy faces "clouds in many directions." *Financial Times,* 18 April.

FT CareerPoint (2001). Tailor-made for lifelong learning, business education. *Financial Times Survey*, 26 March.

HEFCE (2001). *Indicators of Employment*. Bristol, U.K.: Higher Education Funding Council.

Himanen, P. (2001). *The Hacker Ethic and the Spirit of the Information Age*. London: Secker and Warburg.

Kane, P. (2000). Play for today. *The Observer Magazine*, 22 October: 20–30.

Kelly, J. (2001). Tailor made for life-long learning. *Financial Times Business Education Survey*, 26 March.

Maddison, A. (1991). *Dynamic Forces in Capitalist Development*. Oxford, U.K.: Oxford University Press.

Milkman, R. (1997). *Farewell to the Factory: Autoworkers in the Late Twentieth Century*. Berkeley, CA: University of California Press.

Milkman, R. (1998). The new American workplace: High road or low road? In P. Thompson & C. Warhurst (Eds.), *Workplaces of the Future*. London: Macmillan (25–39).

Miller, K. (2001). A run for the money. *Newsweek*, 29 January: 26–28.

OECD (1994). *Economic Outlook*. Paris: OECD.

Pasinetti, L, & Solow, R. (Eds.) (1994). *Economic Growth and the Structure of Long-Term Development*. Basingstoke, U.K.: Palgrave.

Perkin, H. (1989). *The Rise of Professional Society*. London: Routledge.

Poynter, G. (2000). *Restructuring in the Service Industries*. London: Mansell.

Poynter, G., & de Miranda, A. (2000). Inequality, work and technology in the service sector. In S. Wyatt, F. Henwood, N. Miller, & P. Senker (Eds.), *Technology and In/equality*. London: Routledge (172–196).

Reich, R. (1991). *The Work of Nations: Preparing Ourselves for Twenty-First-Century Capitalism*. New York: Vintage.

Robins, K., & Webster, F. (1999). *Times of the Technoculture*. London: Routledge.

Ritzer, G. (1998). *The McDonaldization Thesis: Explorations and Extensions*. London & Thousand Oaks, CA: Sage.

Sennett, R. (1998). *The Corrosion of Character*. New York: Norton.

Solow, R. (1990). *The Labour Market as a Social Institution*. London: Blackwell.

Stewart, T. (1998). *Intellectual Capital*. London: Brealey.

# 5

# Digital Technologies and Competing Models of Higher Education

*Caroline Hodges Persell*

In this chapter I consider the relation of George Ritzer's McDonaldization thesis to the use of digital technologies in higher education. In doing this I stress two distinct dimensions of McDonaldization—namely, "rationalization" and "profit maximization." By digital technologies I mean the relatively new digital information and communication media, including, but not limited to, the Internet, World Wide Web, video conferencing, digitized multimedia, groupware, and the varieties of synchronous and asynchronous computer-mediated communication (Benson et al. 2001).

What is, or might be, the role of rationalization in higher education? Can using rationality increase the effectiveness of learning and understanding, and what are the limits of applying rationality to the design of learning experiences? Clearly, there is a need for surprises, the unexpected, and serendipitous experiences and findings. But there may also be a role for some rational planning and designing of instruction, depending on who is initiating such efforts. The introduction of digital technologies may offer new opportunities for reflecting on what understandings faculty want students to gain, how they might design curricula to help them to learn, and how well students are understanding.

If rationalization is a means, then the questions are: toward what ends is it being directed, and who is doing the directing? In McDonaldization, the purpose of rationalization is profit maximization. One of the profound implications of McDonaldization is its potential to change the mission of higher education through the intrusion of profit maximization and market principles into education. Tendencies toward commercial goals severely challenge higher education's historic mission and alter educational practices. The values and goals of higher education conceived of as a social institution are the creation of new knowledge, teaching and learning, and service, none of which include profit maximization.

## HIGHER EDUCATION AS SOCIAL INSTITUTION OR INDUSTRY?

One of the most dramatic shifts in U.S. education over the past quarter-century is the growing prevalence of the logic and principles of the marketplace, without full consideration of the consequences. The fastest-growing sector of U.S. higher education is for-profit institutions. In 1998, the *Chronicle of Higher Education* reported that there were 564 such institutions, with annual revenues of $3.5 billion (Newton 2000: 4).

The growth of the for-profit sector and the rise of for-profit companies, such as the University of Phoenix, that are building regional and national educational franchises changes the organizational field, in the sense that Bourdieu (1980; Bourdieu & Wacquant 1992) uses the term, within which nonprofit higher-education institutions operate. No longer confined to local, non-degree-granting vocational schools, the new for-profit educational enterprises now offer some bachelor's and master's degrees.

As Schmookler noted in *The Parable of the Tribes* (1984), when new competitors, playing by new rules, enter a situation and seek to claim valued resources, existing groups must respond. According to Schmookler, there are several possible outcomes: the existing groups may be destroyed, be taken over and subjugated, flee to a less desirable place, or they may fight (in which case they need to become more like the newcomers). What is missing from Schmookler's discussion is any possibility of a legal framework or other countervailing forces that limit the means that might be employed by the invading tribe. Is there any evidence that the other 3,500 institutions of higher education in the United States are changing?

Another observer of U.S. higher education has noted that, over the last 25 years, "the dominant legitimating idea of public higher education" has moved away from the idea of higher education as a social institution toward a view of higher education as an industry (Gumport 2000: 149). Conceiving of higher education as an industry involves a set of narrow and particularistic goals. Governed by the value of economic rationality, the institution is organized to maximize its own remunerative success and that of its students, by preparing them for competition in the job market. In this form of legitimation, there is no "provision for public good that may exceed the market's reach" (Gumport 2000: 149).

In light of these developments it is reasonable to ask to what degree technology is a Trojan Horse sneaking market values inside the university's walls. How can we insure that commercialization does not undermine valuable educational conceptions (for example, of knowledge) and practices (for example, of openness)? Can digital technologies be used in ways to foster knowledge creation and understanding, not simply in an effort to maximize profits?

I use the tension between conceptions of higher education as a social institution or an industry to inform the analysis of four contested arenas in which digital technologies and higher education are meeting—namely, competing conceptions of knowledge, contending modes of delivering or distributing knowledge, struggles over learning and its assessment, and shifting faculty roles.

## COMPETING CONCEPTIONS OF KNOWLEDGE

If we posit a continuum, at one end of it is a constructivist conception of knowledge where people learn how to critically assess existing knowledge (ideas and data), pose new questions, gather new data, and develop new theories. At the other end is a conception of knowledge as bounded, fixed, and prepackaged. The latter is very much like a Big Mac in a Styrofoam container in that it allows no room for interaction or creative input.

Digital technologies can provide opportunities to challenge a "packet" conception of knowledge, and they offer the potential for everyone to become knowledge creators to some degree. However, digital technologies may also be used to produce and distribute canned bundles of information. Fixed conceptions of knowledge are easier to rationalize, control, and commercialize, but they are also finite and do not stimulate the expansion of knowledge.

The growth of digital technologies intensifies tensions between conceptions of knowledge as proprietary and knowledge as openly available. Copyright law has struggled for years with the competing values of honoring and rewarding creativity and innovation on the one hand while fostering the benefits of public knowledge, including intensifying the value of knowledge and encouraging its growth and development. In a knowledge economy, the stakes escalate. We can see this in contests over courses, websites, software, and journals.

Will course websites (including syllabi, exercises, readings, and supplemental materials) be public and open to all, or will they be password-protected and limited to students enrolled in a course or to members of a particular university community? Some institutions, like the Massachusetts Institute of Technology (MIT), are consciously taking a stand in support of openness. First, their OpenCourseWare effort "aims to make instructional materials for all of MIT's courses available free on the Web" (Young 2001a: online). The institution "has not ruled out the possibility . . . of licensing its online course materials to for-profit institutions, which might be interested in putting them in products or courses even though the materials are free online. . . . But we would not do that if the condition was that we could no longer make [the material] free and open," according to Steven R. Lerman, "a professor of civil and environmental engineering who is part of the team organizing the project" (Young 2001a). As Young notes, "MIT's plans for the project have sparked widespread interest at other institutions, and many see it as an important statement that course materials should be considered scholarly publications, not commercial products" (Young 2001a). This is a good example of a hybrid system preserving the educational values of a social institution while leaving open the possibility of cooperative arrangements with market institutions.

MIT is also involved with some other institutions, including Stanford University, Dartmouth College, North Carolina State University, in the Open Knowledge Initiative (OKI). This is an effort to design "a course-management system that will be free and whose source code will be made publicly available" (Young 2001b: online). The "open source" nature of the software means that others can freely use or change the computer code if they are willing to share their work with others. It also means that professors can freely chose among various software modules for teaching courses online, to enhance their classroom teaching, and possibly to conduct research on difficulties their students are having understanding key principles. It is not yet clear what the relationship of OKI will be with MIT's OpenCourseWare project.

There are already growing numbers of outstanding websites in the social sciences that are freely available to all. For example, there are the slave narratives, early man in anthropology, the General Social Survey, and many, many others in the public domain. These examples affirm the social institutional values of sharing knowledge and the possibility of social recognition and prestige.

An increasingly contested arena is the discipline-warranted research and knowledge published in journals. In recent years many journals—especially in the natural sciences, but also in the social sciences—have been acquired by for-profit publishing companies, and have raised their prices to college and university libraries dramatically. Indeed U.S. campus libraries spent 152% more to purchase 7% fewer journal titles in 1998 than they had in 1986, according to the Association of Research Libraries. The rapidly escalating costs of for-profit scientific journals have hurt college and university libraries, that are increasingly less able to purchase monographs (often in the humanities) because of the high costs of scientific journals. For-profit publishers may also limit authors' rights to post their articles on their own web pages or to use their work for teaching, research, or other scholarly purposes.

Knowledge producers have alternatives, but as long as the prices charged by for-profit publishers were seen as "reasonable," such alternatives were not vigorously pursued. However, as the fees charged rose and production costs were reduced for work published on the web, reactions developed. For example, SPARC (the Scholarly Publishing & Academic Resources Coalition) established competing online, nonprofit scientific journals and made them available at much lower costs.

Another example is a web-based scientific archive centered at Los Alamos National Laboratory in New Mexico; this allows any scientist or researcher with an Internet connection to post or download the latest research in a dozen disciplines in the physical sciences, including astronomy and astrophysics, condensed matter physics and particle physics, and related fields (Glanz 2001: F1–F2). Founded 10 years ago, the archive attracts some two million visits a week, more than two-thirds from institutions abroad. In fact, to speed communication, the archive has been duplicated on 16 sites around the world. It expects to receive some 35,000 new paper submissions in 2001. The archive is supported by about $300,000 in annual grants from the National Science Foundation, the Department of Energy, and Los Alamos National Laboratory. In addition to spreading new ideas and concepts far more quickly and cheaply than they could be spread by paper journals, the archive encourages multinational collaboration, recognizes outstanding work by unknown scientists in remote regions of the world, and reduces the importance of geography for gaining scientific visibility. In some fields, like string theory, the premier figures read preprints on the archive daily and may contact students who post from distant places. As a professor in Chile said about an email message one of his students received from Dr. Edward Witten, a physicist at the Institute for Advanced Study in Princeton: "Dr. Witten's instant response [to his paper] . . . 'was like having the pope drop by for tea'" (Glanz 2001: F2). The limitations of the archive, in some people's view, is that the papers are not peer reviewed, web access is slow in some countries, and the work of unknown people in unknown places may still be overlooked. Nevertheless, this is an example of how an open knowledge system may contribute to the development of scientific understanding.

Given the potential for free or low-cost ways of distributing knowledge, it is possible that scholars will become more selective about where they donate their efforts as authors, reviewers, and editors. Rather than subsidizing corporations that profit from their efforts while making their intellectual work less available, scholars may decide increasingly to donate their intellectual labor only to nonprofit enterprises. The normative values of a social institution support gift relationships, but the values and norms of for-profit enterprises do not. A conception of higher education as a social institution supports an open conception of knowledge and courseware systems, while a market model of higher education is congruent with closed, proprietary conceptions of knowledge and courseware.

Like society, higher education is becoming increasingly stratified; the idea that there is a common educational core shared by all who experience higher education is gone. People do not encounter the same conceptions of knowledge. "The University of Phoenix does not seek to discover new knowledge but to teach students how to apply existing theory and research to practical situations and real work issues" (Newton 2000: 6). As an institution, the University of Phoenix does not value knowledge, understanding, or learning for its own sake, but only in terms of its pragmatic value. Students (and their employers) are the ones who decide what is needed or useful. While this might be seen as empowering the consumers of education, it limits their choices to what they already understand well enough to think they need. There is no room for "surprises" or for the unexpected, as Ritzer notes about McDonald's. This approach reifies knowledge as a closed and finite system rather than as an open system. Furthermore, knowledge is not only seen as fixed and finite, but only a limited band of the knowledge color spectrum is deemed worth teaching—specifically that which might be applied immediately in one's work situation. Historically, the mission of higher education included more than narrow preparation for a career. Not only might people change careers during their work lives, but they also need to prepare for life beyond work, as citizens of a democracy and as members of families and communities. Many educational thinkers consider the current narrow vocational training to be inadequate preparation for social and civic goals (Persell & Wenglinsky 2001). The question is an epistemological one regarding conceptions of knowledge prevailing in various institutions of higher education. Instead of learning how to become critical appraisers of knowledge and producers of new ideas, some members of society are being taught prepackaged bits of information that may prepare them for the McJobs Ritzer describes (1998: 60). Others are being prepared to become what Robert Reich calls "symbolic analysts" (1991). They are learning that knowledge is a social construction and learning ways to develop and justify new constructions—precisely the qualities needed to maintain control in an information economy. They are also gaining a sense of entitlement, because they are learning that they are experiencing a "superior" education.

## CONTENDING MODES OF DELIVERING OR DISTRIBUTING KNOWLEDGE

The delivery of knowledge is related to who learns what, and the issue is how students encounter various kinds of knowledge. The fast-food mode of delivering nourishment clearly affects the nature of the food offered. It becomes standardized and predictable. While customized gourmet fast food seems a complete contradiction in terms, the potentialities of digital technologies may span learning possibilities that encompass a range of intellectual contents and approaches, from inquiry-based, higher-order thinking and deep understanding to applications and rote learning.

Implicit within questions of "knowledge delivery" is a "packet" conception of knowledge. Does the use of digital technologies to "deliver" knowledge have single, uniform effects on the nature of knowledge and who has access to it? Or, on the degree to which knowledge becomes stratified? Some universities, for example, decide that using digital technology for teaching consists of wiring all classrooms and requiring professors to use presentational software to project the major points in their lectures. Some on-line courses consist only of the typed text of lectures on the screen. On the other hand, some on-line courses have utilized cooperative learning groups where students learned more than in a traditional course because they worked out their understandings of the concepts and principles in conjunction with their classmates (Benson et al. 2001; Jaffee 1997; Schutte 1996). Clearly, the interactive capabilities of digital technologies are among their most promising potentialities, but how we employ those capabilities needs further research.

This range of potentialities is possible because of some of the unique features of digital technologies—including 24/7 availability, speed that is adjustable by the learner, tremendous potential for interaction, the opportunity to make thinking visible to others, and access to vast arrays of data, much of it downloadable and analyzable. These include audio, visual, and ultimately video (in Internet2) archives, datasets of abstracts, on-line full text copies of journals, and simulations, all of which can be searched electronically and reviewed easily. One of the potentialities of digital technologies includes the possibility of slowing down and reexamining faculty educational assumptions, goals, and practices (Bass & Eynon 1998). Whether or not that potential is positive may well depend on who controls the process.

In this way, digital technologies may not only lead us to reexamine what we are doing and why, but provide us with new insights into processes, for example, of student learning that were previously less visible. As social researchers, we should be looking closely at these potentialities.

Before the digital age, information was a scarce resource, located in hard-to-find archives and libraries, or on complicated computer tapes. Now there is a surfeit of information. What becomes even more important is knowledge, understanding, and wisdom. We need more tools for making sense of all the information, knowledge of its epistemological limitations, ways of asking questions about it, ways of framing and thinking about it, and ways of raising new questions, such as: will it help students to identify new problems, issues, and questions, thereby leading to the potential production of new knowledge and understanding?

At the same time, there are some modes of learning that are much more difficult, if not impossible, to replicate through digital technologies. These include the experiences of studying abroad, on-campus living with late-night dorm "bull sessions" with people from diverse backgrounds, service learning experiences, and extracurricular activities. The creeping commercialization in higher education has resulted in some campuses assigning dorm rooms and meal plans to students based on how much they are willing to pay (Kaufman 2001: A1, A6). Such a practice reduces the chances of informal, dorm-based discussions among economically diverse students. These informal curricular components of higher education are unavailable for increasingly larger percentages of students, as the number of part-time, commuting, and older students in higher education grows. The advent of distance education certainly raises new questions, such as how much of an "education" students can really get if they never leave their homes? We would expect that education would become less transformative under such conditions—less of a social institution and more of an industry. A question we can ask about modes of delivery is: for what purposes is a given mode of delivery being used? Is its goal "edutainment" or deep understanding? An edu-

tainment mode of knowledge delivery focuses on making knowledge presentation entertaining and amusing and perhaps not too taxing. Like MTV, critics fear
that edutainment will magnify short attention spans and contribute to more of a
bricolage presentation of ideas rather than to their logical unfolding. Critics also
wonder how edutainment will deal with the mastery of difficult principles.

At the end of the day it is all about who is involved in decisions about the
conditions under which knowledge is delivered. At the University of Illinois, a
yearlong faculty seminar was convened during the 1998–99 academic year in
response to faculty concern about the use of technology in teaching. The seminar
was evenly split between "skeptical" and "converted" faculty. Their focus was
on what made teaching good, whether in the classroom or online.

The seminar concluded that online teaching and learning can be done with high
quality if new approaches are employed which compensate for the limitations of
technology, and if professors make the effort to create and maintain the human touch
of attentiveness to their students. . . . Participants concluded that the ongoing physical and even emotional interaction between teacher and students, and among students themselves, was an integral part of a university education. [University of
Illinois Faculty Seminar 2000]

## STRUGGLES OVER LEARNING AND ITS ASSESSMENT

In the United States "assessment" and "accountability" are the new buzzwords
in education at all levels—a development that has happened simultaneously with
the expanding use of digital technologies. The significance of this is evident in
the difference between educating a fine chef and a McDonald's food preparer.
Chefs are taught to understand basic principles that can then be amended, recom-
bined, or mindfully ignored, including an understanding of the limitations of
those principles. Chefs can be both disciplined and creative, developing innovative new dishes. McDonald's food preparers are taught the unquestioning application of routine protocols, with little or no understanding of why they are done a
certain way or what would happen if the procedures were modified. Thought and
originality are completely discouraged, and no tools or methods are acquired for
developing new understanding or for assessing the potential of new approaches.
This distinction captures well the range of differences in educational goals,
content, processes, and results. The differences are so great that we need different words to describe them. Will we allow this level of polarization to emerge in
the academy?

In the United States assessment has tended to focus primarily on student
outcomes, but it might also be considered in relation to the quality of educational
programs, curricula, courses, and faculty. The rapid growth of satellite campuses, overseas programs, transfer credits, and so forth raises issues of quality
control and acceptance of credits and courses. If credits become standardized
and fungible, what does that do to quality control? In developing countries the

rapid expansion of distance education (much of it not yet digital but still in the form of radio lectures or correspondence courses) has raised serious concerns about quality control among educational officials in some of those countries—for example in Brazil, China, and India (Bollag 2001: A29–A30).

Marketplaces are notorious for producing overblown advertising claims and counterfeit goods that try to simulate known brands with a reputation for quality. As market principles and practices penetrate higher education, we would expect to see more examples of "consumer fraud." One question is: how will "educational consumers" be protected from such instances? How will the rights of students be protected? The growth of an industry model of health-care delivery has led to a call for a "Patient's Bill of Rights" in the U.S. Congress and to growing efforts by doctors to unionize. We would expect that changes in the way higher education is delivered and assessed might lead to various kinds of reactions and resistances.

Research has yielded mixed effects, with a large number of examples available in the "no significant difference" archive (Russell 1999). We clearly need more detailed studies of how digital technologies are being used and what the intended and unintended consequences are. These studies need to consider how digital technologies affect different types of students. For example, current research is often ambiguous. A study by Gay and Grace-Martin found that email and the web offered major distractions to at least some students (Carlson 3/21/2001: online). Flowers, Pascarella, and Pierson (2000) found that email and other digital technologies affected different types of students differently, and Dillon and Gabbard (1998) found that better students benefited more from hypertext than did weaker students.

## SHIFTING FACULTY ROLES

Digital technologies will also impact on faculty roles. Is the role of university professor going to become more like a McJob? While many faculty use email and word processing, considerably fewer use digital technologies in their teaching (Green 2000).

Many U.S. universities are pushing the use of digital technologies in a big way, in the hope of saving or even making money in the long run. To what degree are faculty involved, or are such decisions being made by administrators and/or information technology personnel?

When technology enters the picture, there is a tendency to unbundle the faculty role, with content specialists (faculty), pedagogical specialists, technical specialists, and assessment specialists working together as a team to produce curricular materials. Formerly, all of these roles were played (however well or badly) by faculty. When the roles are separated, there is a greater likelihood that a "work for hire" model of intellectual production may occur (see next section).

Such tendencies might result in the "deskilling" of much of the faculty workforce. If doctors can find their professional expertise contested by health maintenance organizations, as we have seen happen in the last five years in the United States, it is possible that faculty will also find their professional expertise contested.

Another possible lesson from the field of medicine is the way the intrusion of business accounting into the delivery of health care has squeezed such non-billable goods as medical education. In the university, some of our "nonbillable" activities include research and writing, which are subsidized by undergraduate education. If the logic of for-profit industries invades universities fully, we might expect it to squeeze out all nonfunded research and writing, as it tends to already at community colleges, where relatively small numbers of full-time faculty teach five courses a semester.

There is a possibility that faculty could lose control over the means of production and the means of distributing knowledge. Intellectual property rights to course syllabi and other teaching materials have been contested, for example, at UCLA in the United States, where university administrators tried to stake a claim of institutional ownership over all faculty teaching materials. Not surprisingly, one of the sources of resistance by faculty to digital technologies is concern about intellectual property rights. David Noble has vividly described UCLA's attempted "land grab" when they declared that every faculty member must put his or her course syllabus on the web, and UCLA "owned" these intellectual products (Noble 1998). The ensuring furor challenged the university's fiat. The example certainly raises the question of who owns the intellectual products created by faculty and graduate students (Clarke 2000).

A second model of intellectual property recognizes the role of knowledge creators but limits the benefits innovators may gain from their work. This is the "work for hire" model. For example, Boxmind, a British company, offers "Prerecorded Lectures by Big-Name Scholars" (Birchard 2001). Academic scholars are paid a flat rate for their lecture and receive no royalties. A "work for hire" model superimposes a corporate model of creativity on academic scholars and teachers, where any discovery, creation, or invention made while in the employ of the corporation belongs to the corporation.

Digital technologies erode the relative monopoly faculty used to have over exposure to "knowledge." With the widespread availability to students of the World Wide Web, faculty are no longer able to restrict the knowledge about a topic or issue that students see. This erosion began with the invention of the printing press, so it is hardly a new phenomenon, and many in the academic would do not see these tendencies in a negative way. Nevertheless, the trend underscores the importance of teaching students how to assess critically the reliability and validity of content from various sources. It also raises new concerns about student plagiarism. A further issue is the potential for a power struggle between professors and students regarding technology. Many students are more skilled users of technology delivery systems than are many faculty, a situation that turns the traditional power structure upside down (Munitz 2000).

In higher education in the United States there has been a growing use of relatively anonymous, powerless adjunct instructors to answer student inquiries, to grade their work, and sometimes to teach courses (Pannapacker 2000). In 2001 for the first time in a number of years the percentage of teaching done by part-time or adjunct instructors remained steady rather than increasing, so possibly the tendency is leveling off. At some institutions, however, the percentage of courses taught by full-time faculty has shrunk below 50% of all offerings. The presence of so many part-time instructors certainly erodes the time of the remaining full-time faculty for participating in institutional decision making about how digital technologies are being used and for engaging in faculty development to obtain the new knowledge and understanding needed to use technology to enhance student learning.

A second major tendency is the growth of unionization at private and public institutions among part-time and adjunct instructors as well as teaching assistants. Will growing unionization be accompanied by intensified efforts by universities to substitute technology for human instruction? If profit maximization becomes the goal of higher education, efforts will be made to reduce faculty power—for example by reducing their role in decision making, by unbundling their roles, and by seeking to define their intellectual work as "work for hire."

Similarly, students with the greatest social, cultural, and economic resources will be disproportionately represented in the institutions with the richest resources, thereby raising the probabilities that they will be exposed to constructivist conceptions of knowledge and its diffusion and thus be well positioned to obtain dominant positions in the "knowledge economy."

There is therefore a possibility of increased stratification in higher education, just as there has been in food provision, where we have witnessed the growth of standardized, low-cost, profit-maximizing fast food at the same time as there has been a proliferation of high-end celebrity chef restaurants frequented more often by the already privileged and powerful members of society, who may buy McDonald's stock but never eat their burgers. Similarly, this upper 5% of society may invest in for-profit educational firms, but they would never send their children to such schools.

Such tendencies are another reason why making knowledge public is so important. If the new technologies can provide "deeper levels of transparency" into what is taught and learned in various institutions of higher education, that would be an important antidote to closed systems that prevent anyone from seeing what kinds of understandings are expected of students in different institutions.

## CONCLUSION

Is technology a Trojan Horse slipping commercialization inside the walls of higher education? The argument of this chapter is that the threat of McDonaldization for higher education lies less in its rationalizing tendencies than in its push toward profit maximization. Both rationality and technology are tools that can be used in the service of many masters. At issue is who will set the goals they serve. Hopefully, other faculties will follow the lead of the University of Illinois faculty seminar that conducted serious investigations into some of the pedagogical implications of digital technologies. Also encouraging are examples of vigorous efforts to preserve open conceptions of knowledge and its distribution such as the Open Knowledge Initiative (OKI) and the Los Alamos archive. The distinctive potentialities of digital technologies for increased reflexivity about teaching and learning and the emergence of the STL movement and other institutional supports for such concerns constitute a third hopeful trend.

## REFERENCES

Bass, R., & Eynon, B. (1998). Teaching culture, learning culture, and new media technologies: An introduction and framework. *Works and Days 31/32*, 16 (1/2): 11–96.

Benson, D. E., Haney, W., Ore, T. E., Persell, C. H., Schulte, A., Steele, J., & Winfield, I. (2001). Thinking sociologically about digital technology, teaching, and learning: What we know and what we need to know. Paper presented at the American Sociological Association annual meeting, Anaheim, CA, August.

Birchard, K. (2001). British company offers prerecorded lectures by big-name scholars. *The Chronicle of Higher Education,* online edition (last accessed 8 March 2001) <http://chronicle.com/free/2001/0302001030801u.htm>.

Bollag, B. (2001). Developing countries turn to distance education: Enrollments can increase quickly with online programs, but so do quality-control issues. *The Chronicle of Higher Education,* 15 June: A29–A30.

Bourdieu, P. (1980). *Questions de sociologie*. Paris: Editions de Minuit.

Bourdieu, P., & Wacquant, L. J. D. (1992). *An Invitation to Reflexive Sociology*. Chicago, IL: University of Chicago Press.

Carlson, S. (2001). Researchers conclude that wireless technology is a double-edged sword. *The Chronicle of Higher Education* online edition (last accessed 22 March 2001) <http://chronicle.com/free/2001/0302001032101t.htm>.

Clarke, L. (2000). Why do we need coolclass? *The Coolclass Chronicle* 01 (02) (last accessed 4 December 2000) <http://www.coolclass.com/newsletter/vol01no02-clarke.html>.

Dillon, A., & Gabbard, R. (1998). Hypermedia as an educational technology: A review of the quantitative research literature on learner comprehension, control, and style. *Review of Educational Research,* 68: 322–349.

Flowers, L., Pascarella, E. T., & Pierson, C. T. (2000). Information technology use and cognitive outcomes in the first year of college. *Journal of Higher Education,* 71: 637–667.

Glanz, J. (2001). The world of science becomes a global village. *The New York Times,* 1 May: F1, F2.

Green, K. C. (2000). *The 2000 National Survey of Information Technology in U.S. Higher Education* <http://www.campuscomputing.net/summaries/2000/index.html>.

Gumport, P. J. (2000). Academic restructuring: Organizational change and institutional imperatives. *Higher Education: The International Journal of Higher Education and Educational Planning,* 39: 67–91.

Jaffee, D. (1997). Asynchronous learning: Technology and pedagogical strategy in a distance learning course. *Teaching Sociology* 25: 262–277.

Kaufman, J. (2001). At Elite universities, a culture of money highlights class divide. *The Wall Street Journal,* 8 June: A1, A6. Chicopee, MA.

Munitz, B. (2000). Talk given at New York University, 9 March, New York.

Newton, R. R. (2000). For-profit and traditional institutions: What can be learned from the differences? *The Academic Workplace* 12: 4–7. Published by NERCHE New England Resource Center for Higher Education, University of Massachusetts, Boston, MA.

Noble, D. F. (1998). Digital diploma mills: The automation of higher education. *First Monday 3* (1) (last accessed 9 November 1999) <http://www.firstmonday.dk/issues/issue3_1/noble>.

Pannapacker, W. (2000). The adjunct rip-off: 10 reasons why the use of adjuncts hurts students. *The Chronicle of Higher Education* online (last accessed 8 December 2000) <http://chronicle.com/jobs/2000/12/2000120104c.htm>.

Persell, C. H., & Wenglinsky, H. (2001). For-profit postsecondary education and civic engagement. Unpublished paper, New York University.

Reich, R. (1991). *The Work of Nations: Preparing Ourselves for Twenty-First-Century Capitalism.* New York: A. A. Knopf.

Ritzer, G. (1998). *The McDonaldization Thesis: Explorations and Extensions.* London & Thousand Oaks, CA: Sage.

Russell, T. L. (1999). *The No Significant Difference Phenomenon.* Chapel Hill, NC: Office of Instructional Telecommunications, North Carolina State University.

Schmookler, A. B. (1984). *The Parable of the Tribes: The Problem of Power in Social Evolution.* Berkeley, CA: University of California Press.

Schutte, J. G. (1996). Virtual teaching in higher education: The new intellectual superhighway or just another traffic jam? (last accessed 10 July 2000) <http://www.csun.edu/sociology/virexp.htm>.

University of Illinois Faculty Seminar (2000). Teaching at an Internet distance: The pedagogy of online teaching and learning—The Report of a 1998–1999 University of Illinois Faculty Seminar (last accessed 10 July 2000) <http://www.vpaa.uillinois.edu/tid/report/tid_report.html>.

Young, J. R. (2001a). Grants help MIT put course materials online. *The Chronicle of Higher Education* online edition. (last accessed 29 June 2001) <http://chronicle.com>, Section: Information Technology, p. A33.

Young, J. R. (2001b). Universities begin creating a free, "open source" course-management system. *The Chronicle of Higher Education* online edition (last accessed 4 May 2001) <http://chronicle.com>, Section: Information Technology, p. A36.

# 6

## The Online Campus

*James Woudhuysen*

In June 2001 the Open University announced that it would put up 360 Websites for each of the 360 courses it offers its 120,000 online students. It will publish in eXtensible Mark-up Language, or XML, a programming system that allows course presentation to be separated from course content. Coupled to a Dutch content management system and suitably amended, XML should

1. allow academic staff to write courseware for the Web in Microsoft Word;
2. speed workflow, re-use, version control, and the selling on of courseware to other institutions;
3. allow large courses to be broken down into smaller ones with ease;
4. make courses more accessible from television and—significantly—from mobile phones.

Dave Meara, head of online applications at the OU, foresees large savings: "We will be able to handle a bigger volume and turn things around quicker, as there will be less editing needed as course materials will come in tidier. XML forces a structure" (quoted in Amos 2001: 34). Britain's Open University is not alone. Against longstanding OU practice, Barcelona's UOC, the Open University of Catalonia, insists that its 20,000 students need attend only examinations in person (Aldea 2001: 13). Might IT therefore conspire and so be complicit in the McDonaldization of lectures, seminars, and tutorials? In his *The McDonaldization Thesis*, published in 1998, George Ritzer argued: "various nonhuman technologies . . . not managers . . . control employees" (1998: 7, 1999: 87). Meara's remark that XML "forces a structure" upon academics seems to vindicate that argument. Moreover, Ritzer continued: "universities are using some of the advanced technology associated with the new means of consumption (especially television home shopping networks and cybermalls) by beaming courses to television sets or computers in satellite campuses or even in student homes" (1998: 11). Like Big Mac's cousin Domino's Pizza, Ritzer remarked, "universities are increasingly in the business of home delivery" (1998: 11). Barcelona's UOC would again seem to bear him out.

This chapter begins by reviewing the IT dimensions of the paper that Ritzer first delivered at Staffordshire University in 1996. Then, by reviewing both more recent authors on the online campus and some of the real practice in the field, I look at two questions that Ritzer did not directly suggest in the less IT-obsessed world of 1996, but which now seem logical extensions of his ideas.

In 1996 Ritzer said that universities, out to attract and please student-consumers, would want to "go to the students," eliminate as many barriers as possible to obtaining degrees, and so accelerate the inflation of student grades (1998: 156). My first question is: how much of a role does IT play in the dumbing down of higher education? As for my second question: Ritzer wrote in 1998 of "the new American menace"—standardization and control—in Europe (1998: ch. 6). In her chapter of this book, Caroline Persell also asks whether IT sneaks market values inside the university's walls. So: how much is IT a Trojan Horse, already within the hallowed portals of European scholarship and pedagogic excellence, for rampant U.S. standardization, control, and branded commercialism?

## "McUNIVERSITY" MEETS IT:
## HIGH-TECH, LOW-COST, LOW-CLASS—
## A MEDIA BROTHEL EVERYWHERE YOU GO

For Ritzer, the university would want to attract students and parents who had consumer expectations of education. To appear high-tech to students, it would opt for the ATM, the cybermall, and the home shopping network (1998: 151–154). Also, those technologies promised, at a time of relative decline in the funding of HE, to lower the cost of higher education (1998: 154). Ritzer suggested that new technology would make learning a remote affair. Students would not need to go even to geographically local, "satellite" university campuses. Education would become national "and even international" in scope; the electronic transmission of courses would alter the time and space surrounding higher education dramatically and in postmodern style (1998: 157). Ritzer saw the advent of the online campus pessimistically, if idiosyncratically. His was a future which was "class-linked": rather than the poor being excluded from IT (what has now come to be termed the "digital divide"), only Harvard and Oxford would offer most of their education on traditional, physically based campuses (1998: 157). It was a future that would be

- hyper-real: universities could field far-off academics of great renown—whether alive or dead [1998: 158]

- full of instructors more rule-bound, more on-message and thus more in McJobs than ever before [1998: 158]

- bent on reproducing existing knowledge, not engaging in original scholarship and research [1998: 158]

- one in which students worked harder, yet had to transact business impersonally, by smart cards [1998: 160–161]

In his treatment of firms as a model for universities, Ritzer made an important distinction:

It is one thing to turn to prestigious industrial giants like IBM and GM; it is quite another to look to the seemingly far humbler McDonald's or Disney. Universities continue to look to industry for innovations (e.g., TQM—Total Quality Management), but the contemporary university is not primarily a means of production and therefore has more in common with, and to learn from, the new means of consumption. [1998: 153]

For Ritzer, the prime mover behind the online McUniversity was not the branded capitalist corporation in general, but the media multinational in particular: it consisted of firms with the production values appropriate to the "computerized, televised images" universities would be "circulating in hyperspace." Such firms certainly included Big Mac and Disney; but, in Ritzer's vision, they were more to do with MTV and CNN (1998: 159). In a general, Baudrillardian media brothel of signs, then, the online campus would ensure that "since education will be everywhere, since everything will be educational, in a sense nothing will be educational" (1998: 160).

Such would be the logical conclusion of dumbing down.

## ASSESSING RITZER'S VISION

Ritzer was very prescient. He anticipated the British and the Spanish Open Universities' move into home delivery. Today, European universities certainly vie with each other to appear high-tech. They also have to compete with U.S. universities online, as education has, indeed, gone international.

Digital universities would rather globalize branded academic media stars and today's dubious credentials than encourage original research and insight. If students in Britain and the United States have shown the same resistance to smart cards as retailers have in those countries, students certainly register online more and register in person less than they did in the past. If there is no higher-education media brothel everywhere you go, and the influence of the Disney Channel, MTV, CNN, or Home Shopping Network on education remains modest, the advent of digital television in Britain—and, with it, channels such as BBC Knowledge—has enabled education to penetrate new milieux.

Does, however, the modern university use the Web to "go to the students" and win them over? Not really. In the first place, the Web remains a consumer "pull" medium, not a corporate "push" one. In a footnote, Ritzer observes that Internet companies like the PointCast Network were "broadcasting their messages to the consumer's video screen" rather than waiting for surfers to come to them (1998: 162). But PointCast, Spielberg's pop.com, and many ventures like them have collapsed. Universities are indeed out to attract and please student–consumers. Failure to run a decent Website will count against them competitively. But universities have been and are likely to remain unable to use IT to "go to the students."

The online campus has also, so far, not been enough in the British student's face to attract him or her, in Ritzerian style—with the delights of high tech. Clubbing attracts students to a particular university more than does its adroit use of the Web. A Web presence is merely a university's ticket to enter the competitive race.

What about the use of IT to eliminate as many barriers as possible to obtaining degrees—eliminate what Ritzer terms "negativity"? Oddly enough, there is plenty of "negativity" around the student use of IT. There are the costs of

1. hardware and software;
2. compatibility problems;
3. maintenance and repair;
4. online subscriptions;
5. what the inkjet printer industry describes as "consumables" (paper, ink).

*Clearly, parents and students will have to undertake more paid work to meet the costs of "IT and HE."*

In addition, anyone who has experience of IT knows that it can often lead to more work, not less. The forecasters Gartner Group say that most users of IT spend about a third of their time with it reformatting documents and images. All these things make the online campus full of barriers as far as students are concerned. Ritzer could have been speaking specifically of IT when he wrote: "students will be forced to do more of the labor within the new means of education. . . . Students do this work for free" (1998: 161). Today, more work from "consumers"—a pattern first set for shoppers in 1920s America by the pioneering Piggly Wiggly supermarket—means that, for students at the electronic McUniversity, there is more labor to do around IT, but an ever greater proportion of that labor is devoid of academic benefit. Self-service in a supermarket or in a McDonald's outlet is not the same as eating the food. By the same token, students who spend a lot of time fiddling about with the poor interfaces and compatibilities that surround IT will be dumbed down in the process.

In believing that IT could cut university costs, as distinct from student ones, Ritzer has been shown to be charmingly naive. Like companies getting serious about the Web, universities the world over have discovered that programming, design, authoring tools, training, upgrades, and downtime around the Web make it a hugely labor-intensive affair. Nevertheless, in 1997 the doyen of U.S. management theory, Peter Drucker, repeated Ritzer's mistake. Already, Drucker argued, universities could "deliver more lectures and classes off campus via satellite or two-way video at a fraction of the cost" of traditional methods. That was why large university campuses would, Drucker forecast, be "relics" by 2027 (Drucker 1997, cited in Werry 2001).

Therefore, the British electronic McUniversity, at least, is not that high-tech, not that attractive because of its IT, and not really low-cost. It has also yet to involve the lower classes by the million: it is Ivy League universities that have been the most aggressive in promoting the Web. Similarly, at Barcelona's UOC, an amazing 96% of students are in full-time employment (Aldea 2001). Finally, the electronic McUniversity has done little to ensure that students experience time and space in a new way. I can remember late nights in a windowless, fluorescent-lit computer room at Sussex University in the early 1970s, when Fortran and COBOL were the programming languages. Today, apart from those few students working from home using Websites that originate in distant time zones, the weird and wonderful student approach to space and time seems only to have changed quantitatively, not qualitatively.


## IT HAS NOT ALL BEEN BAD . . .

Is, however, IT everywhere and always a force for dumbing down, standardization, and social control? For a start, it is worth asking what Ritzer meant by "nonhuman" technologies. All technology is made by humans; all, too, as the result of human labor, can never be anything else but "nonhuman." As it happens, the Web and Web-based videoconferencing have the potential to be perfectly "human." Although I favor "didactic" forms of teaching, and in particular the formal lecture, I very much approve of the Web as one among many dialogue-based supplements to lectures (I also approve of seminars).

However, in a famous article published in 1997 by the peer-reviewed Internet journal *First Monday*, David Noble, a distinguished historian at Toronto's York university, announced that IT was, indeed, a universal force for evil in HE. He ridiculed North U.S. universities as "digital diploma mills" in which an unholy alliance of corporations and university administrators put students and professors back into an old, coercive era of automation, mass-production, standardization, and commercial interests.

For Noble, IT commoditized instruction into courseware that could be owned and bought and sold in the market.[1] The domination of the university classroom by the boardrooms of companies in IT, edutainment, and publishing—a triad of the kind of media pimps lambasted by Ritzer—would revive "traditional labor issues." Why? Because "as in other industries," IT was "being deployed by management primarily to discipline, de-skill and displace labour." Noble continued:

Once faculty and courses go online, administrators gain much greater direct control over faculty performance and course content than ever before and the potential for administrative scrutiny, supervision, regimentation, discipline and even censorship increase dramatically. At the same time, the use of the technology entails an inevitable extension of working time and an intensification of work. [Noble 1997]

Faculty could expect IT to assist in the usurping of their intellectual property rights. Students could expect the same to happen to them, as well as to pay for costly IT that would track their every move as guinea pigs in "product trials masquerading as courses."

Noble's emphasis on market commoditization and the theft of intellectual property showed a debt, perhaps, to an uncredited Marx—although Marx faulted capitalists, not technology, for the theft, not of ideas, but of surplus value. Despite his references to long hours and intense labor, the attention Noble gave to the control of labor, rather than its exploitation, showed a debt to a reviser of Marx whom Ritzer, in his own treatment of McJobs, explicitly acknowledges as an inspiration: Harry Braverman (1974). Finally, Noble's emphasis on corporations unethically endangering students' privacy by tracking them through IT showed, if not a debt to Foucault, then perhaps one to the communitarian father of anticapitalist paranoia about IT, Howard Rheingold (1994).

But if Noble differed from Ritzer in attributing high costs to IT, he carried through the logic of his predecessor's argument in his charge—made in a final footnote—that IT had won "no significant gains" in "pedagogical enhancement." That was too sweeping.

In a riposte to Noble, Frank White, library director at Marygrove College, Detroit, notes that Web-based instructional tools and applications include

1. Virtual Reality Modeling Language

2. Multipoint video conferencing

3. Teleconferencing

4. Digital video and audio broadcasts

5. Interactive multimedia, self-instruction modules

6. Audio-text lectures

7. Audio-slide presentations

8. Plain text applications

9. Computer-mediated conferencing ("by far the most popular of all higher education tools"). [White 1999]

One does not need to be a booster of IT to believe that, given the right curricular and research directions, some of these tools have, in a minority of cases, brought real pedagogical benefits.

As White accurately notes, Noble failed to adduce real evidence of pedagogical failure with IT. Indeed, while Ritzer felt IT to be a positive attractor of students, Noble's evidence for pedagogical failure was the argument that "students want the genuine face-to-face education they paid for, not a cyber-counterfeit." That argument has not been borne out by events, for, as Ritzer predicted, students now expect education to be online. But in fact Noble's real lapse was worse.

Apart from a few remarks, Noble neglected the whole issue of pedagogy in IT-assisted education. His focus on ideas being ripped off, on traditional labor issues, and on student privacy failed to address the key question: if IT dumbs students down, how exactly does it do that? Yet refusal to discuss in detail the pedagogical merits and demerits of IT is, with Ritzer and a few other honorable exceptions, very common. Britain's Higher Education Funding Council for England (HEFCE), for example, wants to make an e-University operational by the end of 2002 (HEFCE 2001b). But why? In its "Strategies for learning and teaching in higher education: A guide to good practice," HEFCE's treatment of the "strategic implementation" of IT makes no reference, across four bulletpoints and three case histories, to improved pedagogy (HEFCE 2001a). Nobody ever asks: at the online campus, is the highest task to cut and paste bits of the Web and present the result as an original essay?

From the anticapitalist side, Naomi Klein has directly stigmatized IT as a collaborator in "the branding of learning" (2000: ch. 4). Though she notes the invasion of schools and campuses by corporate brands such as McDonald's, Klein does not touch on university websites as a conduit for ads. But when schools and universities "pretend they are corporations," she argues, the deployment of IT that goes alongside this corporatization of teaching has sad results: "as many education experts have pointed out," she announces, "the pedagogical benefits technology brings to the classroom are dubious at best" (2000: 88).

It is true that the historical evidence for pedagogical success with IT, like that for economic productivity with IT, is limited—whatever IT's boosters say. After all, the Web is still in its infancy, and nowhere more so than in HE. But it is poor scholarship to think that one has marshaled all the evidence against pedagogical success with IT by means of a Noblesque footnote or, in Klein's case, an unsubstantiated assertion. IT is a powerful mediator; the arguments around it need to be mediated if they are to be powerful. Here we will touch on a few very simple examples of the pedagogical benefits available through IT.

It is only a trite point, but the fact that Noble published on the Internet aided the discussion of his ideas. The wider access to education that the Web can open up does not, by itself, inevitably result in dumbing down. It does not, either, inevitably result in a better debate; but First Monday alone has sponsored serious discussion of the online campus, and this chapter—which is not published on the Web—has benefited from it.

More substantively, T. Mills Kelly, who teaches an undergraduate course on Western Civilization at the history department of Texas Tech University, has concluded that students who access learning resources on the Web display a higher level of recursive reading than do those with access only to paper materials.[2] Primary sources on the Web were "just a click away": three in every four students went back to them, while just one in every four did the same with documents supplied in a course pack.

That gain was significant. But students engaged in this sort of recursiveness, Mills Kelly reports, did so almost exclusively when assignments were designed in such a way that returning to earlier sources would obviously improve student papers. As Mills Kelly concludes of his research: "Thus, when properly designed, web-based learning resources and assignments do encourage recursive reading among students in an introductory history course in ways that the very same assignments in a offered via print do not."[3]

Nothing is guaranteed with IT: putting rubbish in leads to rubbish coming out. But at the level of research, the success of the Human Genome Project depended, in part, on international collaboration mediated through the Web. That was not dumbing down.

So much for IT's historical record. What about its future potential? Ritzer hints in his chapter in this book that IT could impart a sense of the spectacular if lecturers could use it "live" in lecture halls to interrogate students and be interrogated by them. This must be true. The right lecturer, buttressing his oratorical technique with the right IT, could engage students, improve their curiosity, and put pressure on them in terms of their preparation for the "event." This would not be dumbing down.

## ... BUT MOST OF THE IT INTRODUCED INTO HIGHER EDUCATION TENDS TO REINFORCE UNCRITICAL ATTITUDES

Where Ritzer was emphatically right was in his forecast that turning education into a consumer experience would dumb it down. And the sad fact is that IT has, in the current climate, mostly acted so as to accelerate this process. That IT has often been used and vaunted as a force for customizing the experience of study, rather than simply standardizing it in the way predicted by Ritzer and Noble, paradoxically confirms this. There is a strong tendency for the real educational potential of IT to be squandered in regressive pedagogy.

In 2001, as part of an excellent book of papers about online communities, Timothy Luke evoked his experience of the Cyberschool at Virginia Polytechnic Institute and State University (Luke 2001: 163, 168). In an otherwise fairly balanced paper, he upheld IT both for the "more open, egalitarian, and consensual" decision making he says it can bring to university administration and for the "fresh modes of discourse" it promotes in pedagogy. Let us assess these two claims.

The claim that IT adds to democracy on campus need not detain us long. IT cannot be a force for democracy, because democracy is a political and not a technical question. The problem with IT is not, as Luke suggests, that "there are at least two billion pages on the Web, but the best search engines only capture only about 300 or so million of them" (Luke 2001: 167). Rather, as Chris Werry, one of Luke's coeditors, records in a still more recent paper, "The argument that the digitization of education will democratize learning is often at odds with the idea that in order to move quickly in the Internet-age, deliberative democracy within the university itself must be lessened" (Werry 2001).

But what about the Web as an encouragement to fresh modes of discourse? The Web cannot just be dismissed as advanced technology associated with new means of consumption. It can form an extra channel—no more, but no less either—for research, experiment, and teaching. Like all its predecessors back to the Gutenberg printing press, the Web is never the independent driver of social developments; to believe this is to indulge in technological determinism. But the Web has some special logics of its own, even if it shares much of them with other technologies.

The Human Genome Project shows how the Web offers people a special chance to build collaborations on academic matters that are genuinely constructive. However, even here it is worth noting the words of Dr. Stephen C. Ehrmann:

Most factors affecting the value of technology for collaborative learning do not directly relate to technology. They are the factors that block or encourage people to collaborate. If people do not want to collaborate, or cannot, the technology is of no value. If, on the other hand, they are hungry to collaborate and are good at it, the very same technology can be of enormous educational value. If we had tried to evaluate the technology just by studying the technology, we'd have missed much of what was actually going on. [Ehrmann 2000]

Unbridled technophilia about the collaborative possibilities in the Web serves little purpose.

As a force for interaction and participation, the Web is, again, often overrated: both clicking through images and blabbing through chatrooms can be mindless. Any good lecturer with chalk and talk can be fully interactive and encourage participation without the aid of the Web. It is, however, the way in which it allows students to "customize" learning that may prove to be the special characteristic of the Web that turns out to be most dangerous from an educational point of view.

With every kind of IT, the process "tail"—clicking through forms and tickboxes—can today all too easily wag the outcome "dog" of studying, reflecting, and acting upon genuine content. So today, when most students approach educational customization in the literal manner of customers, they will suffer. Using the Web in a sensible, guided customization of educational content to one's own research interests will be the exception, not the rule.

Claire Fox has contended that "the great celebration of expanding knowledges" in education today neglects knowledge as mankind's "unique capacity to strive towards truths through the application of reason" (Fox 2000). She is right; and the Web chimes all too easily with those uncritical, relativist theories, now so fashionable in education, that she attacks. I have argued elsewhere that the Web, like postmodernism, can fragment inquiry and indeed become a substitute for it; that there is a general "crisis of content" around IT (Woudhuysen 1999). Since the publication of Howard Gardner's *Frames of Mind: The Theory of Multiple Intelligences* (1983) and Diana Laurillard's *Rethinking University Teaching: A Framework for the Effective Use of Information Technology* (1993), educationalists have set a context for the Web that exacerbates its tendency to dumb things down.

The modernizing educationalist's agenda with the Web today begins by contrasting it to lectures gone by.[4] They were "one-way" and "broadcast" in nature, unrelated to students' needs, and often alienating to students. What is now required is a recognition that learning is a joint, interactive construction of and dialogue between the student, his or her peers, and the teacher. Learning cannot be one-way, it cannot concentrate on the linear, printed word as the sole mode of discourse, and the Web is on hand to ensure that these problems need exist longer. Instead, learning must and can now address the needs and educational pace of each individual student; it must and can, in a phrase, be "student-centered."

This is a beguiling doctrine, not least because many of the old lecturers were boring. But the fact is that, mediated by those managers whose role Ritzer dismisses, the student-centered pedagogic approach today converges with "user-centered" IT not just to facilitate the control of university employees and students, but also to dumb them down. Werry sees the claim that online is "student-centered" as "camouflaging shortcomings in models of online education . . . it isn't clear that this necessarily empowers students, provides for a better educational experience, or is really in line with constructivist pedagogy" (Werry 2001).

His only error is to see an opposition between constructivist pedagogy and the "student-centeredness" of online. Constructivists put the different lines of inquiry and forms of discourse that students customize for themselves on the same level as the accumulated wisdom of professors—now renamed "coaches." They are bound to take an uncritical attitude to the Web and ensure that it plays its part in dumbing people down. The canon is no more; the customizing Web takes its place. As Norman Clark, an assistant professor at Appalachian State University, notes of the U.S. educational portal supplier Campus Pipeline, "by customizing each page for each student, Campus Pipeline is actually ensuring that students will have less and less in common to discuss" (Clark 2001: 143).

Mills Kelly, who, as we have seen, is by no means unsympathetic to IT, has eloquently brought out what uncritical attitudes it encourages among students:

... students in my courses, despite going through very specific assignments designed to help them use the web as a research resource, remain disinclined to apply any sort of critical analysis to the sites they visit. Even the very best students simply do not think very much about whether or not a site is a good source of information. The only test most students impose on the sites they visit is a visual one—if the site appears to be very professional, then the information it contains must be valid. [http://www2.tltc.ttu.edu/kelly/Pew/Portfolio/welcome.htm]

HedLines, the higher-education part of the forecasting services provided by Gartner Group, also makes some commendably sober remarks about how, in education as elsewhere, there is indeed a "crisis of content" around IT:

digital delivery technologies have matured much faster than those involved in the production and distribution of content.

... as higher education's focus passes from delivery infrastructure to content management . . . e-learning content—the digital resources, whether commercial or homegrown, that add instructional value to network-delivered courses, including instructor-developed materials, electronic textbooks, library collections, simulation software, and even dynamic online interactions — will help determine both the pedagogical and the economic success of e-learning.

At the same time . . . institutions must maintain a sense of proportion. . . . Even the best content, whether traditional or electronic, cannot automatically make students learn. Perhaps more than ever, institutions must highlight the services they deliver: selecting material, defining programs, setting standards and creating dynamic interaction — all of which make learning happen. [Yanosky 2001]

Too right! Universities, not students, must take the lead in selecting Web materials, defining programs, and setting standards. The "bottom line," as Gartner properly notes, is that "long-term investment in content will far exceed that of delivery infrastructure." For the moment, it observes, Web content for higher education is a matter of "caveat emptor." Likewise, it notes: "the e-library is a great idea and digital collections are growing. Yet we are years away from digital libraries that will support basic higher-education degree programs" (Harris 2001). IT, then, has not caused a dumbing down of education. But, within today's context of bleak educational philosophy, it has given that process extra momentum. IT does not "conspire" or act in a way that is "complicit" in dumbing down. IT lacks, after all, human willpower. But as it is deployed today, IT is an excellent mediator for the forces of relativism in higher education and boasts its own crisis of content there.

## THE PRECAUTIONARY PRINCIPLE
## AND THE ONLINE CAMPUS

*Let's not go too far*. The dot.com era—from 1995 to spring 2000—meant "cash burn," banner ads, and passing fads. The subsequent mood swing about IT—from what Alan Greenspan called "irrational exuberance" to what has been termed "irrational pessimism" about it—is also an example of short-term thinking. Since the millennium, many people have mistaken a decline in the price of technology stocks as a decline in the potential of IT to work as a force for good. Thus although the online campus has, more or less, helped to mediate the process of dumbing down higher education, to conclude from current practice that IT is intrinsically fated to degrade the pedagogical process would be a mistake. It would betray thinking about IT that was as impulsive as Ritzer's hated "fast food" is fast.

Yet that short-term thinking about IT—a kind of alienated response to the alienation it induces—is quite prevalent among educationalists. In 1999 Michael Milken, the junk bond king, Paul Allen, a cofounder of Microsoft, and John Chambers, chief executive of Cisco Systems, all announced that they could make money from online education. Since that time, online education has gained a treatment from academia that is indifferent when it is not hostile.

Joanna Addison has shown that the American Association of University Professors regards IT as merely a delivery mechanism; it neglects IT's wider potential as a supplementary learning environment—one that academics must play a part in designing and modifying, even if companies supplying distance education technology would rather they did not (Addison 2001: 176, 187). The Universitas 21 global online university consortium, which at the time of writing is in negotiation with the U.S. firm Thomson Learning, has been hit by the withdrawal of two founding universities, Toronto and Michigan, which were worried that Thomson might abuse their names (Maslen 2001). The watchword is likewise evolution, not e-revolution, with Sir John Daniel, Vice-Chancellor of the OU for 11 years. Now assistant director general for education at UNESCO, he broadly applauds the way in which assessments of online learning turned "more sober" after the collapse of the dot.com era (Daniel 2001).

Frances Cairncross is management editor of *The Economist* and the latest chair of the Britain's prestigious Economic and Social Research Council. In her famous 1990s paean to IT, "The death of distance: how the communications revolution will change our lives," she pronounced: "in rich countries, more and more higher education and training will probably be delivered long-distance. . . . Distance learning may not have the cachet of a good university name, but it will be as good as, and less expensive than, a mediocre one" (Cairncross 1997: 274).

Now, in an article titled "Net froth is red herring," her tone has changed: "None of the elaborate projects that has sprung up in the United States in recent years to deliver online university education has yet come near to recouping the hefty costs of doing so." For Cairncross, online teaching is no match for the application of IT to university administration: "although it is certainly possible to teach people things online—sometimes with better results than in conventional classes—the main benefit to universities of the communications revolution is unlikely to lie in that area. Instead, for the foreseeable future, the main effect of new technology will be on the administration of universities" (Cairncross 2001).

Werry is also pessimistic. He concludes his recent survey of "the age of the e-college" with a call to be cautious and slow in adopting online techniques (Werry 2001). To be fair, it is only Werry and some of his collaborators who, by targeting the consumerization of the university in a manner akin to Ritzer, make a critique of the Web's effect on pedagogy. Elsewhere, the spread of a kind of precautionary principle in "IT for HE" is founded not on such a critique, but on a faddish, superficial posture against IT.

Although it appears the exact opposite of short-termism in higher education, the precautionary principle neglects the long-term potential of IT. Instead, it makes the worldly-wise observation that IT must be accompanied by other teaching methods. Yet to dismiss IT as merely the "clicks" that must at all moments be accompanied by campus-style "bricks" and faculty "face time" is to abdicate responsibility for research and action around the right question to ask about IT.

That question is simple. "What pedagogical advantages does IT, by itself and in conjunction with other technologies, offer?" The right answer is: given good content and design—it is a big given at the moment and looks like continuing to be one for some years yet—IT can within strict limits be a force for constructive collaboration, interaction, participation, and customization. I turn now from the question of dumbing down to that of commercialism.

## BRANDED AMERICANA
## AND THE RISE OF THE CORPORATE UNIVERSITY

We have seen in our look at customization that the move by corporations into the university world is not merely an economic one to do with standardization and control. As Clark notes of Campus Pipeline, its "revolutionary" aspect is that it has "found a way to convince people in academia, who are traditionally somewhat reluctant to commercialize, to actively participate in the transformation of their community into a consuming audience" (Clark 2001: 145). Clark observes: "When email from a professor comes with an advertisement attached, how much easier does it make it for students to connect consumption with education, to see knowledge as just one more thing that can be bought?" (2001: 148). This is a proper objection to the cult of the market on the online campus.

The online campus is not just about U.S.-led e-commerce commoditizing instruction, or "Michael Milken's plot to eat our lunch." It will also be about the EU trying to sustain its competitive advantages in telecommunications by bringing European education to foreign markets. HEFCE, for example, looks forward to a "future outcome" in which "demand for HE programs both in the UK and overseas" expands through Britain's e-University (HEFCE 2001a). Barcelona's UOC concluded an agreement in 2000 with the Planeta publishing house to offer Spanish-language degree courses throughout Latin America (Aldea 2001).

When I notice such developments, I conclude not that IT is a Trojan Horse for brash American commercialism, but rather, that IT spreads a pedagogic ethos that, emanating as much from the European public sector as from U.S. corporations, seems bent on dumbing down the whole planet.

Following Farrell, Werry, and my colleague at De Montfort university, Stephen Brown, it is possible to classify online universities into different types (see Farrell 1999; Werry 2001). Table 6.1 attempts to do this.

Perhaps the most important development has been that of online corporate universities. Top ones exist in North American corporations: at Anheuser-Busch, Bain, the Bank of Montreal, Cisco, Dell, General Motors, Hewlett-Packard, IBM, Intel, Milliken, Motorola, NCR, PeopleSoft, Sprint, Sun Microsystems, the Tennessee Valley Authority, and Xerox. But corporate universities are also a European creation, and are to be found at ABB, ABN Amro, Alstom, BAE Sytems, BT, Cap Gemini Ernst & Young, DaimlerChrysler, Fiat, Lloyds TSB, Lufthansa, LVMH, Old Mutual, and Volvo. Altogether, their numbers have grown over the past 15 years from 400 to 2,000, with the possibility of 3,700 being around in 2010. On average, each uses about 80 staff to train, for nearly 40 hours a year, 4,000 employees out of a typical corporate workforce of 26,000 employees. About one in four employees trains online, although this figure is set to rise to one in two by 2003 (see Anderson 2001: 1).

Corporate universities try to develop their own revenue streams and keep their own intellectual property. They are in the business of growth, of acquisitions, and, significantly, of educating customers. The Disney Institute is among them; but the list above shows that it is not just Ritzer and Noble's media concerns, but what Ritzer exonerated as "prestigious industrial giants" who are likely to determine much of the agenda in online higher education in future. Already, their influence in business schools is considerable.

However, it is not so much that corporations bring e-commerce to education, as that education has become a corporate discipline, like finance, sales, operations, and IT before it. But what kind of discipline is it? If the British case is anything to go by, corporate universities reveal the prejudices of public-sector educationalists just as much as they exhibit the vulgarities of market forces.

Human Resources departments inside British corporations are very keen on promoting knowledge management. But the cadre for this work frequently hails from the public sector in general and higher education in particular, if only because the education of adults remains a much bigger enterprise in the public sector than in the private one. Backed by a government committed to lifelong

**TABLE 6.1. Classification of Online Universities**

| Type | Characteristic | Example (originating firm or university) | Websites | Remark |
|---|---|---|---|---|
| Mega/Global | More than 100,000 students, many of whom study abroad | OU, UK | | 20,000 of OU's 150,000 degree students study in 100 countries outside the U.K. |
| Broker/Course aggregator | No courses of its own | Western Governors' Hungry Minds | www.wgu.edu www.hungryminds.com | Consortium of 11 western states in the U.S., plus Simon Fraser, Vancouver |
| Commercial | Private supply of education by universities or firms. Firms offer:<br>• courses | Phoenix<br>Melbourne<br>NYU<br>California Texas | www.uophx.edu/online<br>www.muprivate.edu.au<br>www.nyu.edu/virtual<br>www.california.edu<br>www.utsystem.edu | |
| | | Worldwide Learning (News International)<br>Jones International<br>FT Knowledge<br>Sylvan Learning Systems | www.worldwidelearning.com<br>www.jonesinternational.edu<br>www.ftknowledge.com | Jones was accredited in 1999 |
| | • networked informal presentations of work done by students or teaching assistants | InstantKnowledge | www.instantknowledge.com | |

| | | | |
|---|---|---|---|
| | • free education—and a conduit for ads, sales and the collection of customer data … <br> • outsourced portals for educational and administrative services | Campus Pipeline; eCollege | www.powered.com |
| Corporate | In-firm provision of educational services; sometimes, firm delivers to B-school, or forms consortia with more than one to develop courseware | See text below | See text below |
| Consortia | Partnerships—with other universities or with private firms—to create critical mass and spread risk | Unext <br> Eurospace 2000 <br> Universitas 21 <br> Fathom | www.unext.com <br><br> Unext includes Columbia, Stanford, Chicago, Carnegie-Mellon, LSE. Backed by Michael Milken and Oracle CEO Larry Ellison. 'Gold standard' in MBAs |
| Hybrid | Normal university offers some or all of particular courses. Sometimes branded but non-accredited | Hybrid. <br> Carnegie Technology Education <br> Columbia's Morningside Ventures Inc | www.dlcoursefinder.com <br> www.carnegietech.org <br><br> More than 50,000 courses from 65 countries |

learning and the educational merits of "human capital," corporate educational policies betray all the faults that now afflict mainstream universities.

At the Chartered Institute of Personnel Development, an 80,000-strong membership organization for U.K. professionals in human resources, e-learning expert Martyn Sloman upholds a "new paradigm" of "learner centered intervention." The CIPD runs workshops that use music and other performing arts to develop "the listening manager." Likewise, the Industrial Society—a long-standing group of U.K. companies that favor fair, partnership-based management—helps to train company employees with a dozen separate "video dramas" on workplace subjects as varied as AIDS, bullying, and negotiating. In short, the educational agenda in corporate universities is student-centered, thespian, therapeutic, and infantile. It is about soft skills, IT skills, and the winning of credentials. Like higher education, it does not need IT to modularize or customize, in the manner of McDonald's, the choice of sustenance it has to offer.

So: the answer to my second question is that, even inside corporations, IT will act as a Trojan Horse for a perfectly British corruption of education. That corruption ultimately emanates from the state, not the market.

## CONCLUSION

What is on the IT-style "menu" at the online campus today can amount to a triumph of style over substance. Already there are one or two great dishes; but for some time the feast looks like being very movable. The electronic McUniversity fills people up—but, like a Chinese takeaway, it leaves them feeling empty inside after no time at all. It is indeed no substitute for the charismatic lecturer or the proper library of hard-copy books.

The Web is a special monument to collective human ingenuity. But so long as it remains the subject of both irrational government dumbing down and the misplaced fears felt by myopic anticapitalists, its potential will be squandered. Worse still: to the extent that the Web is associated in the public mind with dumbing down, it risks becoming an Aunt Sally.

## NOTES

1. According to Noble, the 1973–74 oil crisis and intensified international competition opened up a first phase in which university research in science and engineering was commoditized from knowledge into intellectual property. A second, current phase is the commoditization of instruction (Noble 1997).

2. <http://www2.tltc.ttu.edu/kelly/Pew/Portfolio/welcome.htm>.

3. <http://www2.tltc.ttu.edu/kelly/Pew/Portfolio/welcome.htm>.

4. See, for example, the influential work of Georgetown University's Randy Bass, and in particular his *Engines of Inquiry: A Practical Guide for Using Technology to Teach American Culture*, a publication of the American Studies Crossroads Project, sponsored by the American Studies Association (first edition, revised, February 1998). See also <http://www.georgetown.edu/crossroads/ctl>.

## REFERENCES

Addison, J. (2001). Outsourcing education, managing knowledge and strengthening academic communities. In C. Werry, & M. Mowbray (Eds.), *Online Communities: Commerce, Community Action and the Virtual University*. Upper Saddle River, NJ: Prentice Hall (175–193).

Aldea, G. (2001). The virtual university campus. *Connectis* (July).

Amos, S. (2001). OU revises Internet strategy. *IT Week*, 25 June.

Anderson, L. (2001). Tailor-made for life-long learning. *Financial Times Survey on Business Education*, 26 March.

Bass, R. (1998). *Engines of Inquiry: A Practical Guide for Using Technology to Teach American Culture*. American Studies Crossroads Project/American Studies Association.

Braverman, H. (1974). *Labour and Monopoly Capital*. New York: Monthly Review Press.

Cairncross, F. (1997). *The Death of Distance: How the Communications Revolution Will Change Our Lives*. London: Orion.

Cairncross, F. (2001). Net froth is red herring. *Times Higher Education Supplement*, 6 April.

Clark, N. (2001). Education, communication and consumption: Piping in the academic community. In C. Werry & M. Mowbray (Eds.), *Online Communities: Commerce, Community Action and the Virtual University*. Upper Saddle River, NJ: Prentice Hall (129–151).

Daniel, Sir J. (2001). Evolution not an e-revolution, *The Times Higher Education Supplement*, 18 May.

Drucker, P. (1997). *Forbes*, 10 March 1997. Cited in C. Werry, "The work of education in the age of the e-college," 2001. <http://www.firstmonday.org/issues/issue6_5/werry/index.html>.

Ehrmann, S. C. (2000). Studying and improving the use of technology to support collaborative learning: An illustration of flashlight methods and tools, 25 April. <http://www.tltgroup.org/resources/F_Illustrative_1.htm>.

Farrell, G. M. (Ed.) (1999). *The Development of Virtual Education: A Global Perspective*. Commonwealth of Learning.

Fox, C. (2000). Knowledge without wisdom. *Times Educational Supplement*, 15 September.

Gardner, H. (1983). *Frames of Mind: The Theory of Multiple Intelligences*. New York: Basic Books.

Harris, M. (2001). The e-library: No shortcuts to quality. *Gartner Research Note TG-13–46331*, May.

HEFCE (2001a). *Strategies for Learning and Teaching in Higher Education: A Guide to Good Practice*. Report 01/37, June. <http://www.hefce.ac.uk/pubs/hefce>.

HEFCE (2001b). *Strategic Plan 2001–06*. Report 01/43, July. <http://www.hefce.ac.uk/pubs/hefce>.

Klein, N. (2000). The branding of learning: Ads in schools and universities. In *No Logo: Taking Aim at the Brand Bullies*. London: Flamingo.

Laurillard, D. (1993). *Rethinking University Teaching: A Framework for the Effective Use of Information Technology*. London: Routledge.

Luke, T. W. (2001). Building a virtual university: Working realities from the Virginia Tech cyberschool. In C. Werry & M. Mowbray (Eds.), *Online Communities: Commerce, Community Action, and the Virtual University*. Upper Saddle River, NJ: Prentice Hall (153–174).

Maslen, G. (2001). Further dissent hits U21 venture. *Times Higher Education Supplement*, 18 May.

Noble, D. (1997). Digital diploma mills: The automation of higher education. <http://www.firstmonday.org/issues/issue3_1/noble/index.html>.

Rheingold, H. (1994). *The Virtual Community: Finding Connection in a Computerized World*. London: Secker & Warburg.

Ritzer, G. (1998). *The McDonaldization Thesis: Explorations and Extensions*. London & Thousand Oaks, CA: Sage.

Ritzer, G. (1999). *Enchanting a Disenchanted World: Revolutionizing the Means of Consumption*. London & Thousand Oaks, CA: Sage.

Werry, C. (2001). The work of education in the age of e-college. <http://www.firstmonday.org/issues/issue6_5/werry/index.html>.

White, F. (1999). Digital diploma mills: A dissenting voice. <http://www.firstmonday.org/issues/issue4_7/white/index.html>.

Woudhuysen, J. (1999). *Cult IT*. London: Institute of Contemporary Arts.

Yanosky, R. (2001). "HedLines: Finding 'contentment' with e-learning content," Gartner Research Note COM-13–6450, 15 May 2001. <http://www3.gartner.com/Init>.

# 7

# From Power Plays to Market Moves: The Standard in Higher Education

## *Alan Hudson*

University attendance might be more common than in the past, but the experience students have today is unlike anything they would have had even a generation ago. The argument that this is a degraded experience is a particular form of the McDonaldization thesis (Ritzer 2000).

While it would be difficult to take exception to the character of this description of the contemporary university, the analytical power of the thesis is more problematic. The thesis in its appropriation and application of a straightforward Weberian model seems to endorse an implicit assumption that there was a golden age of the university before it was disenchanted or "McDonaldized." If this were the case, we should expect to find a university in which critical thinking and the rigorous questioning of inherited wisdom was the norm.

But if we take our Weberian template literally, we should expect to find, prior to the bureaucratization of the university, an enchanted and irrational world of tradition and arbitrary authority. In this enchanted world there is no place for the rational world of the university, nor, in the counterposition of the lost golden age and the contemporary degradation, is there a place for the Weberian sense of the positive aspects of rationality: the elimination of arbitrary authority. Characterization of the university through a systemic model that has such an ahistorical character must serve to idealize the university of the past and, as such, is an additional barrier to an understanding of how the university has become the sort of institution it is today.

Even the most cursory examination of the university experience in the postwar period (I just asked a number of friends who went to university in the 1960s but especially in the 1970s to recall their undergraduate days) reveals that there was no golden age of rigorous critical thinking. There was also no evidence of passionate, but probably platonic, relationships with intellectual mentors in a common search for the holy grail of truth.

Far be it from me to suggest that this would not be a good thing, but in the 1960s and 1970s it was not the case. Most students spent three years, in relatively privileged circumstances, discovering new aspects of the world in the first flush of still unresponsible adulthood. One possible route of discovery was in reading a number of interesting books, but for the majority this was a sideshow and not the main event.

The main function of the university, as it had long been, was the socialization of a new generation who, through their reaction to the experience, were to become the most influential players in government, business, and the professions for the following 30 or 40 years. The big difference was that for the generation that went through the university at this time, the normal socialization process broke down to a certain degree. The society of the elite which they were expected to enter became much less certain of itself, and the predisposition of the new generation to participate in that society became by no means assured. As Bob Dylan sang a few years earlier, as he discerned the shift occurring, about losing control over our sons and our daughters, for "the times they are a-changing."

The purpose of this contribution is to examine the educational forms that the arguments around the unraveling of the traditional role of the university took. I hope to show that the arguments deployed against the traditional elitist organization of the university not only missed the point but, indeed, contributed greatly to the present crisis of the academy.

In order to do this, I intend to present a necessarily schematic, historical view of the development of the university, to the point at which its function as a transmission belt for government and social order becomes challenged. I then wish to look at what I will term the two "progressive fallacies" deployed against the established order: cultural relativism and the association of social justice with economic efficiency. The twin dangers of these approaches come to fruition when they are placed in the pervasive culture of market forces. The result is the phenomenon we are all describing as McDonaldization.

I would then like to try to understand the same process through the way that the discussion of the purpose of education takes the form of different approaches to the curriculum. I do this not only from the point of view of a teacher but also from that of a citizen in the hope of helping to clarify and define what it is I hope the university can be.

## THE HISTORIC MISSION OF THE UNIVERSITY

The historical role of the university has not been to question authority, but to constitute it. The University of Bologna owes its origin to its geographical location: the place where Byzantine diplomats traveling from the Adriatic ports met papal clerks from Rome. Here the two legal traditions had to be reconciled and interpreted.

In England, at Cambridge, in 1316, a college was founded for the special purpose of providing "clerks for the King's service." The clerks were a body of men who codified, explained, and interpreted the authority of the crown in relationship to the divine order. This body of men, among whom we can count More, Wolsey, Cranmer, and Cromwell, were likely to be drawn from outside the landed aristocracy, but they interpreted the world of the nobility and especially the king to him. At an important moment in time they were required to redefine the social relationships of the early modern world for the benefit of the king. As such, although their relationship to the law cost a number of individual and previously influential clerks their lives, that same defining relationship to law and authority constituted the clerk in both his intellectual and his administrative dimensions as a key force in the land.

In order to explain and justify authority, the clerks in the university and in the chancellery had to assimilate and embody the total knowledge of humanity as it was formulated in the classical humanist curriculum. Their learning was the fullest expression of the objective knowledge of humanity, and it was deployed for the most part without any tension in the service of those who founded and funded the universities.

In the medieval university this was not a contentious proposition but the common sense of the natural order of things. It is only when in the scientific sphere the natural world is reconceptualized and in the social world human action is conceived as a more significant agent than divine ordination that the relationship between knowledge and the social order becomes problematic. For the most part the conflict between knowledge and authority takes place both outside and against the university. In the Renaissance this often took the form of a heroic struggle in the teeth of opposition from the Inquisition, perhaps staffed with university appointees. In eighteenth-century France most contributors to the *Encyclopédie,* the storyboard of the Enlightenment, had not only been nowhere near a university chair, but their project was to free the world of traditional obscurantism.

The experience of intellectual life from the Renaissance to the Enlightenment was predominantly outside the university. "You could find out more about Newtonian science in a London coffee house that sponsored weekly demonstrations and lectures than you could in most French colleges before 1750" (Appleby, Hunt, & Jacobs 1995: 8). If the university played any role at all, it was either as a bastion of reaction or as an organizer of knowledge that had become acceptable.

This is not to ignore isolated individuals such as Vico in Naples or influential schools of thought such as the political economists and historians associated with the Scottish Enlightenment, but to assert their exceptional nature. The experience of the universities of Glasgow and Edinburgh in the eighteenth century is a case in point. The excellence of these institutions at the time is closely associated with the theorization of the established commercial supremacy of the new British elite and a commitment to confirming that supremacy through empirical investigation.

At the same time Oxford played a parallel and perhaps more important social function as a rite of passage into the ordered world of the elite. Edward Gibbon said of his experience at Magdalen College, Oxford, in the middle of the eighteenth century that it was "the most unprofitable of my whole life" (Midgley 1996: 104). He said that the majority of students filled their days with drinking and idle chatter until they collapsed into sleep: "From the toil of reading, or thinking, or writing they had absolved their conscience" (1996: 58). Oxford did not suit Gibbon, but that was not its point.

The social habits of the students were part of a wider process of socialization: to become familiar with and accept self-confidently their position in the world, which included the right to rule. But the ability to rule in the modern world became a more complex affair than could be catered for by the habits of an eighteenth-century gentleman. New methods had to be adopted to equip the elite with the tools of their trade: the minority would understand and innovate social policy; the majority would administer it.

The excellence of the Scottish universities was short-lived, and although British universities did provide a grounding in the natural sciences for students such as Charles Darwin, this was not their main function. Darwin, himself, pursued his career outside the academy.

The modern origins of the university dating from the nineteenth century are in a social sense British and in an intellectual sense German. The British university adapted and changed at the end of the nineteenth century incorporating the academic traditions of Germany and adopting them to its own needs. The socialization of the elite remained the primary function of the university, but conducted in an environment in which the social order of the day was elaborated in a new spirit of academic specialization. The majority of undergraduates would imbibe the spirit of duty, piety, and responsibility. A minority would investigate and interpret the world around them.

A society like Britain's, whose elite had already arrived at a viable set of consensual political arrangements, had not previously needed to discuss its own identity or justify the forms the state took.[1] The subjects that reflected these concerns did not play much of a role in the university curriculum. In contrast in nineteenth-century Germany, which lacked any such political institutions, the university philosophized about such arrangements especially through the discussion of history and literature. In the process the German university developed the notions of specialized knowledge, research strategies, and the role of the academic professional that have become integral components of the modern university. At the same time the university was much more directly subordinated to the authority of the state and continued to articulate the need for such subordination and the purposes of the state.

Although the relationship between the university and the state was much more an unspoken one in Britain, it was nonetheless crucial. This relationship is reflected in the continued preeminence of Greats (ancient history, literature, and philosophy) in the Oxbridge (Oxford and Cambridge) curriculum. At the same time the German emphasis on national history and literature intended in Germany to impart a sense of national identity found its way into the curriculum to emphasize and celebrate British supremacy and all that had contributed to Britain's historical mission and triumph. In the twentieth century Modern Greats (at Oxford, politics, philosophy, and economics) played a defining role in the training of the governing elite.[2]

At the end of the nineteenth century the British university had an integrated answer to the following list of questions: why do you educate, whom do you educate, how do you educate? The answers were to provide the personnel who would provide the leaders of society who would preserve and enhance that society. These young men would come from those sections of society who had a stake in its maintenance and order. They would be taught to respect and learn from the past and to apply those lessons to key areas of contemporary public policy. The exemplary method for this was to acquire a critical and rigorous approach based on a thorough subject grounding but in the context of social conservatism.

The special merit of this system was that, allowing for the restricted understanding of the concepts, the university was a civic and public institution, albeit the intellectual discipline required of a minority was subordinate to the unspoken rules of the club. It was only together that the élan and cohesiveness of the elite was constituted.

In Britain the university experience, like the public school that preceded it, was more important for the inculcation, enhancement, and recognition of the cultural capital in which the initiates are secretly equipped.[3] In other university systems, and to some degree in Britain also, the formal recognition of qualifications or credentialing is important.[4] It is worth remarking here that the "credentialing" of civil servants in Britain from the time of the Northcote Trevelyan reforms in 1855 is an important part of the progressive rationalization of the state apparatus. Rational bureaucratic choice of state administrators began to replace arbitrary decisions and patronage.

## BREACHING THE IVORY TOWERS

The relationship of the university to the political elites broke down in the 1960s and 1970s. In the United Kingdom, this was because of the objective decline of British power and a subjective crisis of confidence in the upper echelons. In educational terms, the old order suffered an attack on two fronts. Each front is constituted by what I will call a progressive fallacy. On the one hand, an epistemological attack on the traditional curriculum led to many concessions to cultural relativism, and on the other, to a belief that access to educational possibilities should be justified not only as a matter of social justice but also on the grounds of economic efficiency.

Between the establishment of the modern university curriculum at the end of the nineteenth century and the widening access to university education encouraged in the 1960s and the 1970s, the British elite had come to take a very different view of the world and its own position in it. The general capitalist experience of economic depression and world war and the specific British experience of imperial decline undermined the elite commitment to a world view that emphasized their own political, cultural, and intellectual superiority, predicated on the assertion of an objective foundation to knowledge. In the nineteenth century the university had been able either to assimilate new knowledge or to generate a critique of new social theory largely because of its own belief in objective social progress. The work of Darwin, despite its implications for religious orthodoxy, entered the mainstream of university science. The work of Marx made little impact on Britain's self-confident elite, but on the Continent academic sociology developed rapidly as a discipline to take issue with the possibility of social transformation.

In the twentieth century the experience of chaos and defeat challenged the idea of capitalist social progress. The university became not only a forum in which the old order understood and tried to explain itself in a less confident and much more hesitant way. It also became an institution in which the very premises of the old order were scrutinized, challenged, and often dismissed: "In the twentieth century, Western civilization produced the most technologically sophisticated genocide ever seen in history. Progress, democracy, objective knowledge, and modernity itself no longer seemed to march in step towards the enrichment of humankind" (Appleby, Hunt, & Jacobs 1995: 8).

In their compelling study on history Appleby, Hunt, and Jacobs indicate the link between the loss of faith in progress and the acceptance of relativism in the discipline. The same point holds for the university as a whole. The elite lost faith in the values that the university upheld and their opponents in challenging elitism also challenged the canon that seemed to embody the discredited old order: "skepticism and relativism are two-edged swords. They can be wielded to question the powers that be to provide a greater inclusiveness, but they can also be employed to question any kind of knowledge whatsoever" (1995: 8).

Since the 1960s and 1970s, radical opponents of the status quo have criticized not only the organization of the university as an expression of elite interests, but the curriculum and the ordering of knowledge itself. Without the political, moral, or intellectual authority to challenge this assault, the establishment gave ground on every front and accepted that truth was relative, that the personal was political, and that there was no literary canon except the one that privileged dead white European males.

The close association of the humanist curriculum with an antidemocratic social order led to the simple but erroneous conclusion that the humanist curriculum was itself antidemocratic. Enlightenment rationality, which the university had not originated but had in the nineteenth century appropriated in the pursuit of technical progress and social order, was jettisoned as part of an assault on tradition. This point of view was only encouraged by the embittered and embattled conservative backlash that asserted that only a small number could hope to understand the canon and this was proof in itself that a democratic society was a utopian fantasy (see Bloom 1987).

But the association of the social order from which the university curriculum had emerged with the intellectual substance of the curriculum had a more fundamental flaw. The challenge to the subject discipline of the university curriculum and the preoccupation with the different subjectivities of the academics and students first made communication difficult, then made rigor unnecessary, and finally made the application of standards impossible. There is a compelling discussion of this point in Philip Roth's *The Human Stain* (2001) in which a classics professor is pilloried and ruined for using the word "spooks" to describe two absent, nonperforming students. Unbeknown to the professor since the two students have not attended class, the two students are African Americans. The word condemns the professor and allows the students to escape any consequence for failing the subject.

This, the postmodern progressive fallacy, is not primarily associated with British education, although it is now commonplace. The second progressive fallacy, the pursuit of an instrumental relationship between education, social justice, and economic efficiency, is more directly associated with the British case.

The second progressive fallacy is located in the experience of British society in the long boom of the 1950s and 1960s, in which economic prosperity and technological development were linked to individual opportunity and social mobility. In this period there was a rapid expansion of technical and managerial employment, which, in turn, demanded a workforce with higher levels of hard skills or human capital.

The old system of higher education and elite formation could not handle the numerical demand for such a workforce. The organization of higher education was criticized not only for its social elitism, but also for its economic inefficiency. There was a progressive demand for social justice and social mobility not only as an end in itself, but also to provide skilled labor for the national economy.

But while there had been an increasing demand for technical, managerial, and professional workers, there was assumed to be a limited pool of talent with the intelligence required to maintain the pace of economic growth. This pool of talent needed to be selected and promoted through the education system because, as Halsey and Floud (1961) noted at the time, "education is a crucial type of investment for the exploitation of modern technology. This fact underlies recent educational development in all the major industrial societies . . . education attains unprecedented economic importance as a source of technological innovation" (quoted in Brown & Lauder 2001: 25).

For the first time, the state took a direct interest in education as a direct means of enhancing economic efficiency. The expansion of higher education would ensure a throughput of talent. The content of higher education would be geared to producing a meritocratic and technically sophisticated economy.

The concern to link educational expenditure to economic efficiency and vocational outcome came to national prominence when the then prime minister James Callaghan proclaimed "The Great Debate" on education in a speech at Ruskin College, Oxford, in October 1976. The idea that education at all levels not only should but will lead to economic regeneration has now achieved the status of common sense. Callaghan's contribution is a specific example of the wider belief that education was no longer playing the traditional role of reproducing the elite and at the same time equipping Britain to compete in the world order. But if education in general and higher education in particular have no other function than an economic one, then the function of the university as an institution for elite socialization and also for critical understanding is quickly undermined.

Callaghan's argument is a particularly philistine result of the progressive fallacy that access to education is justified because it stimulates economic efficiency and that an education system linked to individual accumulation of human capital will lead to social justice. As Brown and Lauder argue, this will lead to something very different:

This inevitably led to a rational linkage between intelligence, curriculum, qualifications and suitability for different kinds of work. The organisation of formal education systems according to these criteria provided a rational means of social selection. . . . School and college credentials provided a useful screening device for employers who were concerned that future employees should be inculcated into the appropriate forms of rule-following behaviour, as well as having the knowledge and skills required for their place in the techno-structure. [2001: 64–65]

This is still at least one step away from what we are now calling *The McDonaldization of Higher Education*. The final humiliation for university education, already reduced to validating vocational outcomes assessed by an increasingly narrow set of quantifiable criteria, is when this standardization and mediocrity becomes the mechanism for credentialing jobs that require little in the way of skill but do require conformity to routine (see Brown & Scase 1994).

The full impact of this two-pronged attack on the university has finally been realized through the corrosive impact of the market on higher education. In the past university education had been immunized from the operation of the market due to its restriction to a smaller number of people. To a degree this ring-fencing is reproduced by the market by the financial status of elite institutions, but even such institutions as Harvard and Oxbridge are not immune from the twofold result of a higher-education system that is characterized by an exponential growth of discourses and the bureaucratization of outcomes (the phenomenon of McDonaldization), both operating in an environment that is market-led. The two results are, on the one hand, an esoteric specialization in which more and more indigestible papers are read by fewer and fewer people and, on the other, the mass consumption and regurgitation of gobbits of approved information.

The phenomenon of specialization has its own bureaucratic aspect in the compulsion to produce for the Research Assessment Exercise or for tenure. It also produces a relentless drive to innovate for career purposes. Each generation of academics must define itself in the job market with a new approach. The specialization and career orientation that this induces removes the academic from any engagement with the intellectual life and concerns of society.

The trajectory for the university as a whole is for the unholy counterposition of research and teaching. While the fully credentialed talk to each other, the apprentice professionals induct the student majority into credentials without consequence.

In the 1960s and for a short time afterwards, the hostility to the old order and the widening of educational opportunities to bright working-class students did indeed lend itself to an atmosphere of intellectual curiosity in a social environment colored by a sense of possibility and optimism (see Adonis & Pollard 1997: 22–25). This window of opportunity was closed down not in a conservative backlash but in the working through of the two progressive fallacies now operating in an environment framed by political disillusion and economic recession.

The paradox of this circumstance is that under the influence of the two fallacies the university—after a short period of freedom in which the erosion of deference and the influx of new types of student combined to make the academy an exciting center of critical thinking—is now less socially engaged and more conformist than at any time this century.

The critical edge to academic life has died; the myth of a golden age has been born. In the name of an attack on elitism, students are indulged, not challenged. In turn, the university experience has become a less secure gatekeeper both to and for the elite. This role is now played to some degree by a small number of elite universities, which provide access to prestigious graduate schools in which the right stuff is combined with the hard work of learning the rules. As I discuss below, the sought-after qualities are being redefined even in this environment.

The university is being reconstructed not on the model of the positive elements of its tradition, but on the negative aspect of ordering the experience according to measurable and behaviorally acceptable objectives. Thus through McDonaldizing higher education, a less than self-confident political elite tries to reassert some measure of control in society as a whole through a new form of socialization in the university.

Instead of bemoaning the fact that the establishment wants to reproduce its view of society, we should be looking at how the present regime, in its glorification of the market through performance indicators, emerged so seamlessly from the relentless attack on traditional ideas of knowledge. Earlier in this chapter I suggested that by the end of the nineteenth century the elite had a clear set of answers to the set of linked questions—why, whom and how do you educate? What are the answers now?

## WHAT IS EDUCATION FOR?

In *The Politics* Aristotle noted the following conceptualization of the purpose of education in his own time:

We must not leave out of sight the nature of education and the proper means of imparting it. For at present there is a practical discussion on this point; people do not agree on the subjects which the young should learn, whether they take virtue in the abstract or the best life as the end to be sought, and it is uncertain whether education should be properly directed rather to the cultivation of the intellect or the moral discipline. The question is complicated, too, if we look at the actual education of our own day; nobody knows whether the young should be trained at such studies as are merely useful as a means of livelihood or in such as tend to the promotion of virtue or in the higher studies, all of which have received a certain number of suffrages. Nor again, if virtue be accepted as the end, is there any agreement as to the means of attaining it. . . . [cited in Smith 1957: 11]

Aristotle is reporting the contemporary form of a discussion about education that all societies have. The function of education may be regarded as the pursuit of truth, the socialization of each generation, for example through notions of citizenship and the allocation through training of a social and economic role in the division of labor.

Education can and should be all these things simultaneously, but in our society education is much narrower. In the educational vocabulary of the curriculum, education is an unholy alliance of the two fallacies: an object-based curriculum in which outcomes are quantified and measured in the ludicrous belief that they measure the success of government policy and job opportunity and a process in which students learn how to manipulate their own personality in order to sell themselves and thus meet targets. This is called being empowered. Missing from this formula is education as engagement with the content and discipline of subject knowledge in the pursuit of truth or what Aristotle might call virtue or the good life.

For the majority, access to higher education only plays the role of delaying entry to the labor market but at the same time acquiring habits not of discipline and rigor, but of passivity and conformity: for this you get a degree. For the elite, the traditional balance between what you know and whom you know has become whom you know and how you sell yourself: "[Blair's] *new* Britain is a flexi-economy of endlessly adaptable service sector entrepreneurs who live off their wits, forever upgrading their portfolio careers and never relying on the world to stay the same. Their product is themselves, and they must know how to sell it" (Aitkenhead 2001). This quotation is a suitable paraphrase of the why, how, and who of education today. The elite consists pretty much of the same people but is trained to market itself and to celebrate style over substance, in the university as elsewhere. This should not and need not be the function of the university. But if the university is to change, a good place to start would be to retrace our steps and realize that the worst way to challenge elitism is to attack the pursuit of excellence.

## NOTES

1. When this had taken place in the revolutionary upheavals of the seventeenth century, it had not taken place in the academy. Political philosophers such as Hobbes and Locke were in a relationship of patronage.

2. For a discussion of the redefinition of the university curriculum in the last years of the nineteenth century, see Colls and Dodd (1986).

3. For a discussion of "cultural capital," see Bourdieu and Passeron (1964, 1977).

4. In an important text Collins (1970) explores the use of the university qualification, especially in the United States, as a gatekeeper to a growing number of professions, even though the credential embodies no specialist knowledge in the field.

## REFERENCES

Adonis, A., & Pollard, S. (1997). A *Class Act. The Myth of Britain's Classless Society.* Harmondsworth, U.K.: Penguin.

Aitkenhead, D. (2001). Staffing pupils with facts and ridiculing progressive teaching won't help in Blair's new world. *The Guardian,* 27 September.

Appleby, J., Hunt, L., & Jacobs, M. (1995). *Telling the Truth about History.* New York: W.W. Norton & Company.

Bloom, A. (1987). *The Closing of the American Mind. How Higher Education Has Failed Democracy and Impoverished the Souls of Today's Students.* New York: Simon and Schuster; Harmondsworth, U.K.: Penguin.

Bourdieu, P., & Passeron, J.-C. (1964). *The Inheritors: French Students and Their Relation to Culture.* London: University of Chicago Press.

Bourdieu, P., & Passeron, J.-C. (1977). *Reproduction in Education, Society and Culture.* London & Thousand Oaks, CA: Sage.

Brown, P., & Lauder, H. (2001). *Capitalism and Social Progress: The Future of Society in a Global Economy.* Basingstoke & New York: Palgrave.

Brown, P., &. Scase, R. (1994). *Higher Education and Corporate Realities. Class, Culture and the Decline of Graduate Careers.* London: UCL Press.

Collins, R. (1970). *The Credential Society: An Historical Sociology of Education and Stratification.* New York: Academic Press.

Colls, R., & Dodd, P. (Eds.) (1986). *Englishness, Politics and Culture 1880–1920.* Beckenham, U.K.: Croom Helm.

Halsey, A. H., & Floud, J. (1961). Introduction. In A. H. Halsey, J. Floud, & J. Anderson (Eds.), *Education, Economy, Society.* New York: Free Press.

Lester Smith, W. O. (1957). *Education.* Harmondsworth, U.K.: Pelican.

Midgley, G. (1996). *University Life in Oxford.* New Haven, CT: Yale University Press.

Ritzer, G. (2000). *The McDonaldization of Society: New Century Edition.* Thousand Oaks, CA: Pine Forge Press.

Roth, P. (2001). *The Human Stain.* London: Vintage.

# 8

# Total Quality Control:
# Universities, Language, and Politics

*Martin Parker*

Who could be "against" quality?[1] How could "quality" be refused? It is undeniable that this is a word, and an associated set of practices, institutions, and relationships, that is ubiquitous in contemporary Western forms of organization. Its migration from statistical techniques of process control and production management to seemingly every other part of the private and public sectors has been propelled by a certain righteous inevitability. Quality appears to champion customers of all kinds: employees, citizens, taxpayers, shoppers, patients, clients, purchasers, populations, pupils, and students. Quality stands up against laziness, shoddy workmanship, obfuscation, and occupational self-interest. The battle lines are clear enough for those who crusade for quality.

There is a mythical history here too. With the advent of mass societies, we were held to account by the numbers. *Quantas?* How much? How many? Efficiencies of scale and new technologies encouraged the production and consumption of any color you like as long as it was black. Now, in a post-Fordist world, we are asked to account for the qualitative satisfactions, the unique selling proposition, that can differentiate our products and services from others in a saturated marketplace. So, *qualis?* Of what kind? What, in other words, are you doing to ensure that your customers are happy? This periodization, and all the various stories of liberalization and liberation that underpin it, does not need to be true to be effective. It simply needs to articulate a move toward a different form of accountability, one that makes the Customer King. Once customers comes dressed in such splendid robes, no longer patient to wait for long, then they are hard to ignore. Their imperial demands for information, service, responsivity, accountability and so on get louder and louder (Munro 2001). And what is worse, since you are a customer too, the recognition of these demands becomes an ethical project that rests upon doing unto others what you want done to you. This becomes a stern duty indeed, one that insists on all customers voices being heard, however unpleasant their messages might be to our own comfort.

Oddly though, given the market liberalism that underpins this story, in much of the U.K. public sector (and some of the private sector) customers cannot be trusted to voice their opinions clearly enough. Because of this, a range of regulatory offices and agencies have been created to ensure that someone speaks on their behalf. These representatives are tasked with ventriloquizing the needs of customers, of acting as their advocates and placing duties by proxy on a particular sector of producers. Railways, schools, financial services, and telephones all become areas in which the big producer is articulated as the problem while the regulatory office stands up for the little customers and ensures that they get the quality that they want and deserve. So, for universities in the United Kingdom, we have the Quality Assurance Agency (QAA)—"an independent body funded by subscriptions," whose mission "is to promote public confidence that quality of provision and standards of awards in higher education are being safeguarded and enhanced."[2] After all, billions of pounds of taxpayers' money are spent on universities every year. The future of our brightest young people is in their hands. Auditing the quality of provision is not only sensible—it is a moral duty. And, as the chief executive of the QAA believes, this is a duty that is further shown to be righteous by self-interested academics (like me) not embracing his mission with sufficient enthusiasm (Randall 2000).

Yet there is a problem here. The needs of the little customers of big McDonald's are not ventriloquized by a Burger Quality Assurance Agency. Though the various outlets are undoubtedly monitored by local councils' hygiene departments to ensure that the food is not (immediately) poisonous, there is no mediator that determines the weight of the cheese slice, the number of chips, or the comfort of the seating area. The "quality" of the experience is largely assumed to be guaranteed by a customer's return visit, or not. The McDonald's organization is certainly *surveilled* in other ways—through its financial reports, its adherence to minimum wage agreements, and so on—but none of these is of direct concern to most customers. So why is this? Why are the relations between McDonald's and its customers left to "market" transactions, while the relations between universities and their students are assumed to need a regulatory body? My answer will be focused on the ways in which the QAA has invented a new language for U.K. higher education and has made that language stick. By redescribing universities in terms of customers and accountability, a new centralized regime has been brought into being, huge sums of money are being spent, and new careers are being made. Another word for this kind of macroeducational policy is "politics," and I intend to engage with it as a political matter.

But, perhaps rather paradoxically, in order to do this I am going to assume that the word "quality" means what we want it to mean—that is to say, it does not have an eternal meaning outside its use as a tactical political device. It is an ambiguous word, a "floating signifier," that can be deployed in a variety of ways to sponsor different projects (Kelemen 2000). Because it is vague, it is useful. Or, as Munro puts it, "quality's elusiveness to definition appears to be part of its resource" (1995: 130). Along these lines, I will begin by thinking through how the word "quality" might be deployed if universities were encouraged to be genuinely responsive to their customers in a market environment without regulation—like McDonald's. I will then contrast this rather extreme thought experiment with what the QAA is actually doing, which is to centralize and tighten state control through imposing a model of behaviorist training for work. In other words, I want to show that the QAA's rhetoric about customers is belied by its practice. This is then followed by a discussion of two different contexts for McDonaldization: market efficiency and centralized control. It seems to me that the paradox of current QAA quality talk is that it claims to speak for customers but does so simply in order to legitimate imposing totalizing control systems on producers. The chapter concludes with some thoughts about the likely outcomes for the sector as a whole if universities are completely transformed into training agencies for the capitalist state and with some suggestions for a revised political language for those who wish to save universities from the zombie embrace of the QAA.

## PROVIDING QUALITY FOR UNIVERSITY CUSTOMERS

What do students want from universities? In this section I want to answer this question in as brutally marketized fashion as possible, in parts echoing Ritzer's discussion of how McUniversities might learn from "the new means of consumption" (1998: 151). This involves (for a moment) leaving aside all the liberal enlightenment values to which many academics seem nostalgically to cling (Parker & Jary 1995) and simply treating universities as producers of a certain kind of product and students as their direct customers. I am also going to assume that the state has no interests in introducing market imperfections and that it treats universities in the same way as it deals with hamburger restaurants. Such assumptions might be deemed objectionable by many, but I discuss this further below. For the purposes of this argument I am concerned with thinking through how the quality of the university product might be addressed by its producers. Putting this in the most schematic of terms, there seem to be three likely reasons why students might decide to invest in an university product—hedonism, credentials, or education. I will begin by discussing each of these market segments separately.

1. *Hedonism*—that is to say, a lively social life, which might involve drugs, sex, and alcohol provided cheaply and easily. This is for many ex-students their abiding memory of the university, a site of multiple pleasures that is rarely reproduced in later life, and its importance for defining the university experience

should not be underestimated. While it would not be appropriate for universities to determine what forms of hedonism might be enjoyed, they should engage in market research to ensure that the opportunities they provide fit the desires of most potential consumers. There may be restrictions on what can be provided within the law, so drugs and prostitutes could not be formally advertised. However, as with other holiday camps, the provision of health clubs and sporting facilities, an excellent range of eating and drinking establishments open at all hours, comfortable accommodation, room service, access to a wide range of entertainments would all be viable strategies. Indeed, Ritzer documents that U.S. universities are meeting precisely this demand through "'theme' dorms, fast-food restaurants, souvenir shops and video arcades" (1999: x). Extending this argument, it would help greatly if edutainment centers were underpinned by a guarantee that there would be little or no interference in these activities by the demands of teaching and assessment. Indeed, the competition between different producers may well focus on the quality of their hedonism and the absence of teaching and assessment in order to distinguish one university from another in a crowded marketplace.

2. *Credentials.* At its simplest, this means adding some letters after the customer's name to facilitate his or her upward mobility within the world of work. It would be easy and cheap to establish a small office that simply processed applications for a fee. Many "fictional" universities already exist that do this. The consumer would specify what their credential should evidence, and the producer would (by return of post) send a personalized certificate that could be taken to the job interview. This may well work in the short term, but in order for the credential to have lasting reputational value, it must be backed up by evidence that the student has studied certain things in a certain way. If the producer is to survive, it will need to do something other than simply issue certificates, but instead do (minimally) what it claims to do. Various strategies might be followed here. One would be to develop a institutional "branding" strategy that claimed quality by proxy. This would clearly be in the interests of those at the top end of the market—Oxford and Cambridge, for example. Other corporate brands with existing "universities"—Motorola, KPMG, Mastercard—could easily add their weight to such projects.[3] However, for those producers without brand capital, it would be more credible to establish a semiautonomous body that agrees on minimum standards on what will be taught and assessed for particular credentials. This will mean that producers avoid destructive competition through collectively determining the length and content of their products. This body would have to seem autonomous in order to gain the trust of consumers, and its kitemark would then symbolize the quality and reputational value of particular credentials. Yet—and this is important—the various precepts of this cartel must not be too demanding, otherwise they would threaten the financial viability of producers. Distance learning would seem to be the best delivery strategy for this segment, since it would not require the maintenance of expensive premises. It

must be remembered that the production of credentials is key for this group of consumers, but it must be done in a way that ensures long-term survival for a large number of organizations.

3. *Education.* Consumers might wish to have a sustained engagement with the subject of their fascination. This I will term "education." This may be an unlikely motivation, but it is a market segment that needs to be catered for. In this case a quality strategy would have to focus on the size and range of library holdings, the intellectual capacities of the academic staff, the wide and flexible ways in which thought will be stimulated, the substantial degree of autonomy that students might have, individually and collectively, the amount of time that students and staff spend together, and so on. This third kind of consumer would wish to be assured that they are going to be able to determine what they study; will engage in detailed and complex discussions; be asked to read difficult texts or solve hard problems; have access to the latest ideas and technology in their area, and so on. Distance learning strategies may hence be difficult to employ, but the producers would not need to worry overmuch about the supply of the hedonistic gratifications offered to the consumers in segment one. Neither would they have to worry about issuing certificates at the "end" of a period of study, since the motivations of these consumers are not primarily focused on having letters after their name.

These three versions of the university are intended to clarify what is at stake in meeting and exceeding customer expectations. Each has a different definition of a quality experience. There are still problems, of course. For segment one, there is a clear confusion (in terms of market propositions) between the university and the holiday camp. Either these institutions would have to become holiday camps and drop all pretenses to being universities, or they would have to dilute their strategy of hedonism by accepting credentialism as being part of their mission too. This will mean that they would be likely to join the cartel but not offer distance learning. The market segment would be those consumers who want credentials but wish to enjoy as much hedonism as possible while they are gaining them. The pure credentialists could then simply offer cheaper products, a no-frills version of certification, without damaging either their reputation or their financial viability. Between these extremes, a sliding scale of price and facilities should ensure that all hedonistic and credentialist customers can be catered for. Furthermore, as Klein (2000) has documented, the possibility for other organizations to get involved in cross-branding and sponsorship is huge. Nike, Burger King, Pepsi, and so on are already heavily involved in edutainment, and this trend could easily be accelerated. However, segment three, the education producer, has clear difficulties. Since it might attract a relatively small number of customers, it is likely to be a small market sustaining a limited number of organizations. As a result, some educational establishments might like to offer credentials, or even recreational facilities. These would be small-scale, however, and should not distract from the central desires of this group of consumers.

An interesting form of market segmentation is beginning to emerge here, with a clarity of focus that might allow university managers at strategic level to clarify just which consumers they wish to attract. Rather than attempting to be all things to all people, which is a disastrous move in marketing terms, each institution would make strategic choices based on clear market research and tailor its facilities accordingly. These would be genuine diversities, not monotone universities. Some of these institutions might fail, but their failure can be treated as market research too. Furthermore, the human and physical resources of failed organizations can be bought up cheaply by the remaining producers. This should lower costs all round and further satisfy consumer expectations in all areas. Of course, if this process of concentration goes too far, we will face the problem of *oligopoly* and potential price fixing, but if no market imperfections exist and entry costs are low, new competitors can be expected to challenge on price. In general, the invisible hand will pat the successful on the back and slap down those who are insufficiently responsive.

In sum, there seems to be no particularly good reason why the state would wish to determine what "quality" meant in a completely marketized higher-education system. Apart from general mechanisms of redress that might be adopted for consumer protection reasons, and the matters of employee rights, financial accounting, and so on, Universities Inc. could be expected to be robust and productive. Indeed, freeing universities from the shackles of the state would encourage them to be more entrepreneurial in meeting customer expectations and would allow a considerable amount of taxpayers' money to be saved by closing all the existing regulatory and funding agencies. These would be useless bodies, QAAngos, in a university system that was genuinely responsive to its customers.

## AUDITING THE AUDITORS

The market libertarian thought experiment above is based on treating words like "customer" and "quality" as if they referred to the consumption of (what economists call) "private goods." In terms of this volume, this means treating degrees like hamburgers and hence treating "quality" as if it were a word that stood for what consumer's are entitled to expect. So, find out what your customers want and then provide it as efficiently as possible. But this is not, at present, the state of affairs in the United Kingdom. In practice, since the state provides the funding and regulatory structures for U.K. universities, degrees are actually being treated as "public goods"—as goods that have some shared benefit for many, or even for the population as a whole. By definition, then, this is a macropolitical decision that is being made on behalf of citizens and not a set of market transactions between consumers and producers. Since the QAA does not conduct market research to find out what students want, it must be acting as a market imperfection. This suggests that the state and/or the QAA are representing other interests than direct customers. What seems to have happened here is that the word "quality" has been shifted to a rather different context. After all, as Kelemen puts it, the very ambiguity of the word allows it to be deployed and consumed in many different ways (2000). In this case, I am going to argue that the word is actually standing for the interests of state policymakers, and not the direct customers of HE institutions. To repeat: the QAA does not ask students to define quality—instead, it defines quality on behalf of students. So what does quality mean for the QAA?

In the QAA's *Subject Review Handbook* (QAA 1997), which describes the process of auditing the quality of provision in universities, we are told that the "subject provider" (usually a department) sets its own aims and objectives and will be judged against these. Fair enough—to ask someone to show that they are doing what they claim that they are doing is not an unreasonable request. However, in the 53 pages of the document the claim of evaluating provider aims is systematically disavowed. As the handbook evidences, the QAA actually has very clear expectations and instructions concerning curriculum design, content, and organization; six versions of learning outcomes; innovation; teaching, learning, and assessment criteria; student profiles; progression and completion rates; student achievement; strategy for support and guidance; admission and induction arrangements; academic guidance and tutorial support; pastoral and welfare support; careers information and guidance; learning resources strategy; library services; equipment and information technology; teaching, learning, and social accommodation; technical and administrative support; quality management and enhancement. Furthermore, there are also detailed prescriptions about the self-assessment document; the preparatory meeting; the role of various parties in the visit; the vast range of documentation to be provided; the timing and structure of the visit; the baseroom; meetings with students; observation of teaching; scrutiny of student work; notes on aspect meetings; the feedback meeting; as well as assumptions about the existence of committee structures, minuted meetings, and external examiner's reports.

The point of that long list was simply to demonstrate that, in practice, the judgment of "quality" is not being made on criteria set by either producers (or consumers), but on those criteria already determined by the QAA, a state-appointed third party. In other words, the word "quality" here indexes a department's success or failure at conforming to these highly detailed procedural prescriptions. Failure to comply with all of these protocols will result in a judgment that quality is deficient. Quality is defined as conformity to what has been defined as quality, and there are no alternative institutions to which a producer (or consumer) could appeal. Indeed, the quality control (and hence control over "quality") is gradually tightening. In the new methodology that the QAA has been applying since 2001, "Academic Review," as well as adherence to similar detail (part 1 of QAA 2000a) all programs will also have to conform to a national framework for naming higher-education qualifications (QAA 2000b). Furthermore, all degrees will also have to produce a "program specification" that

details the "learning outcomes" of each program (QAA 2000c). However decep-
tively obvious this may sound, there are some very alarming assumptions being
made here about learning as a form of performance. Essentially this is based on a
policy form of behaviorism that regards mental states as ghosts in the machine.
Unless something can be demonstrated to have been learnt, then there is no
evidence to prove that it has been learnt. Therefore, if things cannot be demonstrated, they cannot be learnt. Unless a subject provider can demonstrate that it
has fully adopted this behaviorist account of teaching and learning, it will have
no evidence to prove that its provision is of high quality. In practice, though
providers are still nominally setting their own objectives, the methodology
brings in key assumptions that effectively determine what the objectives must be
since they must now demonstrate that they are encouraging certain kinds of
behavior from their students. In other words, if you refuse to codify learning as
behavior, then your program is deficient in quality.

As if this were not enough, at the time of writing 22 subject areas have
"subject Benchmark Statements" that determine the minimum acceptable content
for curricula and that must be referred to in the program specification and
integrated into the curriculum. The benchmarks begin to define what the contents of a particular discipline must be and pay no attention to the fact that most
disciplines are continually debating their internal constitutions, appropriate
methods, and boundaries. Revisions of these benchmarks can, in the future, be
expected to further lay out a national curriculum for each discipline. Finally, at
an organizational level and as part of the process of "Institutional Review" (a
separate process from "Academic Review," see part 2 of QAA 2000a), all
universities are visited to ensure their compliance with other "quality" standards
set by the QAA. All institutions must also conform to (currently) nine "Codes of
Practice for the Assurance of Academic Quality and Standards in Higher Education" issued by the QAA. These cover postgraduate research programs; collaborative provision; students with disabilities; external examining; academic
appeals and student complaints on academic matters; assessment of students;
program approval, monitoring, and review; career consultation; and placement
learning. This "suite" of codes can be expected to expand and perhaps also to be
used as criteria to assess departments during academic review.

Universities now have no choice but to spend large chunks of their budgets on
compliance, though the actual costs of regulation are hidden in the system itself.
The QAA's direct budget is currently about £10 million (which it already taxes
from universities and the university funding council). But this figure is so small
simply because the majority of costs are displaced to universities themselves. A
modest estimate of the costs of one visit to one institution is approximately
£200,000 (about $300,000) in staff and administration time for the year up to the
visit, replacement teaching for staff given remission to deal with quality, catering
and stationery, mountains of photocopying, room hire, and so on.[4] Most of the
reviewers are full-time members of staff at other universities, so they are being
paid for time they are not spending on their own universities' business, as well as

getting fees and expenses from the QAA, and hotel bills and training paid for by the QAA. All universities also have departments of several people who are now dedicated to QAA compliance functions, and a small army of consultants and conferences has grown up alongside them. Furthermore, more and more academics and academic related institutions are now preparing benchmark statements or responding to consultation documents, attending expensive training courses, writing program specifications, attending quality committees, and so on. If I only include visits and the QAA's budget, the compliance costs to the sector are now in the region of £110 million (about $165 million) per year (Harrison et al. 2001). If all the other activities were included, the figure would probably be close to £200 million (about $300 million) and rising.[5]

Frankly, it is difficult to conceptualize this gigantic list of documents as "regulatory" and as having anything at all to do with (as the QAA mission has it) promoting "public confidence that quality of provision and standards of awards in higher education are being safeguarded and enhanced." There is no evidence that public confidence, whatever that is, has been diminished in the first place. Though if the public were aware that at least £200 million is being spent enhancing their confidence, no doubt it would be shaken considerably. Taken as whole, since the parts are not optional, they add up to centralized direction (not regulation) over virtually every matter that an university administrator might dream of. Yet—and here is the paradox—despite the frequent use of the word "quality," there is no evidence whatsoever that the QAA has actually attempted to determine what sorts of satisfactions the direct customers of universities might like to see met. Instead, it is simply assumed that students want a form of behavioral training that allows them to become employable, that they want all degrees to conform to a national curriculum, and that they want hundreds of millions of pounds to be spent on compliance and not books or teachers. So "quality," for the QAA, is about restricting areas of university and student autonomy in the name of accountability. It is a series of interrogations stridently justified in the name of nameless others and aimed at the management and enhancement of the regulatory process itself. For this particular way of using language there is actually rather little ambiguity. Quality means what the QAA says it means, no more and no less.

## MARKETS AND HIERARCHIES

In the sections above, I have described two very different versions of "quality"—one market-driven and the other hierarchically driven, one concerned with customer satisfaction, the other with systemic conformance. At this point, I think it would be helpful to turn back to McDonaldization in order to disentangle two rather different models of causation here. According to Ritzer, the rationalization of the world is a process that has its own inexorable logic. It requires that whatever human and nonhuman materials an organization wishes to organize are made efficient, calculable, predictable, and controllable (Ritzer 2000). Yet, in the case of HE, there are clearly two different contexts within which such a process might take place. Within a market, an organization might do everything in its power to engineer its internal processes to maximize profitability. So McDonald's restaurants have detailed guidelines on burger flipping, cup filling, and window cleaning, which are intended to ensure that the maximum amount of money is transferred from the consumer to the producer, at the same time as the minimum amount of labor and materials is used. The "end," profitability, is assumed, and the "means" are continually re-engineered in order that the outcome of the cash/burgers equation becomes more favorable. Other, "external," forms of regulation and intervention (minimum wage agreements, or the McLibel trial, for example) may need to be dealt with if they impact on the organization, but they are not the motive force for rationalization.

However, as the QAA example shows, McDonaldization can also happen within hierarchies—that is to say, even if there is no "market" and "profits" in any meaningful sense, the process of rationalization can be propelled by an assumption that regulation and control are necessary in themselves. The state is a prime mover in such processes, via semiautonomous agencies like the QAA, but the legitimacy for such processes still appears to come from a "zombie rhetoric" of the market. I am calling this a "zombie" rhetoric because even though it appears to be alive to stakeholder concerns, it is dead inside. It involves deploying the rhetorical tropes of the market as its ends—"quality," "customers," "stakeholders," "audit"—at the same time as it systematically disavows them through its means. In practice, the hierarchy spreads its power through tighter and ever more extensive frameworks, precepts, and guidelines. Calls for transparency and accountability are translated into demands for codification—and, since codification is usually incomplete, into further demands for instructions that will cover every single case. Extrapolating the QAA's current trajectory into the not-so-distant future would result in an (almost) entirely unified and uniform multidivisional organization. Though universities may be nominally independent, it would be an independence best characterized as "agency" status for the QAA. There would be a national curriculum for all higher-education courses; standardized learning materials and expected learning outcomes; a centralized examination, assessment, and accreditation process; and even an instruction set for the administrative structure of the university itself. Given such a state of affairs, universities would be better conceptualized as regional delivery centers for a combined funding and regulation agency, in turn funded by the state. "Quality" will be defined as conformity, and customers will be able to choose confidently between one McUniversity degree and another, since the products will be the same.

But perhaps this description of universities being strangled by red tape should hardly surprise us. The QAA proceeds by treating staff and students as if they were in need of more rigorous time-and-motion study in the name of "maximum prosperity" and "national efficiency." F. W. Taylor used these phrases in his 1911 *Principles of Scientific Management* to justify the separation of planning from execution, and to codify the efficient behavioral training of the "first class man" For Taylor, and for the QAA, any protest against this inexorable logic is seen as dysfunctional and as a demonstration that recalcitrant elements have not yet understood that the rules are for everyone's benefit. Yet even conventional management theory has, for many years, been stridently bemoaning this view of employees, and the dinosaur centralization and giganticism that seems to follow from taking bureaucratic methods of control too seriously. Indeed, it seems rather ironic that the QAA's version of managerial modernization looks like General Motors 50 years ago. Even the most elementary "organizational behavior" textbook contains extensive discussions about the problems of centralization, in terms of stifling creativity and flexibility, mistaking means for ends, and adding layers of management who do nothing but manage each other. What is worse for the QAA is that its central brand, the language of "quality," seems to be running into some serious problems too. As Kelemen (2002) documents, there are many commercial organizations that have now decided to scrap their quality management programs on the grounds that there was no evidence that they were doing anything but adding costs. So whatever else we might think of the breathless language of the new "excellence" managerialism, at least it tends to recognize that organizations are not solely constituted by formal rules. In order to keep up with the times perhaps the QAA needs to re-brand itself in terms of "culture," "innovation," or even (irony of ironies) the "learning organization." But since the QAA has already specified in advance what learning outcomes are, the latter seems unlikely.

## REDESCRIBING QUALITY

In a sense, all that I wanted to do in this chapter was to demonstrate that it was possible to be critical of the QAA's definition of "quality" without deploying all the usual nostalgic professional self-interest that academics are rather good at dressing up as reason (Parker & Jary 1995) and which opposition to McDonaldization often trades on (Parker 1998). It is precisely because quality is such a seductive and ambiguous word that it is so powerful as a way to castigate smug professionals in the name of accountability to powerless, voiceless students. But, as I hope I have made clear, the word is actually being used to justify a radical centralization of universities, together with a behaviorist model of learning based on the supposed needs of employers. If quality actually meant being responsive to customers within a marketplace, then radical deregulation and rolling back the frontiers of the state would seem a more credible response. This would, in other words, be a response that made sense in terms of the logic of a marketplace in educational products. But this is patently not what the QAA is doing. QAAuality means conforming to hierarchical direction, and hence it requires a steady increase in the reach and detail of the capillaries of power. John Randall, the QAA's chief executive, is keen on writing about "clear standards," "transparency," "accountability," "impartial evidence," "value for money," and "comparability," as if these terms meant something beyond the ways in which they were being operationalized by the QAA. So, too, does he call on "public confidence," "informed choices," and "stakeholders" and invokes the ghost of a self-serving professoriate intent only on protecting its expert status (Randall 2000, 2001). These are words that force you to be inside or outside, a friend or an enemy.

John Randall claims to know what students want and what all the other stakeholders want too. This is a remarkable achievement, simply because, like many other institutions, the goals and purposes of universities are by no means clear—nor have they ever been. In practice, they are contested between (at least) potential and actual students, parents, FE teachers, university employees, university managers, local and national policymakers, trade unions, potential and actual employers, taxpayers, academics, and so on. John Randall seems not to acknowledge that the understandings of the goals and purposes of universities held by these various groups may be divergent, or even contradictory (Parker & Courtney 1998). So, the question arises, quality for which customers? Fitness for whose purpose? Since this question cannot be answered to the satisfaction of all the interest groups involved, closing down possible definitions by imposing centralized power must involve an act of political will by the people and institutions doing the defining. In this case, it is clearly motivated by an attempt to totally transform universities into arms of the state that function as behavioral training agencies for employers. The success or failure of a university can then be measured by its success in providing learning for labor, of acting as the human resource function for the industrial state. Lawson (1998) characterizes the last century of U.K. higher education as a long debate between culture and utility. If the QAA are to have their way, this debate seems to be drawing to a sadly utilitarian end.

Despite the supposed move from *quantas* to *qualis*, and unless a viable opposition is built, McUniversities will become institutions in which all the colors are black. The desires of the direct (or indirect) consumers will not be listened to but simply assumed through a gigantic act of paternalist mindreading.[6] The language will have changed, since universities will now be spoken of as if they were profoundly democratic and responsive suppliers of consumer goods, but this is now a language that refers to the scientific management of learning outcomes and an accountability that only ever leads upwards to the state, which, is in turn, acting on behalf of the "needs" of capitalism. As one of the arms of this state and claiming to be speaking on behalf of voiceless customers, the QAA is imposing its own version of means and ends in a way that silences the babble of other voices who might actually wish to have something to say about universities. In practice, since nobody else is listened to, the only customer that seems to really matter is an imagined new economy.

So (how) can a viable opposition to the QAA's colonization of quality be built? It is ironic indeed that a marketized McDonaldization would open up definitions of quality in a much more thoroughgoing and diverse manner than the QAA are inclined to do. That would be to extinguish the reason for the

QAA's existence by using the language it has colonized as its own, but it would also involve sponsoring a neo-Thatcherite deregulation of universities that treated education as a private good. The three scenarios of market segmentation I offered above, combined with ever leaner and meaner management strategies, are likely to be the result. I do not consider this to be a desirable outcome. Instead, and following the broad argument about the power and flexibility of language that I have offered here, I suggest using some other words to describe the QAA, words that capture the attempts at total control that this organization is currently sponsoring. These would be words like "centralization," "red tape," and "bureaucracy," phrases like "top-down" and "control freak," and outcomes like "inflexibility" and "lack of choice." The friends of these words must be my enemies. Just as John Randall employs the rhetoric of the free consumer with perfect information, so could those opposed to quality talk about freedom from state interference in what students are taught, how they are taught, and why they are taught. So could "value for money" arguments be turned onto the squandering of hundreds of millions that could be spent on books, or even grants. So could the specter of the "McUniversity"—a splendidly useful term for political polemic—be let loose as a cultural counterweight to treating universities as corporate training agencies.

It does not matter if this oppositional language is imprecise and insufficiently theorized for refined academic tastes. The populist rhetoric of the QAA cannot be effectively opposed through the niceties of intellectual debate. Politics is about redescribing the world and making that language stick for a while. It is not about eternal verities or ultimate truths. Those who wish to defend a liberal pluralist (or even radically oppositional) version of the university against QAA centralization would do well to exploit the distinctions between "freedom of speech" and "state intervention," "democracy" and "bureaucracy," "the individual" and "the corporate." Perhaps the beginnings of this move happened in early 2001, when, in the name of cutting down on bureaucracy, the then Minister for Education announced a new "light touch" regime for visits. The consternation at the QAA was a pleasure to watch. But in case this is taken to be the beginning of the end, it must be stressed that the central purpose of the QAA, as well as all its other activities, were not challenged. Nonetheless, if this anti-bureaucratic populism solidifies into a meaningful head of political steam, then I will enjoy watching the QAA swallow the bitter pill of attaching itself so firmly to its profoundly autocratic version of quality. Let the QAA attempt to demonstrate that this is what students want, or what employers care about, or that they have the backing of the academic community. Let them explain why so much money is being spent on their expanding empire. Let them try to claim that they care about student freedom to think and study, and about the freedom of universities to teach and innovate.

If the QAA's language is politics by another means, and "quality" is the central term of that vocabulary, it can currently only be refused by describing universities in other terms. In an older usage, "quality" was a more neutral noun, which referred to the character or nature of something—its essential or distinguishing characteristic. In this sense, the quality of universities might be a matter for permanent debate, not something that can be defined by fiat in section 101, paragraph 27 of an instruction originating in the Head Office of McUniversities Ltd. John Randall writes about the QAA sponsoring "modern democracies' proper expectations of transparency and accountability" (2000). He must then agree that the QAA should be transparent about its mission of centralized control, colonization of taxpayers' money, and the scientific management of programmed training—unless, of course, he does not really care about quality?

## NOTES

1. Some people who seem to be are the members of Keele's Management Department and Barry Schofield, who commented on an earlier draft of this chapter. Thank you.

2. <www.qaa.ac.uk>.

3. There are already over 100 corporate universities in operation across the world.

4. During our own visit, we also had to rent shelving for the week in order to display the hundreds of files stipulated by the QAA.

5. Probably still an underestimate. PA Consulting's report for the HEFCE calculated £45 million (~$67 million) in direct costs, £100 million (~$150 million) in administration costs, £100 million (~$150 million) in unmeasured costs, and £70 million (~$105 million) in stakeholder costs (2000: 24).

6. It is unlikely that they ever were, but, as I have said, this chapter is not attempting to claim that the past was flawless, simply that the present is undesirable.

## REFERENCES

Harrison, M., et al. (2001). Trial by ordeal. *The Guardian*, 30 January: 12–13.

Kelemen, M (2000). Too much or too little ambiguity: The language of total quality management. *Journal of Management Studies*, 37/4: 483–498.

Kelemen, M. (2002). *Managing Quality: A Multi-Disciplinary Approach*. London & Thousand Oaks, CA: Sage.

Klein, N. (2000). *No Logo*. London: Flamingo.

Lawson, A. (1998). Culture and utility: Phrases in dispute. In D. Jary & M. Parker (Eds.), *The New Higher Education: Issues and Directions for the Post-Dearing University* (273–287). Stoke-on-Trent, U.K.: Staffordshire University Press.

Munro, R. (1995). Governing the new province of quality. In A. Wilkinson & H. Willmott (Eds.), *Making Quality Critical* (127–155). London: Routledge.

Munro, R. (2001). After knowledge: The language of information. In S. Linstead & R. Westwood (Eds.), *The Language of Information*. London & Thousand Oaks, CA: Sage.

PA Consulting (2000). *Better Accountability for Higher Education*. London: PA Consulting Group.

Parker, M. (1998). Nostalgia and mass culture: McDonaldization and cultural elitism. In M. Alfino, J. S. Caputo, & R. Wynyard (Eds.), *McDonaldization*

    *Revisited: Critical Essays on Consumer Culture.* Westport, CT, & London: Praeger (1–18).

Parker, M., & Courtney, J. (1998). Universities or nurseries? Education, professionals and taxpayers. In D. Jary & M. Parker (Eds.), *The New Higher Education: Issues and Directions for the Post-Dearing University.* Stoke-on-Trent: Staffordshire University Press (335–349).

Parker, M., & Jary, D. (1995). The McUniversity: Organisation, management and academic subjectivity. *Organisation,* 2 (2): 319–338.

QAA (1997). *Subject Review Handbook.* Gloucester, U.K.: Quality Assurance Agency for Higher Education.

QAA (2000a). *Handbook for Academic Review 2000.* Gloucester, U.K.: Quality Assurance Agency for Higher Education.

QAA (2000b). *The Framework for Higher Education Qualifications in England, Wales and Northern Ireland.* Gloucester, U.K.: Quality Assurance Agency for Higher Education.

QAA (2000c). *Guidelines for Preparing Programme Specifications.* Gloucester, U.K.: Quality Assurance Agency for Higher Education.

Randall, J. (2000). Quality street. *The Guardian,* 25 April.

Randall, J. (2001). Belief system. *The Guardian,* 6 February.

Ritzer, G. (1998). McUniversity in the postmodern consumer society. In *The McDonaldization Thesis: Explorations and Extensions* (151–162). London & Thousand Oaks, CA: Sage.

Ritzer, G. (1999). *Enchanting a Disenchanted World: Revolutionizing the Means of Consumption.* Thousand Oaks, CA: Pine Forge Press.

Ritzer, G. (2000). *The McDonaldization of Society: New Century Edition.* Thousand Oaks, CA: Pine Forge Press.

Taylor, F. W. (1911). Scientific management. In H. Clark, J. Chandler, & J. Barry (Eds.), *Organisation and Identities* (231–237). London: Chapman and Hall, 1994.

# 9

# The Massification of Higher Education

*Claire Fox*

The coincidence of the mass expansion of HE with a decline in quality has led critics to conclude that, in principle, many cannot study at the highest level without a collapse in standards. In response, supporters of widening access cry "elitism" and mutter of old school ties and social privilege. But this is a false debate. The question is not whether fewer or more people should have access to the ivory towers, but rather what these towers represent in the contemporary context. The key question is: what are today's students being given access to?

The circumstances in which universities have opened up have diminished what any student can gain from undergraduate study. More significantly, these circumstances have contributed to the redefinition of the very idea "the university." Apart from one very obvious problem—that mass access has not been matched by a mass increase in resources (staffing ratios have increased from 8.5:1 at the start of the 1980s to over 20:1 today, while the new universities buy less than one book per student per year), an attendant problem has been a shift in philosophy that has accompanied the expansion. Today's universities are being reorganized around a new agenda, which broadly describes itself as student-centered. This reorientation—whether justified through the new consumer model of education, the emphasis on higher education as a force "for social justice and equity" (Blunkett 2001), or the embracing of new student-centered pedagogies that have affected both curriculum and teaching methods—always presents itself as putting students first. But in the name of student-centeredness, what is offered to those who go to university today is increasingly thin gruel.

## STUDENTS AS CONSUMERS

One way that students have entered center stage is through the marketization of higher education. We are currently seeing the sector aping the market rhetoric of the rest of society. In the past, students had to compete for places at universities, which confidently selected and rejected without apology. Today, the shift in government funding to encourage growth in numbers means that universities desperately compete to recruit new undergraduates. Therefore the key task in every faculty is how to make courses attractive to more students. Students have become consumers, and lecturers have been forced into selling their wares. University management meetings are as preoccupied with advertising campaigns, brand loyalty, and customer satisfaction as any other business enterprise.

The consequences of such marketization when applied to a university means turning education on its head. Students are no longer supplicants who must demonstrate that they deserve to be accepted as apprentices by the most advanced minds and researchers in the field. Rather, students are the masters who must be flattered and cajoled by humble lecturers who are warned that students will take their "custom" to other educational institutions if they are not satisfied with the marks they receive or the way they are taught. Students who feel they have not got what they were promised in the college's adverts threaten to sue, as if they had bought a dodgy television set. The Students' Rights Charter hangs over the head of any academic who does not toe the line. The result has been the introduction of easier assessment methods and the inflation of the number and class of degrees issued, all to ensure that customers' expectations are satisfied. Exam boards are as likely to weigh up a student's welfare and self-esteem as to scrutinize academic achievement. Students who fail are not happy customers.

In order to fund expansion, students now pay their own fees, which also sharply underlines the customer/provider relationship. It is argued that if students are to pay hard cash—or get into debt in order to study—they will expect to get the product they ordered. This is altering all relationships in universities. Power and authority is increasingly derived not from knowledge, specialism, or expertise in the field. Instead, the academic/student relationship is being equalized through a contract, with an emphasis on what students get as consumers. This has increased the tendency to view degrees as ready-made, salable commodities. Customers in University Britain plc demand a worthwhile product.

## PRAGMATISM TO PEDAGOGY

While many in academia are uncomfortable with the language of consumers and the market, they feel at ease with the more politically correct language of student empowerment as befitting the New Labour regime. While New HE is reorientating around satisfying the alleged demands of students rather than the demands of the disinterested pursuit of knowledge by focusing everything on student empowerment, consciences have been salved. Changes are argued for as being in the best interests of students, and contrasted with an elite system in which academics were the only constituency who were satisfied.

This is best illustrated by the acceptance of Labor's social inclusion agenda, which, as I have argued previously, effectively refocuses university around a policy of social engineering (Fox 2000b). In explaining why this government is aiming for 50% of the population to gain a higher-education qualification, then Education Secretary David Blunkett claimed in his seminal "Greenwich Speech" in February 2000 that "widening access to higher education is a key priority and critical to tackling social exclusion" and talked of universities as key players in delivering social justice. Funding through the HEFC is being reorganized with this in mind. Entrance requirements these days are less a discussion about A-level (equivalent to U.S. high-school diploma) results and more about social disadvantage. Universities are being given financial incentives to take the socially excluded, regardless of educational achievement. The government now pays universities extra for each student recruited from lower socioeconomic groups (designated as such according to home postcodes). Performance criteria—so crucial for league table status—includes a breakdown of an institution's intake of nontraditional students from "low-participation neighborhoods." The acceptance of this approach means divorcing the aim of university from any educational outcome—what matter if what's on offer is inferior as long as it is inclusive, if knowledge is sidelined, if more and more students are put center-stage?

This approach has particularly affected approaches to pedagogy. It is worth noting that many student-centered models began as pragmatic responses to the difficulties of overcrowding and the underfunding, which accompanied the mass production of HE. Who has not advocated student-centered self-directed study when faced with cuts in contact time? Peer assessment can look an attractive option when you do not have time to mark those essays. Packing a tutorial off to the Resource Learning Centre—or what Natfhe's general secretary Paul Mackney once labeled FoFo: "F___off and Find out"—has been a staple teaching strategy over recent years (O'Connor 1999).

But this pragmatism has been theorized into a new educational dogma and dressed up as a new student-centered pedagogy for a democratic age. For example, self-directed learning and group-work are often practical responses to the very real problem of not enough staff to cope with students and other demands on academics' time. But these coping strategies are increasingly presented as liberating students from the stultifying limits of what feminist educationalist Professor Dale Spender describes as "a stable body of knowledge which (in the past) universities jealously guarded as custodians and gatekeepers" (Wallace 1998). Another commentator, singing the virtues of tutor-less group-work, describes the learning model based on the "individual and privatized dynamic between tutor and student" as "simplistic and erroneous" (Heathfield 1999). The increasing reliance on new technologies as a substitute for face-to-face teaching is dressed up as empowering students; one consultation document is entitled "Point and Click—ICT learners in the driving seat."

Similarly, student-centered assessment has moved away from being a coping strategy and is now contrasted positively against its more testing traditional methods. These new educational assessments are certainly more student-centered than they had been in the past, inasmuch as they now accommodate every student's dream: easier exams. Only a minority of students in the best universities relies on that three-hour ordeal to get their degree. In fact, "open book" exams are now routine, and exam questions are regularly issued in advance to help students to prepare. Exams and competition are castigated as elitist as new assessment methodology increasingly strives to reward rather than to challenge—as though students cannot make the grade without changing the grading system. Continuous assessment by course-work and seminar performance is a common experience.

Inevitably, this approach moves pedagogy to accommodate to the limits of knowledge as it is constituted in the student body, rather than expanding what is known. Students themselves are even asked to draw up the basis on which they should be judged. One proponent of this approach in relation to group work argues: "students, of course, are the best people to know what are the important criteria and benchmarks for grading group work processes" (Heathfield 1999). Meanwhile education Professor Richard Winter argues for a new form of "collage or photomontage" style assessment to be used as an alternative to traditional essays. His proposition is that these "patchwork texts" help "broaden access to higher education qualifications for the large number of students who do not lack the ability to write but for whom the essay form is alien" (Winter 2000).

## STUDENTS AS FOCUS GROUP

Accepting student-centeredness means adopting a focus-group approach to what happens within universities. One expression of this is the new fad for student satisfaction surveys. These are now routinely used to ascertain how students feel about the success of lectures, course content, and even how they are assessed and examined. But while taking on board the views of students sounds very progressive, what does it say about education when the people asked to rate the quality of HE are the students—the least educated constituency in the university and the least likely to be able to judge what they should be getting from lecturers? Courting student approval is unlikely to be a useful way of establishing what constitutes a quality education. Satisfaction surveys at best produce banal complaints of the "not enough handouts . . . too few seminars" variety and confuse quantity with quality. Even more understandably perhaps, undergraduates complain of rigor and testing as problematic. What student spontaneously welcomes the pain and effort of being intellectually stretched? Ask students about their lecturers and listen to the moans about bumbling, boring academics droning on and sending everybody to sleep. But these stock images of other-worldly professors, swotty academics, and nerdy researchers, usually associated with a philistine response to academia, now seem to inform public policy.

Surely the moans of students who might prefer study to be easy and to fit in with their social life should not be taken too seriously. But today they are, and the prejudices of those fearful of being put to the test are accepted as good practice. Instead of students dreading exams, lecturers live in dread of end-of-term student assessments. Witty lecturers do well, while others are written off as boring. But HE is supposed to be more than entertainment. Many of my own students described me as tedious because the text I was teaching was difficult; but it was just a phase—once the education started and they learnt how to appreciate the material, I became popular. It does not do to lose one's nerve.

## STUDENT-CENTERED TEACHING

Pandering to the lowest common denominator in the name of listening to students has dire consequences for what a higher education really amounts to today. A more specific example of the consequences of organizing HE around students' demands is the new Institute for Learning and Teaching, set up following a recommendation by Sir Ron Dearing in his report of 1997 *Higher Education in the Learning Society*. Its stated aim is to improve teaching methods and to take responsibility for new teacher-training qualifications for lecturers. But on what did Sir Ron base his assertion that lecturers are not teaching properly? One of the key groups consulted on the question of lecturers' teaching abilities was students. Their perceptions have been used to justify the new emphasis on teaching techniques.

The Dearing Report cited a Policy Studies Institute survey of 1,200 students, in which almost a half of those who responded are cited as being less than satisfied. In its contribution to Dearing, the National Union of Students (NUS) complained of a slowness in introducing new teaching methods and bemoaned the fact that funding mechanisms reward good research much more than good teaching. After publication of the report, the NUS boasted that the student voice was heard and was central to the report's findings. The report itself claimed that it "puts students at the centre of the process of learning and teaching" (Dearing 1997: 8 sec. 35). David Blunkett, then U.K. Secretary of State for Education and Employment, also infamously used his own son's experience to endorse the ILT because he felt that his son was not being taught properly and that university teachers were more interested in their own research than in teaching (Hodges 1998).

Breaking the link between university teaching and research represents an assault on the very idea of higher education and shows how the language of empowerment is being used to give the ever-growing number of students an inferior university experience. The traditional belief that research and teaching must be closely linked reflected a view of universities as special places of scholarship and knowledge, where academics were at the cutting edge of intellectual progress, expanding ideas and researching new areas.

Undergraduates were educated by interacting with the people who were pushing society's intellectual boundaries outward. The education process lay less in the technical teaching of subjects and more in allowing the new recruits to academia access to the greatest minds in the field. This was not school, but an apprenticeship to becoming independent thinkers.

The essence of university education is giving precedence to research. The relationship of research to good teaching is the understanding that what inspires young people is the stimulation and challenge of dealing with new and difficult ideas, the intellectual excitement that emerges from an atmosphere of originality and scholarship. If they are to be university teachers in any meaningful sense, lecturers need to have the opportunity to pursue an active and creative research relationship with their subject.

## RELATIVIZING THE MASTER/PUPIL RELATIONSHIP

The new approach to teaching, which allegedly puts students at the center of the process, is also helping to undermine one of the most valuable ideals embodied by the university—that of the master–pupil relationship. Whether it's the slick Powerpoint delivery of information by new ILT-credited unicrats or the DIY educational model of students being left to their own devices (usually in front of a PC monitor), both threaten the intimate one-to-one relationships that can be achieved when the "apprentice" encounters the expert. While the awe and reverence inspired by being instructed by a "great master" was often more an ideal than the reality, it was a worthy one, which regularly produced a palpable educational engagement and development. This aspiration, which was embodied in one-to-one tutorials and the model of university teachers who were the leading researchers in their field, is being undermined. This is not solely by overcrowded seminars and teaching that relies on technique rather than depth of knowledge. There is also an ideological assault on the ideal. The ideal of institutions dedicated to expanding the sum totals of human knowledge through research, committed to the passing on of all the best that has been known and thought to date, to new generations of novices, with the underlying belief in the possibility that we might arrive at truths through the application of reason, dispensing with hearsay and superstition—all this is now contended within academia itself. It is difficult to lay a claim to being a truth-seeker without raising a snigger; when last year I talked about imparting a body of knowledge to my students at an education conference, I was accused of arrogance. Who was I to define what knowledge is? (see Fox 2000a: 70–72).

This attitude is partially a consequence of the cultural leftism that has gained supremacy in academic and intellectual circles since the 1960s. The enduring legacy of this movement has been its hostility to the idea of objectivity itself. As well documented and partially endorsed by Professor Ron Barnett in his book *Realizing the University in an Age of Supercomplexity*, there is a general antipathy to any assertion of truth or knowledge with a capital K (Barnett 2000). Metanarratives are rejected as manipulative and ideological. Cultural relativism, storytelling, and subjective interpretation is the new discourse. Expressed in various forms, Foucauldian theories of power relations, postcolonial and feminist theories, and postmodernism have undermined every attempt at objective truth and universality. With such a relativist view of knowledge so prevalent, it becomes understandable that many in academia have been incapable of a robust defense of their own special role as senior to their students. They themselves concede that Knowledge per se is problematic and that they know little more than their charges.

In this context, it is unsurprising that Oxbridge tutorials are now regarded as sites of bullying—the very pressure of exposing ignorance to knowledge is demonized as unfair. The very suggestion that the academic is a senior partner or that the apprentice has a lot to learn is viewed suspiciously. Even individual relationships between lecturers and students are deemed potentially abusive and run counter to the notion that everyone should be treated equally for fear of accusations of bias. This means that the tutor now treats tutees with kid gloves, and these relationships have become safer, predictable, samey, and, indeed, deadening. The NUS campaign for anonymous marking, cravenly backed by the Association of University Teachers (AUT)—increasingly found hanging on the student union's coattails—makes the point well (Pakes 1999). Tomorrow's students are likely to face impersonally marked scripts, with no individual feedback. Worse still is the fake intimacy that seeks to court students rather than risk real relationships with them. In one piece of advice to lecturers, under the heading "How To . . . Give Students the Big Picture," it is proposed that learning outcomes are empowering for students, lecturers are advised to avoid using the word "students" in documentation: "It is much better to use the word 'you' (as) students need to feel that learning outcomes belong to them, not just to other people" (Race 1998).

## LOVE AFFAIR WITH A SUBJECT

What is being lost through the leveling out and relativizing of the status of academics and students is passion. One of the mainstays of the master/pupil idea is that it is like a love affair—not between the participants (although that is sometimes a byproduct), but a grand passion with the subject and the discipline.

Who can forget how the wonders of Shakespeare were revealed to them by a wizened old man who was transformed into a dashing hero through the insights he revealed after 50 years of scholarship? What room for dreaming do we allow today's undergraduates if we rob them of the hours spent mulling over the finer points of Ibsen with the favorite lecturer in European theater who knows the playwright's work intimately.

What cemented this love affair was love for a subject. But as many of today's academics have lost confidence in their role as masters or intellectual leaders, the center of academic life has moved from expertise and subject knowledge to the students themselves. There is an unhealthy trend to do what pleases rather than what the curriculum or pursuit of higher knowledge requires. In this respect, student-centered HE means a loss of intellectual coherence, especially when applied to course design. We have recently witnessed Oxford and Cambridge English departments debating dropping Anglo-Saxon on the basis that it may put off potential students. Who cares if the students would have a more coherent grasp of the subject by studying a difficult and unattractive, but nonetheless valuable aspect of literature? That 44 universities do not make Shakespeare compulsory on English courses points to an abdication of responsibility—a refusal by academics to indicate which writer is better, more important, canonical, and so on (Simons 1998: 164). While the masters shy away from leadership, students are treated as equal stakeholders who should have an equal say in what their education should consist of. But at what cost? Take the example of pick & mix, modular, interdisciplinary degrees that have particularly plagued the humanities. How can students choose when through no fault of their own they do not know how to construct a meaningful syllabus? They need guidance as to what makes up a discipline. But if it matters so little to lecturers what one subject should add up to, how can we expect students to immerse themselves sufficiently to become critical thinkers? The result is Jacks of all trades, masters of none.

## CORE SKILLS, NOT CONTENT

What love affairs are on offer to today's students to replace the passion for a subject? Surely the new vogue for a core skills is poor substitute. Apart from the obvious point that these skills are often imparted inherently when studying, for example, history or English, no one is likely to get too passionate about Information Retrieval Skills, employability, or the ability to work in groups. But one way that the content of subjects is being marginalized is through the educational establishment's passionate embrace of the jargon-laden "generic transferable skills" agenda. Inevitably this is justified as yet another student-centered initiative: we are told it is these skills that will enable graduates to fit their degrees into the demands of the knowledge economy.

The core/soft skills agenda has been readily accepted by an academia that now views the passing on of knowledge as only one outcome of HE, alongside achieving social justice. This explains why helping students to get jobs rather than an education has become an ever-acceptable core part of university life. The one love affair that is now positively encouraged within academia is that between the workplace and higher education. Speaking at a conference launching "benchmarks" in May 2000, then education minister Baroness Blackstone said:

"Making standards explicit is a key part of ensuring that graduates are prepared for the world of work" (Russell 2000).

Of course, there is little point in mastering a subject if the new role of universities is as agencies for credentializing skills for work. This incorporation of employability skills into HE means that students can forget truth and beauty—they are now being groomed as marketable employees. When the Universities of Strathclyde and Paisley announced that they would be issuing laptops to undergraduates, Paisley's Dean of Faculty, Alan Roach, explained that this was to "to equip them with cross-disciplinary skills that make them extremely appealing to employers" (Wojtas 2000). That studying at a higher level is increasingly hemmed in by utilitarian and instrumental considerations is bad enough. But the core skills agenda is also facetious. Students are in danger of being sold a pup if we allow the curriculum to be dominated by the abstract learning outcomes that present themselves as student-centered. A popular new learning scheme, labeled Integron, illustrates the point. One model describes students filing into a lecture theater. They are unable to go to their accustomed seats because they have been painted or have signs on saying they have. Obviously those who are on time sit in other seats at the front of the theater, but "The latecomers . . . have to decide which is correct, their own sense of touch or the 'Wet Paint' signs." This, we are told by Professor Barbara Gorayaska, is a "subtle and powerful way to help somebody fully understand, and reflect on, the power of symbol" (Gorayaska & Lonsdale 2000). This learning to learn approach not only degrades the content of education, it leaves no room for master/pupil relationships: "there are no 'teachers'. Individuals responsible for running a course are learning facilitators. Everyone is seen as a learner" (Gorayaska & Lonsdale 2000).

## STUDENT-CENTERED NARCISSISM

One other acceptable love affair open to today's students is a narcissistic relationship with themselves. Student-centeredness is easily translated into a curriculum that puts students' own feelings, experiences, and lives on a pedestal. The new learning journeys of discovery are less driven by the external criteria derived from a discipline or method and more about self-discovery. This content-free model of self-expression is put at the heart of, for example, art, drama, and creative writing courses, at the expense of mastering a technique or studying "The Greats." Standing on the shoulders of giants and looking on astonished and in awe has been replaced by self-flattery encouraged by sycophantic academics. As usual, this does a disservice to students. They are denied the chance to discover that they are unlikely to do anything new or interesting unless they've absorbed the achievements of their predecessors and have realized what it takes to be creative. In the same vein, students' ill-formed opinions are frequently credited with insight as lecturers embrace all ideas as having some merit. But if education is to go beyond the rote transmission of received opinion, surely it involves challenging students' accustomed beliefs and attitudes to allow them to determine which hold up under pressure and which need to be rethought, improved, or junked. The subjective impressions of self-expression often leave students none the wiser.

## STUDENT-CENTERED KNOWLEDGE

This embrace of students for themselves in preference to transforming them has contributed to how we view knowledge. The everyday acquisition of experience and skills is now honored with the knowledge tag. This was codified by Gibbons and associates in their influential book, *The New Production of Knowledge*, which characterized Knowledge 1 as essentially theoretical knowledge inside the university sector and Knowledge 2 as essentially "knowledge-in-use" produced outside the university (see Gibbons et al. 1994). Now Knowledge 2, which comprises the banal routines of home and work and affords them equal status with philosophy and chemistry, is being internalized within the university sector. The Action on Access team is arguing that a more inclusive model of HE with a "larger, more diverse student base" must acknowledge "the transformative impact that . . . workplace-led learning will have over the sector" (Layer 2000). Professor Ivor Crewe, Vice Chancellor of Essex University and Chair of the working group designing foundation degrees, has stated that applicants will be able to sign up without formal qualifications and will, for example, "to be able to gain accreditation for skills learnt at work" (Hodges 2000). There is currently a move to credit the alleged learning that students get from the part-time jobs they have been forced to do in the absence of grants, and to use these to enhance their employability after graduation (Moon & Bowes 1998). The much-vaunted, government-backed Learndirect scheme boasts that it is "based on the premise that people don't always need to go to college or university to learn because the process of learning . . . is part and parcel of everyday working life" (Learndirect 2001).

## FEEL AT HOME

The argument that one can gain a university degree without ever leaving work or actually going into a higher-education institution is the logical conclusion of a philosophy that shapes itself around students and their lives rather than seeking to transform them. This is mirrored in the present obsession with making universities less alien to potential students and more like the rest of their lives. It is argued that what holds many back from going into HE after school is that campus life is too distant and far removed from everyday experience to appeal to the majority.

The original idea of the ivory tower as a separate world (or campus) was that the pursuit of knowledge should be disinterested and done for its own sake. For the entirely justifiable pursuit of academic autonomy, universities were to be one step removed from the influences of society, outside the immediate demands of politics or commerce. Although an ideal that was all too frequently compromised, today it is no longer an ideal but, rather, a notion seen as too exclusive, insular, and irrelevant to the modern world. Once universities are about the pursuit of students rather than the pursuit of knowledge, it is hard to justify their other-worldliness.

The contemporary demand is that universities should model themselves on their would-be students' prior lives. The Open University's Judith George and Ewan Gillon, in research presented to the European Access Network in July 2001, criticized the "enormous differences between the approaches and cultures of community education, further education and higher education" (Wojtas 2001). So in order to attract "alienated potential tertiary entrants from nontraditional backgrounds," universities should become more like the local tech. Backing up the OU research, the National Association of Teachers in Further and Higher Education's (Natfhe) Liz Allen complains that "higher education fails to cater for nontraditional students" because it is "a daunting experience for the uninitiated" with its culture and foreign traditions (from the gowns to the architecture) seen as both "alien and intimidating" (Allen 2001). So what is to be done? The solutions put forward consist of ways of making HE closer to students' familiar experiences. This can lead to some patronizing and crass campaigns to sell HE. Cambridge University's Group to Encourage Ethnic Minority Applications (GEEMA) Coordinator, Joy Wheeler, suggested in an article in *The Guardian* that one reason working-class black youngsters are deterred from applying to Cambridge is because there is no night life. Needless to say, they were assured that there are "plenty of ragga, soca and hiphop bands on offer" (Gold 1999).

The most common initiatives consist of selling HE to would-be students as an easy extension of school. Many of the new universities are forming partnerships with primary schools in disadvantaged neighborhoods to such an end. John Knowles, school liaison officer at Lincolnshire and Humberside University, runs courses to enthuse children as young as nine about campus life. He explains the philosophy behind the lectures about Guy Fawkes, witchcraft, and horror movies: "The idea is that they go back to the schools and tell all their friends what fun they have had there" (quoted by Utley 1999). So universities are reduced to playschool status. David Littlefair of Teeside University's Meteor program, which targets inner-city primary schools, explains the strategy: "We are trying to empower children . . . to let them know it is not an alien environment" (Utley 1999).

But if universities are not alien to primary-school kids or everyday life, what is their point? And there is a danger here that molding HE around the familiar will leave new generations within the confines imposed by their social circumstances, from which university should offer an escape. Willy Russell's Rita recognizes that taking education seriously means breaking away from her own culture. Even though she is intimidated by the world of literature and donnish dominion, it is worth it, or she will forevermore be frustrated by the familiar but intellectually stultifying world of the hairdressing salon. When universities organize "Feel at Home" days and summer camps, I shudder. The last thing I wanted when I went to university was to feel at home—a place that limited any possibilities for me to develop my mind, pursue my passion for poetry, or have space to think and contemplate.

So much for university being a life-changing experience. Now it is the universities that we expect to change, to resemble life more closely. But for university to have the potential to act as a challenging educational experience, it has to overturn all that is familiar, introduce alien ideas and foreign concepts, and liberate students from the parochial and commonplace, precipitating them into the unfamiliar worlds that new ideas and knowledge opens up. To allow universities to ape the well-known world of the everyday means leaving students in the very place education should allow them to escape from.

Universities shaping themselves on the world that students already inhabit rather than introducing them to new worlds helps to explain why that weasel word "relevance" now haunts the curriculum. One of the DfEE's preelection stunts this year was the launch of a new qualification in Real World Mathematics, which aims to teach with reference to the mathematics used by individuals in their day-to-day life such as household finance, building work, and so on. Adapting to the relevant presents the danger of reining in the imagination (the very quality needed to pursue new areas of investigation) and confining it to the students' immediate reference points, whether that be pocket-money numeracy or popular culture.

This year, the University of Cambridge used a quote from the lyrics of "Tragedy," sung by the Bee Gees, a band more popular in the 1980s than today, in the English compulsory paper in an attempt to make the concept of tragedy more relevant to modern life. While choosing the Bee Gees indicates that English dons are more in touch with literary classics than with youth culture, what is indeed a tragedy is this feeble attempt at denuding one of the most complex and fascinating aspects of literature by reducing it to the banal in the name of student-centered education (see Bennett 2001).

## TRANSFORMATION

In conclusion, it is worth reflecting on what education can offer when removed from the vicissitudes of student subjectivity and the narrow confines of utilitarian ends. In a heartfelt reflection on the dropping of compulsory Anglo Saxon at Oxford, Graham Holderness, Dean of Humanities, Languages and Education at the University of Hertfordshire, draws out what unexpected consequences education can offer: "Had I not been obliged to learn it (old English at Oxford), I . . . doubt that 35 years later I would have found myself publishing verse translations and a book on Anglo-Saxon poetry. The long term benefits of education are far less quantifiable than is dreamt of in the skills agenda" (*THES.* Letters. 19 May 2000).

Meanwhile, in Jonathan Rose's new book, *The Intellectual Life of the British Working Classes*, a wonderful study of turn-of-the-century education, he quotes a cowman's son on discovering the joy of literature through reading Tennyson:

The coloured words flashed out and entranced my fancy. They drew pictures in the mind. . . . My dormant imagination opened like a flower in the sun. Life at home was drab, and colourless, with nothing to light up the dull monotony of the unchanging days. Here in books was a limitless world that I could have for my own. It was like coming up from the bottom of the ocean and seeing the universe for the first time. [quoted in Rose, 2001: 127]

In today's mass student-centered university we would leave this agricultural worker on the seabed. We would deprive him of those irrelevant novels, disguise the universe as a farm to make him feel at home, assess the prior learning and transferable skills involved in milking cows and award him a degree in rustic studies.

The faults and foibles of the traditional university, with its old-school-tie ethos, snobbishness, and cavalier attitude to its own mission, deserve a savage critique. There is no room here for rose-tinted sentimentality about the good old days. But bearing in mind babies and bath water, we throw out the knowledge-centered Western ideal of the university at our peril. For those of us who have fought long and hard to open up access to the ivory towers to allow more and more people to share the liberation of developing the critical and analytical powers that accompany studying at the highest level, we must acknowledge that in the guise of student-centeredness we are in danger of destroying precisely what it was that was worth gaining access to. The transformative aspect of education means forcing students to struggle with the sometimes uncongenial, the markedly different, and the unfamiliar. Without these challenges, higher education is a paltry, passionless affair—less love affair, more one-night stand and a disaster for the student experience.

## REFERENCES

Allen, L. (2001). Retention please . . . *THES*, 20 July.

Bennett, J. (2001). Why I . . . . *THES,* 20 July.

Barnett, R. (2000). *Realizing the University in an Age of Supercomplexity.* Buckingham, U.K.: Society for Research into Higher Education/Open University Press.

Blunkett, D. (2000). Reaching out to make society just. Speech to the annual council of the Association of University Teachers, Eastbourne. Reprinted in *THES*, 12 May.

Dearing, R. (1997). *Higher Education in the Learning Society.* London: HMSO.

Fox, C. (1997). The dumbing down of higher education. *LM*, 104 (October).

Fox, C. (2000a). Knowledges, knowledges everywhere. *Last Magazine* (Summer): 70–72.

Fox, C. (2000b). Education: Dumbing down or wising up? In I. Mosley (Ed.), *Dumbing Down: Culture Politics and the Mass Media.* Thorverton: Imprint Academic.

Gibbons, M., Limoges, C., Nowotny, H., Schwarzman, S., Scott, P., & Trow, M. (1994). *The New Production of Knowledge: The Dynamics of Science and Research in Contemporary Societies.* Thousand Oaks, CA, & London: Sage.

Gold, K. (1999). Rainbow warriors. *Guardian Higher,* 16 March.

Gorayaska, B., & Lonsdale, C. (2000). The integron effect. *THES,* 3 March.

Heathfield, M. (1999). How to . . . assess student group work. *THES,* 26 March.

Hodges, L. (1998). Sending the lecturers back to school. *Independent Education,* 9 July.

Hodges, L. (2000). Is there anyone out there who wants a degree? *Independent Education,* 6 April.

Layer, G. (2000). Facing the challenge on widening participation: Action on Access team report. *THES,* 25 February.

Learndirect (2001). Want to learn through work and get a university qualification? Promotional brochure, University for Industry.

Moon, S., & Bowes, L. (1998). Earning, learning, spending, fending. *The Lecturer* (December).

O'Connor, M. (1999). What happens when students assert their consumer rights? *The Lecturer* (December).

Pakes, A. (1999). Pride and prejudice. *THES,* 19 March.

Race, P. (1998). How to . . . give students the big picture. *THES,* 13 November.

Rose, J. (2001). *The Intellectual Life of the British Working Classes.* New Haven, CT, & London: Yale University Press.

Russell, B. (2000). Scrap university degree system, inspector urges. *The Independent,* 18 May.

Simons, J. (1998). Reading and the University. In B. Cox, (Ed.), *Literacy Is Not Enough: Essays on the Importance of Reading.* Manchester, U.K.: Book Trust/Manchester University Press.

Utley, A. (1999). Universities set primary targets. *THES,* 12 November.

Wallace, J. (1998). Sheila still making waves. *THES,* 13 November.

Winter, R. (2000). How to orchestrate cerebral cells. *THES,* 24 November.

Wojtas, O. (2000). Job skills boosted with free laptops. *THES,* 8 September.

Wojtas, O. (2001). Experts on access lay blame on campuses. *THES,* 6 July.

# 10

## Taking the Hemlock?
## The New Sophistry of Teacher Training
## for Higher Education

*Dennis Hayes*

There is no reason to think that, in general, university teaching is inadequate. There is no reason to think that there is a need to reform, reorganize, and make accountable the sort of teaching that goes on in universities. There is no reason to think that courses of teacher training are necessary for university lecturers. There is no reason to think that such training programs will benefit university lecturers or their students. There is no reason to think that there is a need for a professional body to promote the status of university teaching. There is no reason to think that university lecturers need to adopt a new ethic or vision to complement, supplement, or resist the impositions of such a body.

It is important to put these assertions boldly because the opposite views are held to be quite reasonable, particularly by the government. All the unnecessary initiatives implied in the paragraph above are being pursued by the Department for Education and Skills or the various higher-education funding bodies, with support from other so-called "stakeholders," such as "the public" and "the students." Only a few isolated academics and a declining number of "elite" university vice-chancellors are prepared to hold out and argue against these initiatives. The opposition is mostly silent and restricted to the senior common room or the coffee bar. However, as a correspondent remarked after I made similar points about teacher training for university lecturers on a previous occasion, "in private, most, perhaps all, agree." It is to that silent group that this chapter is addressed, to alert them to how arguments and initiatives aimed at improving teaching skills, or at reconstructing or professionalizing university teaching, are really about laying the foundations for what I will call the *therapeutic university*. But what is stated so boldly must also be argued for and, if possible, explained.

## CHANGING SCHOLARS INTO TEACHERS

Why not make sure that the teaching of all university lecturers is up to scratch? After all, moves are underway to improve primary and secondary teaching, so why not university teaching? These naive questions are illuminating. They rest on mistaken but commonplace ideas that appear in many discussions about university teaching.

The first question presupposes a view of the university that makes "teaching" a function that can be simply separated from the essential work of the university in advancing knowledge. This is a debased idea of the role of the university that is facilitated by those who talk of a "teaching" and "research" divide in which both of these are seen as functions of equal value. The old-fashioned term "scholarship" indicated the unity of teaching and research, as well as many other things. Adopting it temporarily, we can say that a university is a place of scholarship, a "community of scholars," in which teaching and research are both part of a scholar's life. This is not to argue that there is a "scholarship" of "teaching" equal to academic scholarship, this is just playing with words (Gibbs 2000; Nicholls 2001). To separate out these two elements is to treat them in a way in which they begin to have aims and objectives of their own. "Research" becomes separate from "teaching," and it is a short step to "funded" research projects with limited and fixed objectives. Furthermore, it is often "researchers" who have no interest in teaching who undertake it. Likewise, "teaching" becomes an independent process of passing on already existing knowledge. But "teaching" in a university is one aspect of the processes that advance knowledge. Even 18-year-olds attending their first lecture could and should experience a tutor challenging them to question old ideas and struggling with new ones beyond the confines of current knowledge. It is tempting to say that there is an asymmetry here with "research" being the dominant aspect, but this argument does not go far enough. It would not show that attempts to isolate "teaching" are necessarily artificial and formulaic. It is better to think of the total integration, or harmony, of "teaching" and "research" in the search for knowledge. Teaching is part of the processes in which tentative knowledge is made public for discussion and in which knowledge claims are judged. Therefore, the starting point for any discussion of teaching must be the process of advancement of knowledge, whether in a subject or field. This priority is often recognized, but then in the process of presenting strategies for professional development, it is almost always qualified or severely weakened (see Brookfield 1995b; Nicholls 2001; Nixon 2001; Nixon, et al. 2000; Rowland 2000).

What I am arguing here, and throughout this chapter, is that there is a profound misunderstanding behind any moves to develop, deliver, and to encourage or require university lecturers to participate in teacher-training courses. Universities are simply not about teaching as it is ordinarily understood. This is because the university since the nineteenth century has become *the* social institution that is primarily concerned with what Anthony Giddens, speaking to a meeting of the

Convocation of the University of London, described and defended as *"the pursuit of knowledge without fear or favour"* (1999: 37, italics added). There are echoes in this phrase of Matthew Arnold's famous description of the essentially human instinct that prompts us to: "try to know the best that is known and thought in the world, irrespectively of practice, politics, and everything of the kind; and to value knowledge and thought as they approach this best, without the intrusion of any other considerations whatever" (1864: 10–11). Arnold and Giddens both stress the disinterested character of inquiry, but Arnold makes clear in his belief that the "disinterested love of a free play of the mind on all subjects, for its own sake" is an ethical value, what he called "a high and fine quality of man's nature" (1864: 10). Arnold's statement is doubly useful as it emphasizes the need to "learn and know the best that is known and thought." This is the task of both lecturer and student. A body of knowledge, a subject, must be mastered and continually engaged and re-engaged with before we can begin to talk about "fresh knowledge" and "ever fresh knowledge" (1864: 24).

Part of the contemporary anxiety about this view of the university is the belief that its monopoly as the site of knowledge production is being challenged. Such claims are sometimes matters of definition in which the word "knowledge" is played with after the fashion of Humpty Dumpty to mean whatever they want it to mean. "Knowledge" becomes anything we learn, and serious academic subject knowledge is said to be just one sort of knowledge. Therefore, as study is only a part of life, it is "challenged" by the knowledge that exists in other areas of life. However, once the term is allowed to cover any sort of learning or skill, it ceases to have any meaning. The assertion that the things we call "knowledge" are equivalent, crudely equates such things as learning skills on the job with knowledge that comes after years, perhaps a lifetime, of study. This attempt to assert an ethical equivalence between different sorts of knowledge serves to undermine the emphasis on the higher and finer qualities of humanity exhibited in the disinterested pursuit of knowledge in the university.

The more serious claim about the challenge to the university monopoly is that there are rival sites of knowledge production, and the university is just one among many. This anxious claim is often made, but never seriously examined. Writers who declare the university to be dead never consider if the facts bear out such a wild assertion. As I have argued elsewhere, when such an examination is undertaken, the conclusion that has to be drawn is that the university has a growing monopoly of knowledge production and that production by potential rivals, such as industry, is declining (Hayes 2000).

These arguments about challenges to the monopoly of knowledge production often rest on more general arguments that the world about us is changing or in a condition of constant change, so that teachers also need to change in response to them (Hargreaves 1994). Occasionally, they go further and argue that part of the university's role is to help us live with, and even to celebrate, change and uncertainty (Barnett 2000). Of course, Socrates' famous refutation of one Heracleitean view applies here: from the premise of constant change everything follows, but equally nothing follows (*Theaetetus*: 183a). Once again, the idea that the world is changing fast, because of technological revolution, is simply never examined. It remains an assertion, a statement of a modern secular faith. When the facts are examined, change is seen to be slower than in the recent past (Woudhuysen 1997, 1999). One could make the mundane and obvious observation that contemporary universities and higher-education institutions have changed and now fulfill several functions (Natfhe 1999a). But this overtolerant and nominalist position simply avoids the question of what is essential to the idea of a university. It is of no use in any argument about the true nature of a university.

The second question presupposes that university teaching is an aspect of a generic activity that goes on in a variety of other settings, such as primary and secondary schools. But there is an essential difference. Teaching in the schooling phase (primary, secondary, and much of further education) must incorporate and utilize knowledge of developmental processes and of learning how to learn. Therefore, some understanding of a field of knowledge called "education" is quite rightly required of all trainee schoolteachers. This is an addition to the knowledge they have of the subject or subjects they hope to teach. This would involve at least some understanding of the insights available from psychologists, sociologists, historians, and philosophers who have written on the subject of schooling and education. This is the proper business of teacher-training departments in universities and colleges. This is not necessarily what they do, of course, as the content of their programs is determined by government and consists largely of experiential learning and the acquisition of skills supplemented by "third way" moralism about issues such as citizenship.

It would be difficult to identify, and even harder to justify, a similar necessity for knowledge of such a discipline to be a requirement for all university lecturers. Although university students may learn much, their maturation and cognitive development processes are effectively over by the time they enter the university. There is no field of knowledge here involving the acquisition of learning skills, of learning how to learn. There is a subsidiary topic in the field of education that involves the study of the processes of adult learning for those turning or returning to university education late. But this is a quite different matter and once stripped of any political pretensions is clearly nothing more than an effective and appropriate form of remedial education.

The specialist study of the university and its achievements would not provide a field of knowledge for all trainee university teachers because its field would simply be that of human knowledge. Likewise, any study of the university within the disciplines, such as a sociological investigation of university students as a subculture, would be just a study in the discipline of sociology. Knowledge of it would have no special consequence for lecturers, although it might be of general interest to those not studying in that discipline.

There is of course a growing literature discussing student learning. This literature is produced by professional staff development organizations and student unions, but most is produced by universities themselves in the annual round of student course evaluations and student satisfaction surveys. By comparison with much of this work, consumers' reports and customer surveys are models of science. Yet student views on teaching are often taken as authoritative, especially by college managers and government. A recent example is an intervention by Owain James, President of the National Union of Students, in the debate about the setting up of the Institute for Learning and Teaching in Higher Education (ILT). He represents what he sees as the consumers' perspective: "With changes to the funding system students are increasingly moving towards seeing themselves as consumers, and so expect the best services that money can buy. Good quality teaching comes top of the list" (Spöring, Toner, & James 2000: 7). James and the NUS want 100% participation of staff: "from research students to established professors . . . as only 100% participation can guarantee a competency standard that students expect and deserve" (2000: 7). The question as to whether there is any evidence that teaching needs to be improved is not discussed, and, in any case, further collection of the views of students would be a useless activity the more that they come to see themselves as consumers. A university education is not a commodity to be consumed. Being the result of a developing relationship between the student and the lecturer and the subject, it cannot be determined in advance. To get to know a subject requires submission to the guidance of someone who has academic authority because of his subject knowledge. This is why student evaluations are entirely, and logically, restricted to the *form* and not the *content* of what they experience. I say "logically," because to be able to criticize the content of an academic course would require that the students had knowledge beyond that of the academic lecturers. Students by definition cannot have this knowledge. They are, therefore, restricted to superficial judgments about the *edutainment* value of their courses. Would students ask to be made to work harder? Does a student evaluation exist that that identifies the need for a compulsory course in *logic* for all first-year undergraduates?

Generalizing from this, we can say that although university administrators and lecturers may think that making university lecturers accountable to student opinion is egalitarian and democratic, the consequences of giving it credence can only hinder the pursuit of knowledge. What is even more important is that a preoccupation with evaluations keeps university lecturers away from research activities while they collate and respond to these evaluations and then spend time brushing up on their jokes and PowerPoint skills.

The fact that no second field of knowledge can be identified has led many university staff developers and teacher trainers to argue that teacher educators should not take the lead in the development of teacher training at university level (Kelly 1995: 185–186). This negative consequence would be a happy one if the task were just given to subject specialists to initiate neophytes into their profession. This is not even considered to be an option. Instead there is a growing agreement that there exists a "professional crisis" in the university (Nixon et al.

2000: 5), that academics "have to face change" (Nicholls 2001: 12). and that it is time to put "the teaching relationship first" (Nixon et al. 2000: 13), to move from a "Culture of Scholarship" to a "Culture of Teaching" (Brookfield 1995b).

## FROM THE ADVANCEMENT OF KNOWLEDGE
## TO THE THERAPY OF ADVANCEMENT

### A Golden Age?

To see the significance of this supposed crisis, it has to be put into a historical context. It is important to remind ourselves that there was a distinct but short historical period when Western economies could afford increased spending on public services and, as part of this, to offer a university education to more young people. Some figures will remind us of what was the longest period of boom in the history of capitalism. Between 1950 and 1973, industrial output in the advanced capitalist countries increased by 180%, average growth was 4.9%, and jobs increased by 29%. Real wages increased at about 3.5% a year, and welfare expenditure increased from 15% to 24% of GDP (Brown & Lauder 2001: 15–19). Interestingly, this period of boom was based on low-skill but high-wage jobs (2001: 19).

Eric Hobsbawm reminds us that the expansion of university education in this period was an "explosion." Before the Second World War, Germany, France, and Britain "with a total population of 150 millions, contained no more than 150,000 or so university students between them, or 0.01% of their joint populations. Yet by the late 1980s students were counted in millions" (1994: 295). Throughout Europe the number of students tripled or quadrupled between 1960 and 1980 (1994: 296), and the number of university lecturers in just seven countries reached 100,000 (1994: 296). To accommodate the increased numbers of students, the number of universities in the world more than doubled in the 1970s (1994: 297).

The first generation of new students was the most radical. Hobsbawm suggests that the reason for this radicalism was the sheer explosion of student numbers: "The number of French students at the end of the second world war was less than 100,000. By 1960, it was over 200,000 and within the next ten years, it tripled to 651,000" (1994: 300). This pressure of student numbers provoked an interest in teacher training (Beard 1970: ch. 1). But it is reasonable to suppose, despite the negative examples based on subjective experience and the need for society to shift to a meritocratic system of selection for middle-class occupations (see Hudson, chapter 7, this volume), that these students were exposed to an education that was clearly rooted in the subject disciplines—something quite different from what students will receive in the current phase of expansion. They were given, whether they saw it and valued it or not, "a deep, empathetic but critical understanding of what they read and hear, and the ability to express that understanding in a manner adapted to whatever audience they have to reach" (Ryan 1999: 138). Whether or not this was yet another cause of student radicalization, it is certainly arguable that this sort of liberal education was a basis for its articulation. In passing, it is worth noting that optimists such as Alan Ryan (1999: 130) and Joanne Finkelstein (chapter 13, this volume) argue that simply because of this expansion, some increased exposure to liberal education must be going on.

The contemporary phase of expansion in student numbers is as dramatic as that earlier one described by Hobsbawm. By 1990, in Britain, there were some 600,000 students in higher education, and a million by the middle of the decade (Smith & Webster 1997: 2). By the end of the 1990s, some 1,600,000 students were receiving some form of higher education (Ryan 1999: 136). This expansion is of higher education in general and includes numbers receiving higher education in a variety of institutions, including further education colleges. Indeed, to meet its arbitrarily set targets for a further expansion in student numbers of 500,000 by 2002, the government has been forced to count further education as part of this figure (Smithers 2001: 422). Set this expansion in the context of real cuts in resources per student since 1970 of 40% (Ryan 1999: 135), and it is impossible to argue that the education on offer is not qualitatively different from that offered in the 1960s and 1970s.

Without nostalgia, and as a corrective to revisionists, I would claim that this earlier period amounted to something like a "golden age" or "first way" for the university. In historical terms, this was a very short period, lasting from the end of the immediate phase of Second World War reconstruction up to and beyond the publication of the Robbins Report in 1963. Its high point is the founding of the Open University in 1969, and its nadir is heralded by Callaghan's speech at Ruskin College in 1976, which marked the transition to the Thatcherite "second way" by putting education at the service of business and the economy.

I take my example of the uniqueness of this period and its importance for the pedagogic memory from Australia (see a short parallel history of higher education in Australia in Joanne Finkelstein's contribution, chapter 13, this volume). The Australian philosopher John Anderson defends the university as a critical community of scholars in various papers (1980: chs. 7–10, 13). Anderson saw the academic not as a private individual, but as one with a public role of "troublemaker" and critic. His job was to argue against all aspects of commercialism and in particular against the "pseudo-academic philistines that saw students as 'job fodder'." Anderson believed that "opposition has been the task of genuine academics in all ages" (1980: 221) and expected that "It would be especially on *education* that strong academic pronouncements would be looked for" (1980: 216). This is not a psychological trait but is a consequence of the academic life: "The work of the academic, qua academic, is criticism; and, whatever his special field may be, his development of independent views will bring him into conflict with prevailing opinions and customary attitudes in the public arena and not merely among his fellow-professionals" (1980: 214). Academic freedom for Anderson did not consists of any special rights but was a recognition of academic authority, that academics have "a special province, a field in which they can say '*We* are the experts here; *we* can tell you (the Law, the State) what has force, what *runs*, in this department of social activity'" (1980: 220).

This is a powerful and confident account of what it is to be an academic, and Anderson's own writings revealed that few of his contemporaries lived up to it. This does not matter. What matters was that the essential idea of a "university" and what it was to be an academic was something held to be worth defending as important in itself. Anderson held that educational study was best thought of as philosophy, as clarity of thought about educational issues. His only discussion of practical teaching is a defense of the lecture as "the central feature of any course of higher study"; the suggestion that there should be more seminars and tutorials he saw as "spoon feeding" as students progress more by thinking over the lecture-material themselves and discussing it with one another (1980: 148–149). The lecture is the vehicle for the presentation of new or developing knowledge and ideas. Such an idea is unacceptable today, when the focus is on student opinion and skills such as problem-solving (Gibbs 1995: 21–22). Anderson's view is based upon the intimate relationship of teaching to the development of critical thought. A few academics still hold to these views:

The research–teaching–study nexus has been central to the identity of the university. Whether or not the nexus is supported by empirical evidence is irrelevant, the ideal form sustains the symbolic distinction between universities, vocational colleges and schools. In this form, the relationship between teacher and student is "sealed by their common pursuit of knowledge . . . [they] engage in research in close cognitive and physical proximity" (Clark 1994: 11). The loss of distinctiveness of the university as a learning community is changing partly as the nexus weakens, but also as the significance of the social nature of learning is challenged. [McInnis 1995: 45]

McInnis' remark about the loss of distinctiveness of the "community of learning that is the university" is an unfortunate one. "Learning" is almost always discussed in relation to teaching and "knowledge" in relation to research. Thus, such an expression could carelessly perpetuate this dichotomy, and therefore "community of scholars" is a better expression. However, given this qualification, he is right about the challenge to the significance of scholarship.

Another challenge to scholarship comes from revisionists who see the golden age as a myth used to defend privilege. Peter Wright, Assistant Director of Development of the Quality Assurance Agency for Higher Education (QAA), in a reply to Gillian Evans's argument for increasing downward accountability in the academy, says that "her analysis of current developments is undermined, in my view, by her account of the past state of U.K. universities. When, if ever, were universities self-regulating communities of scholars unconstrained by external forces?" (Wright, 2000: 32). But there was something approximating this, so we do not have to rely entirely on the argument that this is an ideal form to which universities aspire, irrespective of the empirical question of the actual or historical existence of any such community.

Anderson promoted the critical approach of Socrates, but only in a period of affluence could any society tolerate more than one Socrates in its midst. Tolerance of even an approximation to the academic ideal form ends in the 1970s against the background of world economic recession, experienced in Britain as the "oil crises." Essential texts on innovation in university teaching, written over the last three decades of the last century, chart its decline.

## A SADDER BUT A WISER TIME?

In 1974, just at the time when the long postwar boom had clearly ended, a series of case studies was put together by a study group set up by the Society for Research into Higher Education (SRHE). The theme of this work, which devotes a whole chapter to "Promoting Innovation in University Teaching," is the need to experiment and provide an objective scientific evaluation of teaching innovation. The work is of its time in seeking planned change. Its editor argues that "Since 1945 there has been a growing consciousness of the need for human civilisation to control its own development and evolution." Although "modern technological resources have enabled man to land on the moon. There is a deep sense of disjunction between men's powers in the field of engineering and [their powers] in the field of social improvement" (Collier 1974: 7). This work still celebrates the potential of higher education, but there is a feeling of urgency and threat, that time was running out, just as the electricity was in Britain in the early 1990s.

In 1983, another SRHE collection tells everything about that time through its title: *Innovation through Recession*. A "sadder and wiser" (Squires 1983: 4) approach to innovation is proposed throughout the book as a conscious attempt to maintain quality in a time of substantial cuts in funding. Innovations in teaching were twofold, involving "a shift of responsibility from teachers to students; and . . . a shift from teachers to technology" (Squires 1983: 6). The innovations in teaching methods illustrated include the involvement of students in self-assessment and the use of teaching "laboratories." Squires characterizes the recession as both economic and a "recession of hope" (Squires 1983: 6). The economic recession continues to occupy academics who face the increasing casualization of working conditions, the loss of ownership and control over the products of their work, and the onslaughts of corporate and bureaucratic management. What is missing is any negative consciousness about the dual shift in responsibility, which is no longer seen as an unfortunate necessity, but rather as something positive. It is more the recession of hope, set in the context of the end of an historic expansion of university education, that determines the contemporary consciousness of the state of higher education. The recession of hope is primarily a retreat from the social, from any view of the university as the place of scholarship having a real role in society. It is about the retreat from any progressive view of the need to aim at the achievement of excellence in the university. To the extent that academics lost their vision or their hope, they became ripe for therapy.

## TOWARD THE THERAPEUTIC UNIVERSITY

Therapy is the focus of John Cowan's *On Becoming an Innovative University Teacher: Reflection in Action,* published in 1998. Cowan reverses the role of technology from something that is used in a conscious way to initiate change to one where its influence will change our consciousness. Cowan's main themes are how the new technologies "provoke" reflection and how his personal and collaborative reflection has improved aspects of university teaching. The influence of Carl Rogers' therapeutic "person-to-person" approach to learning is explicit and recommended (Cowan 1998: 142–146). Cowan identifies three conditions to be met if Rogerian "growth promotion" is to be successful: (1) Teachers must "unearth their immediate thoughts and feelings, and . . . make these available to their students without editing or censoring" (1998: 143). (2) Teachers "make themselves transparent to the learner, who can then see right through to what the teacher actually is, within their relationship" and equally that they have "a positive and accepting attitude to whatever the student is, or is thinking or doing, at that moment. It is a prizing of learners as imperfect human beings" (1998: 144). (3) The teacher "accurately senses and assimilates the feelings and personal meanings which the student is communicating" (1998: 144).

The notion behind such an approach is the reconstruction of the teacher/ student relationship to focus on building up the self-esteem of both. Rogerian therapy sees the self as something to be "esteemed, actualized, affirmed, and unfettered" (Nolan 1998: 3). It is "liberating" because in a quasi-religious way it sees all human beings and their impulses as essentially inclined toward good (Nolan 1998: 4). We are a long way from Anderson's concern with subjects and the self-denial required to be a critical thinker. His dismissal of any concept of innovation in the methodology of teaching as "spoon-feeding" has been replaced by an obsession with building up student self-esteem.

The language is not always overtly therapeutic, but the therapeutic approach lies behind the current vogue for talking about "reflective practice." This is true even if we talk of "critical reflection" that recognizes the existence of particular power relations in reflective practice (Brookfield 1995b: 130). The relocation of the discussion of "power" to person-to-person relationships within a classroom is part of the "liberating" (transformative, empowering, emancipatory) language of therapy whether or not that debt is recognized:

critical reflection is inherently ideological. It is also morally grounded. It springs from a concern to create the conditions under which people can learn to love one another, and it alerts them to the forces that prevent this. Being anchored in values of justice, fairness, and compassion, critical reflection finds its political representation in the democratic process. Since it is difficult to show love to others when we are divided, suspicious, and scrambling for advantage, critical reflection urges us to create conditions under which each person is respected, valued, and heard. In pedagogic terms, this means the creation of democratic classrooms. In terms of professional development, it means an engagement in critical conversation. [Brookfield 1995a: 26–27]

Two of the important features of critical reflection listed by Brookfield are that it avoids self-laceration and grounds us emotionally (1995a: 23, 24). It also fosters trust by treating students as adults and by acknowledging peer learning. His discussion of critical reflection culminates in a purely therapeutic model of practice: "A teacher who encourages students to point out to her anything about her actions that is oppressive and who seeks to change what she does in response to their concerns is a model of critical reflection. Such a teacher is one who truly is trustworthy" (1995a: 26).

The emphasis in reflective practice is to treat lecturers and students as academic equals. "Education" is defined as a dialogue among equals and: "Through this dialogue, students are helped to name, honor, and understand their own experiences. They do this using categories of analysis that they have evolved themselves rather than those that have been externally imposed on them by the dominant culture" (1995a: 208–209).

This overturns what is normally thought of as education, which involves acquiring a culture—striving to learn and know the best that has been thought and said. Love of subject is replaced by the love of individuals, and the true equality in the search for truth is replaced by a purely subjective valuing of experience. This may well build up student self-esteem, as they no longer have to study to understand the best that is known and thought, but it is a destructive experience for staff.

Engaging in critical reflection might, at least initially, make us actually feel worse as teachers "more doubt-ridden, puzzled, sadder perhaps. After all, sadness and wisdom are not incompatible" (Jackson, quoted in Brookfield 1995a: 239) and Brookfield's own experience has been one of "sustained epistemological demolition, as my certitudes are constantly crashing to the ground" (1995a: 115: 239–240).

This therapeutic undermining of academic confidence is held to be a defense of cooperation and collaboration in the face of rampant individualism in the university, where the culture is individualist and the model is the "Lone Ranger." Not surprisingly this approach is resisted by the Lone Rangers themselves (Brookfield 1995a: 260–263), and Brookfield argues that the solution is an institutional reward system to encourage critical reflection as a "normal and desirable professional habit" (1995a: 252). This idea is becoming the norm, even if formal reward systems are absent. Interestingly, it is unlikely to be challenged by institutions as the therapeutic impulse locates discussions of power solely at the level of tutor/student relationships. Such a relocation of power is entirely to the advantage of those who hold the real power to hire and fire who can intervene in any conflicts at this level in a seemingly neutral and supportive way.

However, this would not necessarily be a cynical move on the part of any institution. All institutions are susceptible to the therapeutic impulse since it allows them to develop new forms of legitimization when old values no longer connect with a disenchanted public (Nolan 1998: 40–45).

What has given the shift toward the therapeutic view of the university some influence in Britain is a debate about the consequences of the formation of the Institute for Learning and Teaching (ILT). Its founding purpose, derived from the Dearing Report, is to provide "professional standing for teachers in higher education comparable with that in other professions" (ILTPG 1998: sec. 4). It aims "*to redress the balance between teaching and research* by providing a national focus for teaching" (ILTPG 1998: sec. 5) and to "enhance the status of teaching in higher education" (ILTPG 1998: sec. 9) by putting "students at the centre of the process of learning and teaching" (Dearing 1997 Summary Report: s35; see Fox, chapter 9, this volume). The ILT is concerned with this as another imbalance, and we have seen that this is to misunderstand the nature of teaching in a university.

With no facts to support its position, the ILT saw a possible role in providing "a level of protection against poor quality teaching" (ILTPG 1998: sec. 7). During the four years since it was first proposed, it has been the focus of constant debate about whether it will enhance "professionalism" by focusing on teaching (Allen, 1999, 2001; Natfhe 1999b) or whether it is a pointless bureaucratic imposition (MacLeod 2000; Toner in Spöring et al. 2000; Unwin & Hodgkins 2000). Most of the debate has been about the ILT's function of distributing a sort of "license to practice" (ILTPG 1998: secs. 18–24). The two lecturers' unions in Britain, the Association of University Teachers and the National Association of Teachers in Further and Higher Education (Natfhe), were supportive even if their membership was not (Brown, Bucklow, & Clark 2001). Natfhe, above all, was and continues to be enthusiastic (Allen 1999, 2001; Natfhe 1999b, 2000). Natfhe, of course, had much to gain in that its membership was based largely in the teaching-orientated sector of the new universities and in further education colleges. Its attitude to the research focus of the old universities was always ambiguous. For a short period the AUT even considered setting up a rival institution (Baty 2001a, 2001b). Academic critics also argued that some other, less bureaucratic alternative is preferable (Nicholls 2001). These debates do not address the central issue and do not question the fundamental basis of the ILT. This is partly because the ILT has always argued that it should be a practitioner body, regulated and owned by its members (ILTPG 1998: sec. 25). It has a long way to go before achieving this status. Since it came into existence on 1 April 1999, it has had only 5,500 membership applications, 39% from old universities (Allen 2001), but this is out of a possible membership of over 160,000 (Bett Report 1999: 13–21). There would be some force behind a general initiative to develop teacher-training courses if they were of any value. This is debatable, and even the evidence from evaluating existing courses is limited (Rust 2000). A recent survey of 24 universities in eight countries suggests that training improves student learning (*THES*,

31 August 2001). But this is not the test. Even if all student results were raised by such courses, the only test is the long-term and qualitative one of the development of knowledge. This development will gradually become apparent both inside the university, when students become the next generation of lecturers, and, to a lesser extent, in the wider world, when students become writers, creative workers, scientists, politicians, and businesspeople. The argument of this chapter remains that they will necessarily be damaging to the university in the pursuit of knowledge.

A more serious debate about the ILT focused on whether it will lead to the imposition of a "skills-based" view of university teaching. Given that school teaching and further education are dominated by a view of training that is built around the acquisition of subject and generic competencies or "standards," this seems to be a model that would simply be applied to university teacher training. The challenge for those professionally interested in such training was how to avoid just this model of teaching that reduces it to technical skills and "refuses to acknowledge the passion for knowledge which is at the heart of learning and teaching" (Rowland in Rowland et al. 1998: 140). Rowland's solution is to advocate a therapeutic approach: "My argument is . . . that university teaching in general, and educational enquiry on the part of university teachers in particular, can usefully draw upon therapeutic insights" (2000: 107). However this is done, it must take us away from the business of developing subject knowledge. Rowland argues that many "experts" in teaching and learning have expertise in no subject and are like "experts of love who have no lover" (1998: 135). Brookfield goes further in suggesting that there is a need to "demystify, debunk and deconstruct the notion of the expert" (1995a: 260). However, amateur teacher/therapists are experts, and part of their expertise is just this denial of the role of the "expert"—meaning any subject expert, confident in their knowledge and abilities. Therapists are, however, much more powerful, because they exercise their trade by sleight of hand. It would be naive to see therapists as any different from Rowland's "experts." The consequences are as bad for the love of one's subject. Stretching his analogy with a lover, his proposals are a form of teasing, and, like Marvel's "coy mistress," they declare love but keep us from satisfying our desire. This is even more clear when Rowland suggests a further therapeutic activity that requires our personal commitment to examining the "multiple selves" that constitute their identity: "One of the aims of enquiry into our teaching is to come to know these different identities, to bring ourselves into a closer harmony with our selves and thus into more authentic relationships with our students. This is a personal as well as a professional project" (Rowland 2000: 114).

The prospect of undergoing this sort of therapy might lead anyone to embrace competence-based training. In fact, the two alternatives are not contradictory but complementary. Competencies can be defined and imposed centrally, whether or not by the ILT, but this direction can coexist with a local freedom of delivery through more humanistic or therapeutic methods. This is certainly what happens in teacher training in further education, where the addition of humanistic notions is precisely what gives the notion of "competene" its seductive power (Usher & Edwards 1994: 110).

Ultimately, it is the seemingly radical and liberating therapeutic alternatives that will come to dominate teacher training for the university sector. Precisely because they adopt a radical or liberating rhetoric, they will be attractive to many new university lecturers, as they seem to be "oppositional" or subversive. However, that "opposition" is entirely destructive of the project of the university. In attacking individualism and academic authority (expertise), acknowledging the value of subjective experience, accepting failing and frailties and bringing in uncertainty and doubt, they undermine the central ethical value of the university—namely, the disinterested pursuit of knowledge. Prioritizing any other values diminishes this value precisely because the pursuit of knowledge then becomes "interested." If we set therapeutic or any other conditions to the pursuit of knowledge, we, in part, predetermine the outcome of inquiry.

The sort of inquiry the therapeutic university would engage in would be determined by therapeutic values. These values are becoming mainstream values. The state, in all its institutional forms, can and will appropriate them. The university, because of the independence of mind brought about by expertise in a subject area, once produced academics who were natural critics. New or experienced university lecturers, put through this sort of therapy, rather than becoming practiced in the denial of self and others in the pursuit of knowledge, may love and respect their students and colleagues, but they will be diminished figures compared with Anderson's academic—an uncompromising and public critic of societal trends. This diminished self will be reflected in the graduates of the therapeutic university who will be the employees and citizens of the future. The consequence will be passivity, as a diminished and uncertain self can pose no challenge to anyone.

Passivity also characterizes the modern university at a time when it is faced with tremendous challenges that may alter it out of all recognition (Smith & Webster 1997). If the rise of the therapeutic university is to be resisted, academics must regain the confidence to speak out against the new Sophists who are setting about redressing the balance between teaching and research in the university. This means primarily taking up the arguments that are put forward in favor of any form of teacher training or development for university lecturers. Adopting this confident, if negative, position rests on the certainty that any university worthy of the name pursues knowledge without fear or favor. Its role is not teaching, as we ordinarily understand teaching. Winning this argument now means that the university as we know it may have a future.

## REFERENCES

Allen, L. (1999). ILT: Get involved from the start. *The Lecturer* (December).
Allen, L. (2001). A professional body for professional people. *The Lecturer* (July).
Anderson, J. (1980). *Education and Inquiry* (ed. by D. Z. Phillips). Oxford: Blackwell.

Arnold, M. (1864). The function of criticism at the present time. In *Essays Literary & Critical*. London/Toronto: J. M. Dent, 1906 (1–25).

Barnett, R. (2000). *Realizing the University in an Age of Supercomplexity*. Buckingham, U.K.: Society for Research into Higher Education/Open University Press.

Baty, P. (2001a). Union launches plot to usurp learning institute. *The Higher*, 6 April.

Baty, P. (2001b). ILT rival is set to bow out of battle. *The Higher*, 6 July.

Beard, R. (1970). *Teaching and Learning in Higher Education*. Bath, U.K.: Chivers–Penguin.

Bett Report (1999). *Independent Review of Higher Education Pay and Conditions*. London: HMSO.

Brookfield, S. D. (1995a). *Becoming a Critically Reflective Teacher*. San Francisco, CA: Jossey-Bass Publishers.

Brookfield, S. D. (1995b). Changing the culture of scholarship to the culture of teaching. In T. Schuller (Ed.), *The Changing University?* Buckingham, U.K.: Society for Research into Higher Education/Open University Press (128–138).

Brown, P., & Lauder, H. (2001). *Capitalism and Social Progress. The Future of Society in a Global Economy*. Basingstoke & New York: Palgrave.

Brown, S., Bucklow, C., & Clark, P. (2001). ILT: The real picture. *AUTLOOK* (January).

Clark, B. R. (1994). The research–teaching–study nexus in modern systems of higher education. *Higher Education Policy* 7 (1): 11–17. Cited in C. McInnis, Less control and more vocationalism. In T. Schuller (Ed.), *The Changing University?* (38–51). Buckingham, U.K.: Society for Research into Higher Education/Open University Press.

Collier, G. K. (Ed.) (1974). *Innovation in Higher Education*. Slough: NFER.

Cowan, J. (1998). *On Becoming an Innovative University Teacher: Reflection in Action*. Buckingham, U.K.: Society for Research into Higher Education/Open University Press.

Dearing, R. (1997). *Higher Education in the Learning Society* (The Dearing Report). London: HMSO.

Gibbs, G. (1995). Research into student learning. In B. Smith & S. Brown (Eds.), *Research Teaching and Learning* (18–29). London: SEDA/Kogan Page.

Gibbs, G. (2000). Is research the important piece of the teaching jigsaw? *AUTLOOK*, 216 (October): 8–9.

Giddens, A. (1999). The future of universities: Address to a Meeting of Convocation, University of London, 11 May. *Minutes of the Meeting of Convocation University of London*, 9 May 2000: 31–38.

Hargreaves, A. (1994). *Changing Teachers, Changing Times: Teachers' Work and Culture in a Post-Modern Age*. London: Cassell.

Hayes, D. (2000). Confidence and the Academy. Paper presented to the *BERA Annual Conference*, University of Cardiff, Cardiff, U.K., 7–9 September.

Hobsbawm, E. (1994). *Age of Extremes: The Short Twentieth Century 1914–1991*. London: Michael Joseph.

ILTPG (1998). *The Institute for Learning and Teaching: Implementing the Vision*. Institute for Learning and Teaching Planning Group. *CVCP* (October).

Kelly, T. (1995). The relationship between staff and educational development. In B. Smith & S. Brown (Eds.), *Research Learning and Teaching in Higher Education.* London: SEDA/ Kogan Page (176–186).

MacLeod, D. (2000). Judgement days. *The Guardian,* 9 May.

McInnis, C. (1995). Less control and more vocationalism. In T. Schuller (Ed.), *The Changing University?* Buckingham, U.K.: Society for Research into Higher Education/Open University Press (38–51).

Natfhe (1999a). *Higher Education: Strategy and Perspectives.* London.

Natfhe (1999b). New Institute Opens for Business. *The Lecturer* (October).

Natfhe (2000). ILT: Tackling the issues. *The Lecturer* (April).

Nicholls, G. (2001). *Professional Development in Higher Education.* London: Kogan Page.

Nixon, J. (2001). A new professionalism for higher education? In G. Nicholls, *Professional Development in Higher Education.* London: Kogan Page (73–88).

Nixon, J., Marks, A., Rowland, S., & Walker, M. (2000). *Towards a New Academic Professionalism: A Manifesto of Hope.* Paper presented to BERA Annual Conference University of Cardiff, 7–9 September.

Nolan, J. L. (1998). *The Therapeutic State: Justifying Government at Century's End.* New York: New York University Press.

Rowland, S. (2000). *The Enquiring University Teacher.* Buckingham, U.K.: Society for Research into Higher Education/Open University Press.

Rowland, S., Byron, C. Furedi, F., Padfield, N., & Smyth, T. (1998). Turning academics into teachers? *Teaching in Higher Education,* 3 (No. 2, June): 133–142.

Rust, C. (2000). Do initial training courses have an impact on university teaching? The evidence from two evaluative studies of one course. *Innovations in Education and Training International,* 37 (No. 3, Summer) (& online).

Ryan, A. (1999). *Liberal Anxieties and Liberal Education.* London: Profile Books.

Smith, A., & Webster, F. (Eds.) (1997). *The Postmodern University?* Buckingham, U.K.: Society for Research into Higher Education/Open University Press.

Smithers, A. (2001). Education policy. In A. Seldon (Ed.), *The Blair Effect.* London: Little, Brown and Company (405–426).

Spöring, M., Toner, J., & James, O. (2000). ILT examined. *AUTLOOK,* 216 (October): 4–7.

Squires, G. (Ed.) (1983). *!nnovation through Recession.* Guildford: SRHE Proceedings, 6.

Unwin, T., & Hodgkins, R. (2000). Refuse ILT's invitation to join. *The Higher,* 4 February.

Usher, R., & Edwards, R. (1994). *Postmodernism and Education.* London & New York: Routledge.

Woudhuysen, J. (1997). Before we rush to declare a new era. In G. Mulgan (Ed.), *Life after Politics.* London: Demos & Fontana Press (352–360).

Woudhuysen, J. (1999). *Cult IT.* London: Institute of Contemporary Arts.

Wright, P. (2000). Accounting for lost communities of scholars. *The Higher,* 21 April.

# 11

## Did I Sign Up for This?
## Comments on the New
## Higher Education

*Mary Evans*

At the Labour Party conference of September 1999 a commitment was made to bring 50% of 18–21-year-olds into higher education. This commitment (to "education, education, education," and not, as Professor John Bayley had remarked, to "learning, learning, learning") now provides the goal for English higher education. In this agenda, however, I shall argue that there is both an "assault" on many of the values and practices of higher education and also a process of transformation which will ensure the maintenance of structures of power and privilege (Ryan 1998). Higher education in England, while offering wider access, is at the same time becoming more *actively* involved than at any time in this century in assisting the reproduction of class and gender inequality. Furthermore, for many of us employed as academics in English universities, the "new" higher education is increasingly a place dominated by what Marilyn Strathern has described as an "audit culture" (Strathern 1997): Academics have had to accept a level of audit that intrudes into all aspects of university life and that—as Strathern has argued—is "deliberately built on the conflation of measures with targets" (1997: 312).

The present expansion of higher education in England dates from the Robbins Report of 1963, which noted the limited access to universities of young people in England (then 6% of the age cohort) and advocated a program of the expansion of both student numbers and the number of universities, which was duly implemented. At that time, there was no state commitment to ensuring that universities should contribute directly to profitability, nor was there any explicit attack on university autonomy. The concept of extending higher education was, in 1963, in tune with the ideology of technological innovation and modernization. Nevertheless, by the late 1970s, as Desmond Ryan has pointed out, the demand that universities directly serve industry and commerce was being explicitly made. Thus in 1976 Baroness Gaitskell asked Lord Robbins, in a House of Lords debate on education, why the expansion of higher education had not been followed by greater industrial productivity (Ryan 1998: 15).

This instance serves to emphasize the identification of both Labour and Conservative Parties with the view that universities have a crucial role in maintaining and indeed increasing profitability. While the imposition of externally organized bureaucratic controls is a legacy of the Thatcher years, there is no evidence to suggest that the Labour party significantly dissents from a model of universities as training grounds for the interests of the state, a training ground in which, specifically, vocational skills are taught alongside socialization in what Alasdair MacIntyre has described as the "fetishism of managerialism" (1994: 107). In this process—in which the former Secretary of State for Education, David Blunkett, spoke openly of "training" at universities—the academic functions of universities are increasingly in contest with those that explicitly serve commercial interests.

In any discussion of universities (as in the case of the discussion of other social institutions) there is, perhaps, particularly in England, a drift toward nostalgia and a perception of the past as a golden age. Here it is worth emphasizing the complexity of previous perceptions about the universities: Kingsley Amis, for example, may well have said "more will mean worse," but at the same time he was the author of a definitive satire about universities, *Lucky Jim*. Published in 1954, *Lucky Jim* took to task the incompetence and pedantry of university practice and suggested—in much the same way as Evelyn Waugh had done in both *Decline and Fall* (1928) and *Brideshead Revisited* (1945)—that cultural creativity lay outside rather than inside universities. Neither Amis nor Waugh went so far as to say that the great meta-narratives that have disturbed the bourgeois order (Marxism, psychoanalysis, and feminism) have come from outside universities, but what they recognized, if only by implication, was the role of universities (most specifically in the humanities and social science) as agencies of the systematization of knowledge. Nevertheless, belief in the pursuit of knowledge and scholarship is actively embraced by many on both the political Left and Right. The conservatism of English universities became a theme in the discussion of English culture through the essays of Perry Anderson, yet at the same time other voices on the Left—most notably E. P. Thompson in England and Naom Chomsky in the United States—have passionately resisted the acceptance by universities of managerial and industrial agendas (Thompson 1970).

These resistances, which were part of a more general examination of the culture of England and the United States, remain prescient. Throughout the 1970s and 1980s the number of students in higher education did increase—dramatically—but this generally, if not universally, welcomed wider access was accomplished through the creation of two forms of control on academics: the Quality Assurance Agency (responsible for the assessment process known as

Teaching Quality Assessment—TQA) and the Research Assessment Exercise. Both these exercises were legitimated and explained in terms of "value-for-money" and "public accountability." The definition of "the public" was hardly pluralistic: "the public" was the taxpayer as the provider of resources, rather than "the public" as both a consumer of university education—in the widest sense—as well as a financial resource. Both the exercises—the TQA and RAE—have made English higher education subject to a degree of surveillance unparalleled in the West—but they were implemented alongside a third form of change that has been no less negative—that of the introduction of internal markets in universities. Through this now widespread organization of university funding, individual departments in individual universities acquire a budget, which is then assessed in terms of its performance as a "surplus budget" or a "deficit budget." Throughout English universities, academics in the same university can find themselves working in more—or less—well-resourced environments according to their department's profitability. In many universities what has evolved is a managerial structure in which a central management maintains overall financial *control*, and *responsibility* for income generation is devolved to individuals or individual departments. These individuals, it is worth remembering, are not accountants: the people responsible for budgets, audits, and the whole panoply of "financial planning" are actually academics. People who have made careers out of the study of diverse (and often obscure) subjects find themselves involved in a managerial culture that only recognizes profit and loss, budgets and deficits. In this, the very skills that academics are encouraged to pursue, of differentiation, of intellectual independence and originality and what can generally be described as skills of heterogeneity, are relegated to a second place in favor of skills that are essentially homogenous.

Anecdotes about the working of internal markets in English universities are now legion. Everyone who works in English universities knows of stories about institutions that charge their employees for the use of space and the pressures on staff to recruit students both within and from outside institutions. Yet while this process—as much part of the new order of universities as it has been part of other public institutions such as the National Health Service and the BBC—has effectively created differential working conditions and increased stress, perhaps more significant in their long-term effects are the TQA and the RAE. The greater impact of these exercises is that both contribute to maintaining and increasing differentiation between universities and the process of what has been described as the "dumbing down"—or the "McDonaldization" of universities (see Halliday 1999; Ritzer 1998). The negative impact of the TQA has been to impose on universities a model of learning that prioritizes the acquisition of "key" and "transferable" skills. Effectively, this emphasis marginalizes the importance of the curriculum and dismisses the idea that skills of learning are actually embedded in course content. The "language of learning" of the TQA—in which teachers become "knowledge providers" the process of teaching become "learning outcomes" and modularized courses acquire "aims" and "objectives"—suggests a world in which packaging, rather than the product, is central (Evans 1996). This process of audit is entirely self-referring, in that the institution being audited ideally parrots back the expectations of the central auditing body. To quote Strathern here: "of course, all the new quality control body will have to do is make sure that its clones, the quality control bodies replicated within each institution, respond appropriately to the parent body" (Strathern 1997: 311). Although inspection by the QAA is now to be decreased, there has, as yet, been no suggestion that the blueprint of the organization of knowledge that it has imposed is to be challenged or overturned.

It is not the case that the TQA has been widely welcomed by the "old" (that is pre-1992) universities. Indeed, Oxford and Cambridge have still largely declined the attentions of the TQA assessors, with their demands for "base" rooms and extensive documentation. But welcomed or not, the TQA has become an intrinsic part of teaching practice in contemporary universities, in the same way that the RAE dominates publication and research. This exercise—originally intended as a means of assessing the research output of expensive-to-run departments of science and technology—now dominates the lives of academics in that inability not just to publish, but to publish four separate items in five years, is the criterion both for appointment and for continuation in employment. For many academics, publication—as communication—was always voluntarily chosen, but the distinction is now emerging between an intrinsic wish to communicate ideas and engage in debate and a forced participation in a particular form of academic engagement, that of publication in what are known as "refereed journals." These journals—about which it is estimated that the average article is read by four people—occupy a central role in the minds of the members of RAE panels. A curious process seems to be at work in which the likelihood of the widespread distribution of ideas (through publication in books) becomes suspect, at the same time as the function of higher education is assumed to be to widen access to informed discussion. It may, of course, be argued that academic journals represent a retreat from the market economy, a place untouched by the demands of the cash nexus. Yet what the RAE effectively does—through the financial rewards associated with success in its assessments—is to bring yet another form of academic activity (publishing in scholarly journals) into the marketplace.

It is through the RAE that league tables of universities have now been constructed in which differences in success in this process of assessment are made transparent. The table includes 104 universities, ranging from the universities of Oxford and Cambridge in places 1 and 2 to the University of Luton at bottom place. More or less exactly half-way down the table there is a break between the old and the new universities. As all vice chancellors (and particularly those who belong to the self-appointed "Russell Group") have recognized, position in this league table has an economic value: students, particularly given the new considerable personal cost of higher education, will choose to go to the university, and the department, where validated excellence will later have a financial reward. In this, Oxford and Cambridge retain the privileged position that they have always had in English higher education (and their association with private secondary education), but further elite institutions are also created. For these institutions, the attractions of privatization are already openly discussed: given the degree of externally imposed bureaucratic control, the flight to the private sector seems to offer that illusion of freedom that the constraints of the market have already created.

In *Love's Work* Gillian Rose described herself fulfilling her role as an academic as a perfect bureaucrat, "with anger or enthusiasm" (1995: 72). This sense of fulfilling a function—of meeting the demands of an unnegotiated and largely unchosen agenda of performance—suggests that there are questions to be asked about the present—and future—role of English universities. It is not enough, I would argue, to settle for the complacent, if comfortable, view that through such practices as the TQA and the RAE universities are doing their best to guarantee high standards for mass education or accept the platitudes of John Randall, Chief Executive of the Quality Assurance Agency, that this agency "commands the confidence and support of the sector, its funders and stakeholders" (QAA 1999). Many individuals, whether academic or not, may well endorse the idea of the wider access to universities, but that in itself need not imply that we do not have to examine the part that the "new"—in the sense of newly constituted—universities play in the social world.

That certain patterns persist in higher education has already been suggested. Oxbridge continues to dominate the academic world, even if that domination—at least as far as the students are concerned—is increasingly threatened by public perception of a far from generally acceptable process of social selectivity. Nevertheless, Oxbridge goes on fulfilling its traditional role of the education of the sons (and now the daughters) of the British elite. Other universities, however, are educating (with some idiosyncratic individual variations) a much wider section of the middle class. Most significantly, the proportion of men and women undergraduates is now more or less equal. The qualification to this is that men are still in the majority as university teachers (dramatically so as professors and vice chancellors) and that the sexes are still divided in terms of subject recruitment. Despite real shifts in the curriculum in certain subjects (notably English Literature) the university curriculum remains largely taught and written by men and about a world in which gendered distinctions between the public and the private and objectivity and subjectivity persist.

Discussion about gender and the university curriculum has taken place elsewhere (see Stanley 1997). In this context, the relationship between gender and higher education lies not in the curriculum, but in the changing function of universities. Fifty years ago English universities existed to educate men, in the context of a culture that remained, in its public form, explicitly masculine. That form of masculinity, now only publicly visible in the Conservative party, has been replaced by a feminized version of public and workplace behavior, in which expectations about individual performance include those attributes traditionally associated with women—attributes of consistency, caring, and concern for others. Michelle Fine, Carol Gilligan, and others have written of the ways in which women police their own academic performance in order to avoid confrontation, and this evidence can be placed in the context of the new expectations about student abilities—that they learn, while at university, not (or only incidentally) a particular subject but a set of transferable skills (Gilligan 1982). This form of education very closely fits the demands of the labor market: that women—and a large number of men—will occupy jobs in administrative, middle-management, and service sector jobs in which the *process* of decisionmaking is of paramount importance. Women are allowed, as Mike Savage has pointed out, to demonstrate "skill," but they are almost never allowed to hold power (Savage & Witz 1992). The "new" universities—and the form of their curriculum and their expectations about learning—produce the ideal skilled functionaries of middle management. These people are literate and able to process information, but their function is not to think critically.

In a discussion of women's attitudes to sexuality, Beverley Skeggs has written of women's intense concern with "respectability," a concern in which women are both agents and victims of their constructed identities (Skeggs 1997). She has linked this pattern to Bourdieu's ideas about human capital and shown how the construction of a "respectable" heterosexual identity is, for working-class women, the construction of a commodity (Bourdieu 1986). If this construction is hardly novel (and eighteenth- and nineteenth-century English fiction is replete with examples of women's attempts at maintaining the "value" of appropriate models of sexuality), it is both resonant and relevant to the contemporary world of universities, in which a model of "the graduate" is being actively pursued. Precisely because higher education has become so widely available, there is more concern with the nature of the product, and in this concern there is the tacit recognition that "to graduate" needs clear definition for both the potential consumers of higher education and the requirements of the labor market for that product. Edward Said has asked the question, "What has kept the Western contract together?" and part of the answer must be a certain concept of "woman" in which women serve, care, and socialize (1978: 700). Women's economic independence (however limited) crucially undermines the secure basis of that function in the private world of the household. Societies therefore attempt to extend to the public world the values and virtues once located within the household. "Feminization" is thus about the movement of women into particular forms of employment (and importantly so since women's economic autonomy helps to maintain consumption) but also about the transformation in the expectations of behavior of individual people in employment.

In the current emphasis on the importance of acquisition of "transferable skills" in higher education what we can see at work is the transformation to the public sphere of skills once associated with the private world. These skills are not literally the same, but are similar in terms of the qualities and aptitudes expected of the individual. The skills are essentially those of behavior and organization of the self. As such, they can have a neutralizing effect on the content of the material (the academic curriculum) through which the skills are required. But as such, they also serve to perpetuate and to renew class and gender inequality: mass higher education extends to the majority of universities the responsibility of socialization once assumed to be the preserve of schools and allows a minority of already privileged institutions to continue to engage with intellectual debate and discussion. Those institutions remain, as much in 2001 as in 1950, largely the preserve of the socially privileged. Even if access to that privilege has been extended to more women, what remains, in the guise of the "new" mass higher education, is a system that is as systematically geared to the reproduction of social inequality and the values that inherently produce that inequality as it ever was.

Comments on the "new" higher education need to remain intensely aware that universities are not changing (and have not changed) from institutions wholly committed to the disinterested pursuit of truth and wisdom. As suggested earlier, universities were always flawed, and it would be incorrect to suggest that what universities have become is a radical departure from a perfect model. Universities were always imperfect places, in the sense that they continued, like other institutions, corrupt practices and questionable behavior. The difference between "old" and "new" is not about looking backwards and mourning a lost paradise. It is about looking at the "new" and defining the ways in which what was of value has been attacked or undermined and what is being imposed is negative. Crucial to this examination must be the recognition that the motives driving the bureaucratization of universities have been mixed. The genuine desire to extend access and diminish privilege has been accompanied by envious attacks on liberal ideas about teaching. (Mrs. Thatcher's famous remark about a degree course in History being a "privilege" is an instance of that particular sentiment.) Equally, envy has often fueled the attacks by "new" (post-1992) universities on the "old."

But this recognition also has to return to the nature of practices and expectations imposed by the QAA. Central to that body's model of learning are what are described as "learning outcomes." This idea is the academic equivalent of what the catering industry describes as "portion control"—the measurement of the product to be consumed so that both sides (customer and provider) can assess the success or failure of the process of purchase and consumption. Mass higher education, like mass catering, needs "portion control," in that the only way to demonstrate that customers—that, is students—have been educated is by demonstrating that they have received the correct "portion." Within the QAA there is apparently a "Learning Outcomes Movement," a body of truly nightmare possibilities. The nightmare, of course, lies in the standardization that "learning outcomes" explicitly condone. It is a prescriptive and authoritarian process that challenges the essence of higher education, that of debate and discussion. In being asked to state what our students should know, we, as academics, are being asked to draw limits and boundaries on knowledge in quantifiable sound-bites and appropriately sized portions. The thesis of "McDonaldization" suggests standardization and conformity. In the context of higher education, I would argue that both these processes are being allowed to occur, and that what is being offered as a real meal is nothing more than fast food.

## REFERENCES

Amis, K. (1954). *Lucky Jim.* Harmondsworth, U.K.: Penguin.

Bourdieu, P. (1986). *Distinction: A Social Critique of the Judgement of Taste.* London: Routledge.

Evans, M. (1996). The language of learning. *Women's Philosophy Review,* 16 (December): 10–11.

Gilligan, C. (1982). *In a Different Voice.* Cambridge, MA: Harvard University Press.

Halliday, F. (1999). The international role of universities. *International Affairs,* 75 (No. 1, January): 99–120.

MacIntyre, A. (1994). *After Virtue.* London: Duckworth.

QAA (1999). Bulletin. *Quality Assurance Agency for Higher Education,* 5 May.

Ritzer, G. (1998). *The McDonaldization Thesis: Explorations and Extensions.* London & Thousand Oaks, CA: Sage.

Rose, G. (1995). *Love's Work.* London: Chatto & Windus.

Ryan, D. (1998). The assault on higher education. *New Left Review,* 227 (January/February): 3–32.

Said, E. (1978). The problem of textuality: Two exemplary positions. *Critical Inquiry,* 4 (4, Summer): 673–714.

Savage, M., & Witz, A. (1992). *Gender and Bureaucracy.* Sociological Review Monograph. Oxford: Blackwell.

Skeggs, B. (1997). *Formations of Class and Gender.* London & Thousand Oaks, CA: Sage.

Stanley, L. (Ed.) (1997). *Knowing Feminisms.* London & Thousand Oaks, CA: Sage.

Strathern, M. (1997). Improving ratings: Audit in the British university system. *European Review,* 5 (3): 305–321.

Thompson, E. P. (Ed.) (1970). *Warwick University Ltd.* Harmondsworth, U.K.: Penguin.

Waugh, E. (1928). *Decline and Fall.* London: Chapman & Hall.

Waugh, E. (1945). *Brideshead Revisited.* London: Chapman & Hall.

# 12

## Feminist Education: Rebellion within McUniversity

*Jane A. Rinehart*

It is not hard to locate significant points of disagreement between the principles of McDonaldization applied to universities and the ideals of feminist education.[1] Ritzer's characterization of the continuing emergence of McUniversity (1998) highlights the ascendance of the student consumer and the business model. According to Ritzer, student consumers seek ease of access, low costs, and "quality" products (Ritzer 1998: 152). All of these goals have the potential of conflict with the aims of feminist educators. One way to increase access is to promote distance education, thereby limiting the possibility for building a classroom community through conversation and focusing on one-sided input from the instructor that contradicts the feminist emphasis upon mutual learning through dialogue. Lowering costs may translate into increased reliance upon adjunct instructors (Ritzer 1998: 158) and higher student–teacher ratios; both of these work against feminist aspirations for strong bonds among faculty and between faculty and students and threaten the academic freedom of teachers. While Ritzer does not give "quality products" a specific meaning in relation to higher education, his general treatment of McDonaldization (Ritzer 2000) suggests that quality is redefined in terms of efficiency, predictability, calculability, and control. If these are what student consumers seek—course credits that are delivered in the same fashion as fast-food burgers—then descriptions of feminist pedagogy as creative, spontaneous, attuned to local classroom dynamics and needs, and facilitative rather than managerial in style point toward the likelihood of conflict.

As a business, the university must attract/please customers (increase revenue) and minimize expenses. The former fosters grade inflation and reduced requirements, and the latter leads to increased reliance on temporary faculty and technology. In contrast, feminist educators strive to challenge students rather than to please them, making them dependent upon the protections of tenure and academic freedom. They are also committed to teaching methods that depend upon face-to-face classroom relationships, meaning that they are less amenable to construction as online or video courses. The differences indicate that feminist educators have entered the university at a particularly inopportune moment. If Ritzer is correct that the forces associated with McDonaldization will increasingly shape higher education, this forecasts considerable trouble for instructors committed to feminist scholarship and pedagogy. But it is also possible that these teachers may create trouble for McUniversity.

Trouble is also widely documented in writings by college teachers who do not explicitly identify with feminist pedagogy (Delucchi & Smith 1997a; Eisenberg 1997), so it would be incorrect to identify feminist educators as the only faculty members struggling with the terms of McUniversity. These general problems center on the tensions between the university's commitment to cultivating the student consumer's satisfaction and the view of many teachers that treating education as a product and teachers as sales clerks corrupts (or even destroys) the mission of a university. However, it is not only that students increasingly regard themselves as consumers of what the university is selling that creates difficulties, but also the gap between what the student customers want and what the faculty believes they ought to want. This is seen most clearly in writings by teachers who complain that students demand easier courses (less reading, rigor, and depth), seem uninterested in academic goals other than "good grades," and punish teachers who disappoint them (Trout 1997). While feminist educators may share this view that student consumers are often hostile to such academic values, there are also additional points of conflict with student consumers generated by feminist commitments to developing a critical consciousness toward society and culture, engaging in collaborative classroom learning, and linking knowledge to political praxis.[2]

## DEVELOPING CRITICAL CONSCIOUSNESS AND POSITIONALITY

Critical consciousness is based on achieving distance from received knowledge and developing the capacity to question dominant ideas, images, and values—the cultural stories that preserve the status quo. These are the model stories present in a culture: its representations of certain kinds of lives as exemplary, its version of how the society has changed, and its cautionary tales about what to avoid. Cultural stories express the normative order, the understandings about how things work and how they are supposed to work (Richardson 1995: 211–212). Ritzer's theory is such a cultural story because he presents McDonaldization as normative, necessary, and inevitable, albeit also undesirable in some respects. University education assimilated to the rules of McDonaldization brings universities into a dominating cultural narrative in which success is tied to conformity to the consumer society. Collective stories contest cultural stories by voicing the experiences and perspectives of "those who are silenced or marginalized in the cultural narrative" (Richardson 1995: 212). In the collective story, the focus is on the social category to which an individual belongs and on the capacity to transform the conditions of its exclusion. Collective stories are critical of the status quo.

Feminism is such a collective story, and feminist teachers have written numerous descriptions of their work as a type of critical or liberatory pedagogy (Hoffman & Stake 1998), although not without challenging some of the assumptions, aspirations, and methods associated with this position and refashioning it for feminist goals (hooks 1994; Luke & Gore 1992). "Positional pedagogies" represents one such reformulation, based on the insight that subject positions and understandings are more multiple and contradictory than critical pedagogy's division between the oppressed and the oppressor, liberating truth and distortion (Ellsworth 1992). This insight entails a commitment to a continuing practice of reflexivity. In teaching that foregrounds positionality, students and teachers work to understand how their ideas and those expressed in the course texts are influenced by their locations—historical, social, cultural, and political—and are therefore partial, relational, and oppositional (Luke & Gore 1992; Maher & Tetrault 1994). In Haraway's (1988) term, all of us are "situated knowers," but awareness of such grounding is often blocked by universalizing ideologies, insistence upon objective truth, and constant pressure to regard the world we are in as given and unquestionable rather than socially constructed.

Ritzer's theory of McDonaldization both describes a dominating aspect of our historical situation and denies our capacity to oppose it effectively, thereby limiting opportunities for genuine critique.[3] Positional pedagogies, on the other hand, strive to expand awareness and resistance while also recognizing that academic courses, although they can become political communities, are not the same as social movements. Positional pedagogies disturb the cultural story's dominance by constructing messier and unstable knowledges that emerge within continuing conversations. Positional pedagogies create opportunities for collective stories to develop that connect members who inhabit different social situations, acknowledging both differences and commonalities that can bridge these. Feminist teachers who practice these classroom strategies acknowledge that discovering ways to link these classroom stories to political movements for social change is a pressing challenge to feminist educators. Feminist pedagogues do not claim the ability to undo McDonaldization, but their work is an example of resistance to its effects within universities.

The negative images associated with feminism in popular consciousness indicate its ability to elicit defenses from those who are comfortable within the cultural story—a category that includes many, perhaps most, of the students enrolled in universities. Feminist education, then, is one of the ways that many students encounter a disruption in their consumer role.[4] In challenging cultural narratives that leave women out or avoid consideration of the effects of gender/class/race/sexuality, feminist teachers attempt to shift students away from acceptance of these exclusions to critical reflection on their consequences. This kind of shift is unsettling because it entails movement off the "paths of least resistance" (Johnson 1997) that allow for ease of passage into accepted social roles and the comforts these provide. The acceptance of consumerism as the paradigmatic mode of public participation for most Americans means that social critique, the presentation of collective stories that contest the hegemony of the existing social arrangements, is risky. Blistering attacks on women's studies (Denfeld 1995; D'souza 1991; Lehrman 1993; Patai & Koertge 1994; Sommers 1994), the prime university location for feminist scholarship and teaching, provide ammunition for student customers who want to avoid the anger and confusion that accompany changing one's mind; such attacks are frequently reinforced in mass media portrayals of all feminists as man-hating extremists (Beck 1998; McDermott 1995; Rhode 1995). In McDonaldized America and McUniversity, anger, confusion, and extremism are problems to be managed and preferably eliminated.

Most students have been trained to be cool consumers of various products, and this consumption requires a lot of looking and making individual choices based on personal preferences. Edmundson has written a description of his students as "nearly across the board, very, very self-contained. On good days they display a light, appealing glow; on bad days, shuffling disgruntlement. But there's little fire, little passion to be found" (1997: 41). This can be attributed to pervasive cultural messages "from consumer culture in general and from the tube in particular" (1997: 41). These messages communicate that the best way to be in our society is to be self-interested, laid-back, tuned into irony, and turned off by big causes. The laid-back quality and the belief that choices are manifestations of personal opinions that cannot be challenged means that many students find intense discussions of their views worthless. They just do not see the point.[5] When these cool customers are buying a university education, the same habits operate and are often reinforced by universities sensitive to marketing and retention. Teaching that is critical of coolness, consumerism, and individualism can prompt a negative reaction. Students may rate more highly teachers who demonstrate the "customer-service traits" they expect, such as friendliness, concern, sensitivity, understanding, and support (Baker & Copp 1997). Customers do not expect store clerks to be subversive of their ideas, to expose them to challenges and unsettle them.

If professors are categorized as sales clerks, this creates problems for teachers who refuse to be helpful assistants to student shoppers, who, instead, raise discomfiting questions about equating social participation with cruising the mall. There are important differences between learning and enjoying, between learning and feeling safe, and between learning and liking the teacher: "I began to see that courses that work to shift paradigms, to change consciousness, cannot necessarily be experienced immediately as fun or positive or safe and this was not a worthwhile criteria [sic] to use in evaluation" (hooks 1988: 53). McUniversity does not offer either resources or a rationale for contesting consumer choices;

instead, it is a place designed to offer students "positive" experiences. While Ritzer offers grade inflation, increased emphasis upon student retention, and fewer curriculum requirements as examples of how universities seek to become "positive" environments (1998: 156), it is also plausible that this list of measures to eliminate negativity might include avoiding teaching perspectives that evoke student complaints. This is the context in which feminist educators meet their students.

Ritzer states that he expects universities to maintain many of their traditional components and not become exactly like fast-food restaurants and malls (1998: 161). However, it is not clear how he believes universities can reconcile their adherence to academic values with their adoption of the principles of McDonaldization—in other words, at what point does a McUniversity cease to be a university—a place where the dominant cultural story can be analyzed and contested and students are invited to become critical and reflexive thinkers (Delucchi & Smith 1997b: 337)? Feminist education is necessarily committed to this understanding of the university because feminist scholarship and action are subversive of established knowledge and structures. Such subversion does not mean the imposition of a different set of authoritative "truths," but the practices of continuous critique and exploration (Lather 1991). Although feminists within the academy have often been accused of undermining its commitment to rigorous inquiry, the ideals of feminist education—if not always the practices—express a firm belief in careful scholarship and open-minded dialogue in the midst of differences (Nussbaum 1997: 202–215).[6]

## COLLABORATIVE LEARNING

Labels for different views (such as conservative/traditionalist versus radical/feminist), whether given to us or assumed by us, mask the complicated mixture of ideas and feelings that each of us brings to our conversations. The labels are more likely to stand, even to become more fixed and rigid, when the teacher presents an argument for one position to student listeners. This structure invites simplification and polarization. Distributing responsibility for talking and working to identify points of agreement and disagreement does a much better job of waking everyone up from the hypnotic spell of the status quo. That spell depends upon most of us being either out of the game as spectators on the sidelines, or in the game as advocates for one side of a dichotomy in a debate that only one side can win. The focus on winning demands domination, and domination depends on forgetfulness of our hesitations, blind spots, inconsistencies, and questions. Winning also means that we have to pretend not to be connected with our opponents, reinforcing denial of our interdependence.

Collaboration is a different design. Collaborative learning is not about a feminist teacher lecturing to students who are for, against, or undecided and moving some of those in the latter two categories into the former. It is not about changing conservatives into liberals or progressives. It is a continuing practice of subversion through questioning and experimenting with various strategies for understanding in the context of a learning community: "feminist education holds out the potential to reinforce understandings that all knowledge, including that which is inspired by emancipatory fervor, must be questioned" (Bauer & Rhoades 1996: 107). In this kind of classroom, truth is not the possession of the teacher, but a shared accomplishment that acknowledges its partiality and incompleteness. Subversive teaching is "not the transmission of ready-made knowledge, but the creation of a new condition of knowledge" (Felman 1982: 31).

Collaborative learning constitutes students as citizens, rather than as consumers. These are highly contrasting social positions and roles. Consumers expect to express preferences and whims, to be courted, even coddled. Consumers make demands, so that parking and purchasing on credit become necessities instead of amenities. There are also responsibilities attached to consuming, such as paying (eventually) for one's purchases and performing various kinds of self-service in McDonaldized settings, but these are not highlighted in the social construction of the consumer's role. Advertising promotes consumption as easy and fun, not as a set of duties, and retailers have adopted various strategies to maximize these aspects, such as "Happy Meals" with toys and playgrounds as part of fast-food outlets and shopping malls. Ritzer points out that the same emphases on comfort and pleasure penetrate university campuses: "Many student unions are already being transformed into minimalls with the inclusion of ATMs, video games, and fast-food outlets. The future of the university may be found, at least in part, in its current student unions" (Ritzer 1998: 155). When students move from such settings into collaborative learning classrooms, consumer expectations and demands are contested by rules about a different form of social participation: citizenship.

In the United States, citizenship is anemic because individualism is so highly prized, and individual well-being is defined in terms of rights rather than obligations: "If the entire social world is made up of individuals, each endowed with the right to be free of others' demands, it becomes hard to forge bonds of attachment to, or cooperation with, other people, since such bonds would imply obligations that necessarily impinge on one's freedom" (Bellah et al. 1985: 23). Furthermore, the agendas of individuals are increasingly identified with the pursuit of occupational success and consumer satisfactions, framed by a refusal to question the economic and political systems in which "individual" wins and losses take place. That refusal to question is connected with the absence of opportunities to question: "We live in self-imposed exile from communal conversation and action" (Borgmann 1992: 3). A university might be expected to be an exception, but often it is not. Students are constructed as private individual consumers, rather than as participants in shaping a common life based in sustained conversations about ideas and their consequences.

Ritzer emphasizes McUniversity's individualizing qualities, especially in relation to technologies of instruction that offer students maximum efficiency and control by sacrificing symbolic exchange. The interactions between teachers and students that have traditionally defined learning will increasingly be replaced, Ritzer predicts, by interactions between individual students and televised or computerized images (Ritzer 1998: 160). These kinds of learning situations are presented as desirable because of the "freedom" they offer to students, such as the freedom from required classroom attendance that ties them to specific times and places. Throughout his discussion of McUniversity, Ritzer assumes that students will demand such options and be tough judges of their quality in terms of "production values" familiar to them from CNN and MTV (Ritzer 1998: 160). Thus, Ritzer claims that most universities (with the exception of the highly prestigious) are, and will continue to be, pressured into adopting formats for learning that meet their customers' expectations; these expectations are formed by broader cultural options for being informed and entertained by technologically mediated communication.

Feminist educators are in a difficult spot. The view from the trenches of women's studies, for example, highlights struggles with limited resources (of budget, faculty, autonomy) and unsupportive administrators (Clark et al. 1996; Martin 2000; Mayberry and Rose 1999). For the most part, women's studies, as well as other disciplines (humanities, social sciences, education) where feminist teachers are likely to be located, are not in a position to refuse participation in the university's efforts to attract and retain students—for example, with technologically enhanced instruction. At the same time, feminist teachers are also likely to be invested in teaching that highlights face-to-face social interactions between teachers and students and among students. They are likely to favor collaborative learning strategies. These methods actively promote the development of the classroom as a learning community that practices shared inquiry and constructs knowledge together—in contrast to a "banking model" (Freire 1970: 58), in which knowledge is passed from the expert teacher to the ignorant student.

The difficulties in combining such a collaborative model with technologically framed instruction are revealed in Rose's discussion of her initial experience offering a feminist theory course within the compressed video/distance learning format (1998). Nevertheless, Rose believes that "distance education is one way in which those offering women's studies programs can collaborate to pool resources and serve our students better" (1998: 127). Avoiding an all-or-nothing stance, she recommends some strategies for reducing the distance of students at the remote site and advocates teacher resistance to some features of distance education (1998: 128–129). Hopkins offers a more emphatic endorsement, based on five years of teaching a live cablecast women's studies course (Hopkins 1999). While she concedes that such teaching departs from feminist principles in its reliance on the lecture format and the absence of direct interactions with students in the classroom, Hopkins asserts that both of these challenges can be managed. Instead of being coopted by McUniversity's reliance upon technologically assisted forms of education, both Rose and Hopkins model an alternative response in which the technological means does not eliminate feminist ends. They show that there is considerable space within a McDonaldized setting for feminist ingenuity. This is both similar to and different from Ritzer's discussion of skunk works—non-rationalized niches within McDonaldized systems in which people are encouraged to innovate and create (2000: 225). McUniversities might regard women's studies programs as sources of positive nonconformity that enliven the organization. Feminist educators take a different view, considering their work not as a niche that serves the organization by being different, but as a space that nurtures resistance to its expectations and demands.

Their hopefulness may be well founded, if Bauer and Rhoades are correct in describing students as "longing for some sort of cooperative or collaborative structure within which to work, a framework which inevitably contradicts their insistence on individualist values." At the same time, however, this longing may be the basis for student criticism and resistance as "students are disappointed that feminism has not yet changed the world" (1996: 103). The meanings of changing the world are various, but the commitment of feminist teachers to connecting theory and praxis, the classroom and the world beyond it, is integral to their conception of teaching and learning as political acts.

## POLITICS AS KNOWING AND ACTING

Feminist teaching is grounded in a mission of social justice, although the definitions of this are multiple (Ropers-Huilman 1998: 150–153). Within this multiplicity of perspectives on what constitutes social justice and how to foster it in classrooms and beyond, feminist teachers share a dedication to eliminating gender inequalities that involves engaging students in critical thinking about existing social arrangements and envisioning other possibilities. Women's studies owes its existence to the women's movement, so it is rooted in efforts to bring about social and political change in societies. Referring to feminist "working papers" produced during the late 1960s and early 1970s, the editors of an anthology of memoirs by feminist activists state: "In fact, women's studies began here, with the scrutiny of gender institutions and practices" (DuPlessis & Snitow 1998: 13). The forms of this scrutiny varied, and not all feminists, then or now, have extended their critique to the problems posed by Ritzer. Still, feminists share a desire to question what exists and pose alternatives. This contrasts with McUniversity's acceptance of prevailing business practices as necessary in order to compete successfully for student (or parent) dollars. Often this acceptance entails the view that the practices and principles of McDonaldization are not political choices but economic realities; as such, they are regarded as objective facts. The sheen of objectivity, then, leads to a presumption in favor of neutrality in which universities can claim to be adjusting to the way things are rather than deciding to take a political (evaluative) position. Feminist teachers are more likely to present all positions as expressing politics—values and interests—and to question the possibility and desirability of neutrality.

Ritzer's stance on this in relation to McUniversity is ambiguous. He identifies his basic premises this way: "the university is a means of educational consumption . . . and students are adopting a consumerist orientation to it" (1998: 153). He writes, "Educators are being compelled to recognize this new reality," preceding a quote about how the expectations of student customers will change how the faculty teach (1998: 152). These, and similar assertions, suggest that he has adopted a neutral descriptive posture regarding the shift to McUniversity. However, he also presents a chapter on ways of dealing with the new means of consumption, including educational consumption, that assumes their negative qualities. Ritzer's general analysis of McDonaldization relies upon a Weberian perspective that "calls attention to the dehumanizing and irrational sides of McDonaldization and forces us to articulate a standpoint of critique and to think of forms of resistance and alternatives" (Kellner 2000). Still, Ritzer indicates that a modern response to McDonaldization is accompanied by the "sense that many of these problems are irresolvable and that they must persist;" and "ultimately this perspective tends to lead to a feeling of resignation" (1998: 163–164). He believes that postmodern perspectives, drawn especially from Baudrillard, offer alternatives to resignation by asserting the fragility of McDonaldized systems.

Ritzer bases his view of McUniversity's fragility on the one-sided exchange that it fosters between students and those who work to please them. Student silence and inertia will reveal the impossibility of McUniversity's terms. If it seeks to "please" the student consumer, the McUniversity will be impossible to sustain because all responsibilities for teaching and learning will be placed on the faculty and staff; it will self-destruct (Ritzer 1998: 169–170). Ritzer uses a surprising metaphor to convey the power of students' nullification of meaning, their fatal silence: "In their mindless, limitless increase the student masses will destroy the educational system in the same way that cancer cells destroy the physical body. . . . McUniversity will not be destroyed with a bang, but in a series of whimpers" (1998: 171). While this imagery is shocking, its practical import is not clear in the sense of offering a detailed prognosis of specific actions and their impact. Ritzer seems to be arguing that McUniversity's characteristics—its lean organization, emphasis upon fun and excitement, lowered standards, reliance on technological means of instruction, proliferation of satellites, and efficient means of handling student consumption—will transform the customer into a relentless, deadly enemy. As students adapt more fully to their role as consumers of education, their facility in playing this part will overwhelm the capacity of their "host"—McUniversity—to satisfy them.

Even though Ritzer presents a variety of micro-forms of resistance that might be deployed in fast-food restaurants, he puts McUniversity students into the same category as credit card users. Neither resists; rather, both accept every new enticement to consume. Their lack of resistance lures "the system into riskier and more desperate forays . . . the system grows so reckless and overextended that the slightest disruption would cause it to collapse" (Ritzer 1998: 172). Meanwhile, intellectuals (faculty) are advised to expose the contradictions in the new means of consumption and develop maps that will help us to find alternatives.

None of this is helpful, even in the limited way of Ritzer's final chapter in *The McDonaldization of Society* (2000), where he presents some individual and collective forms of resistance. Ritzer concedes that "the postmodern perspective does not lead us to a clear and coherent set of procedures," providing, instead, "theoretically informed hints" (2000: 173) and a sense that change in the new means of consumption will be created not by self-conscious agents but by consumers who bring about its collapse by their conformity. He ends the chapter on dealing with the new means of consumption with the suggestion that "a modernist" might want to search for ideas that would mobilize "agents against the excesses of the new means of consumption" (Ritzer 1998: 173). It is curious that he identifies such a desire only with modernists, because he acknowledges that the postmodernists Derrida and Foucault suggest strategies for everyday forms of innovation and resistance (Ritzer 1998: 170–171).

The argument of this chapter is that such agents are already mobilized, many under the sign of postmodernist ideas about knowledge and power. Feminist educators are one example of this mobilized resistance to McDonaldization. Their curriculum materials and teaching methods are both critical and transformative. Feminist education is a political practice of active resistance that aims to foster a sense of agency—the capacity to act—and some research suggests that it succeeds (Lovejoy 1998; Musil 1992). One of the reasons that students may fear feminist education is reluctance to gain critical insights that will lead to feelings of hopelessness (Bauer & Rhoades 1996: 105) and isolation (hooks 1994: 117). These fears reveal the power of "the world as it is" to seem "the world as it must be"—a translation that Ritzer's work on McDonaldization may strengthen. Although his new edition of *The McDonaldization of Society* includes a more extensive discussion of how people can work together to create non- or less-McDonaldized alternatives (Ritzer 2000: 202–222) and presents reasons why such struggles are worthwhile (2000: 232), Ritzer still asserts that "no matter how intense the opposition, the future will bring with it more rather than less McDonaldization" (2000: 232). Feminist education, and the larger effort of feminist activism in which it participates, become, in Ritzer's analysis, small havens of escape (niches) and ennobling but futile struggles.

These terms of existence are unacceptable. Why put forth the strenuous effort entailed by critical consciousness and collaborative learning if not for the belief in the potential of such work to undermine pessimism and to nurture hopes? Practicing freedom from McDonaldization within McUniversity is not the same as creating a non-McDonaldized society, but it is one of the steps toward building the social movements that might accomplish this. Kellner suggests that "Ritzer's critical analysis . . . of McDonaldization . . . forces us to articulate a standpoint of critique and to think of forms of resistance and alternatives . . . to consider precisely what form of society, values, and practices we desire" (2000: 13). A different reading suggests that Ritzer's work might have the opposite effect, instilling resignation to an irreversible social trend (Rinehart 1998). Feminist education is one means for challenging such passivity: "The classroom, with all its limitations, remains a location of possibility" (hooks 1994: 207). These words of a women's studies student are one example of the possibilities: "Women's studies has opened up whole new areas to question myself about. Questions like: 'Well, how is this useful for activism? How is this going to change the world?. . . . Am I working hard enough to change the world?'" (Lovejoy 1998: 129).

## NOTES

1. For the purposes of this chapter, "feminist education" refers principally to the pedagogies and content of women's studies courses, but it may also include courses not listed under this program but taught by professors who identify their aims as feminist. This follows the practice of Hoffman and Stake, who investigated feminist pedagogy practiced within both women's studies courses and courses taught by the same teachers under other disciplinary headings (1998).

2. My formulation of the distinctive characteristics of feminist education differs only slightly from the definition of feminist pedagogy used by Hoffman and Stake: participatory learning, validation of personal experience, encouragement of social understanding and activism, and development of critical thinking and openmindedness (1998).

3. For examples of such criticisms of Ritzer's theory of McDonaldization, see Alfino, Caputo, and Wynyard (1998).

4. Women's studies is sometimes dismissed by parents of students as a "nonmarketable" subject (Martin 2000: 112), suggesting that these courses are also regarded as detrimental to preparation for work in the McDonaldized economy.

5. This is one professor's explanation for students' failure to see the point: "They are, after all, the products of a culture committed to entertaining them 24 hours a day, and of a high school system committed to providing a 'comfortable,' stress-free academic environment, one largely stripped of academic pressures and demands (little or no homework, no flunks) and marked by therapeutic praise and inflated grades" (Trout 1997: 30). The relationship between this assessment and McDonaldization is obvious.

6. One feminist educator, while conceding that "criticisms of some women's studies work are not without basis," also points out that many of those who criticize women's studies as intolerant rely on anecdotes and small samples and fail to acknowledge that "problems of shoddy scholarship and intolerant classrooms cut across all disciplines" (Rhode 1997: 226).

## REFERENCES

Alfino, M., Caputo, J. S., & Wynyard, R. (Eds.) (1998). *McDonaldization Revisited: Critical Essays in Consumer Culture*. Westport, CT, & London: Praeger.

Baker, P., & Copp, M. (1997). Gender performance matters most: The interaction of gendered expectations, feminist course content, and pregnancy in students' course evaluations. *Teaching Sociology,* 25: 29–43.

Bauer, D., & Rhoades, K. (1996). The meanings and metaphors of student resistance. In V. V. Clark, S. N. Garner, M. Higonnet & K. H. Katrak (Eds.), *Antifeminism in the Academy*. New York: Routledge (95–113).

Beck, D. B. (1998). The "F" word: How the media frame feminism. *NWSA Journal,* 10 (1, Spring): 139–153.

Bellah, R. N., Madsen, R., Sullivan, W. M., Swidler, A., & Tipton, S. M. (1985).

*Habits of the Heart: Individualism and Commitment in American Life.*
Berkeley, CA: University of California Press.

Borgmann, A. (1992). *Crossing the Postmodern Divide.* Chicago, IL: University of Chicago Press.

Clark, V. V., Garner, S. N., Higonnet, M., & Katrak, K. H. (Eds.) (1996). *Antifeminism in the Academy.* New York: Routledge.

Delucchi, M., & Smith, W. L. (1997a). A postmodern explanation of student consumerism in higher education. *Teaching Sociology,* 25: 322–327.

Delucchi, M., & Smith, W. L. (1997b). Satisfied customers versus pedagogic responsibility: Further thoughts on student consumerism. *Teaching Sociology,* 25: 336–337.

Denfeld, R. (1995). *The New Victorians: A Young Woman's Challenge to the Old Feminist Order.* New York: Warner Books.

D'souza, D. (1991). *Illiberal Education: The Politics of Race and Sex on Campus.* New York: Free Press.

DuPlessis, R. B., & Snitow, A. (1998). *The Feminist Memoir Project: Voices from Women's Liberation.* New York: Three Rivers Press.

Edmundson, M. (1997). On the uses of a liberal education: As lite entertainment for bored college students. *Harper's Magazine* (September): 39–49.

Eisenberg, A. F. (1997). Education and the marketplace: Conflicting arenas? *Teaching Sociology,* 25: 328–332.

Ellsworth, E. (1992). Why doesn't this feel empowering? Working through the repressive myths of critical pedagogy. In C. Luke & J. Gore (Eds.), *Feminisms and Critical Pedagogy.* New York: Routledge (90–119).

Felman, S. (1982). Psychoanalysis and education: Teaching terminable and interminable. *Yale French Studies,* 63: 21–44.

Freire, P. (1970). *Pedagogy of the Oppressed.* New York: Seabury Press.

Haraway, D. (1988). Situated knowledges: The science question in feminism and the privilege of partial perspective. *Feminist Studies,* 14: 575–599.

Hoffman, F. L., & Stake, J. E. (1998). Feminist pedagogy in theory and practice: An empirical investigation. *NWSA Journal,* 10: 79–97.

hooks, b. (1988). *Talking Back: Thinking Feminist, Thinking Black.* Toronto: Between the Lines.

hooks, b. (1994). *Teaching to Transgress: Education as the Practice of Freedom.* New York: Routledge.

Hopkins, A. (1999). Women's studies on television: It's time for distance learning. In M. Mayberry & E. C. Rose (Eds.), *Meeting the Challenge: Innovative Feminist Pedagogies in Action.* New York: Routledge (123–140).

Johnson, A. G. (1997). *The Gender Knot: Unraveling Our Patriarchal Legacy.* Philadelphia, PA: Temple University Press.

Kellner, D. (2000). Theorizing/resisting McDonaldization: A multiperspectivist approach. *Illuminations* (retrieved 30 August 2000) <http://uta.edu/huma/illuminations>, pp. 1–16.

Lather, P. (1991). *Getting Smart: Feminist Research and Pedagogy with/in the Postmodern.* New York: Routledge.

Lehrman, K. (1993). Off course. *Mother Jones* (September/October): 45–68.

Lovejoy, M. (1998). "You can't go home again": The impact of women's studies on intellectual and personal development. *NWSA Journal,* 10: 119–138.

Luke, C., & Gore, J. (1992*). Feminisms and Critical Pedagogy*. New York: Routledge.

Maher, F. A., & Tetrault, M. K. T. (1994). *The Feminist Classroom*. New York: Basic Books.

Martin, J. R. (2000). *Coming of Age in Academe: Rekindling Women's Hopes and Reforming the Academy*. New York: Routledge.

Mayberry, M., & Rose, E. C. (Eds.) (1999). *Meeting the Challenge: Innovative Feminist Pedagogies in Action*. New York: Routledge.

McDermott, P. (1995). On cultural authority: Women's studies, feminist politics, and the popular press. *Signs: Journal of Women in Culture and Society,* 20: 668–684.

Musil, C. M. (Ed.) (1992). *The Courage to Question: Women's Studies and Student Learning*. Washington, DC: Association of American Colleges.

Nussbaum, M. C. (1997). *Cultivating Humanity: A Classical Defense of Reform in Liberal Education*. Cambridge, MA: Harvard University Press.

Patai, D., & Koertge, N. (1994). *Professing Feminism: Cautionary Tales from the Strange World of Women's Studies*. New York: Basic Books.

Rhode, D. L. (1995). Media images, feminist issues. *Signs: Journal of Women in Culture and Society,* 20: 685–710.

Rhode, D. L. (1997). *Speaking of Sex: The Denial of Gender Inequality*. Cambridge, MA: Harvard University Press.

Richardson, L. (1995). Narrative and sociology. In J. V. Maanen (Ed.), *Representation in Ethnography*. London & Thousand Oaks, CA: Sage (198–221).

Rinehart, J. A. (1998). It may be a polar night of icy darkness, but feminists are building a fire. In M. Alfino, J. S. Caputo, & R. Wynyard (Eds.), *McDonaldization Revisited: Critical Essays on Consumer Culture*. Westport, CT, & London: Praeger (19–38).

Ritzer, G. (1998). *The McDonaldization Thesis: Explorations and Extensions*. London & Thousand Oaks, CA: Sage.

Ritzer, G. (2000). *The McDonaldization of Society: New Century Edition*. Thousand Oaks, CA: Pine Forge Press.

Ropers-Huilman, B. (1998). *Feminist Teaching in Theory and Practice: Situating Power and Knowledge in Poststructural Classrooms*. New York: Teachers College Press.

Rose, E. C. (1998). This class meets in cyberspace: Women's studies via distance education. In G. E. Cohee, E. Daumer, T. D. Kemp, P. M. Krebs, S. A. Lafky, & S. Runzo (Eds.), *The Feminist Teacher Anthology: Pedagogies and Classroom Strategies,* New York: Teachers College Press (114–131).

Sommers, C. H. (1994). *Who Stole Feminism? How Women Have Betrayed Women*. New York: Simon and Schuster.

Trout, P. (1997). Conflict in the college classroom. *The Cresset: A Review of Literature, Arts, and Public Affairs* 60: 28–36.

# 13

# Novelty and Crisis
# in the World of McKnowledge

*Joanne Finkelstein*

The novelist, Bret Easton Ellis, later to be famous for *American Psycho* (1991), began an earlier novel, *The Rules of Attraction* (1987), with the opening sentence: "and it's a story that might bore you. . . ." The sentence began without capitalization; it was as if the reader had simply been dropped into the narrative at random. By way of explanation for this unusual beginning, Ellis had used the following as an epigraph: "The facts even when beaded on a chain, still did not have real order. Events did not flow. The facts were separate and haphazard and random even as they happened, episodic, broken, no smooth transitions, no sense of events unfolding from prior events (Tim O'Brien *Going After Cacciato*)." The signposts at the opening of *The Rules of Attraction* all pointed to an absence of rules, coherence, and direction. The reader was quickly immersed in a world of detail and action without much sign of conventional authorial control and narrative direction, without much "sense of events unfolding from prior events."

## NOVEL IDEAS

These literary devices, new at the time to the reader of popular fiction, remain part of a larger legitimation crisis collectivized under the rubric of the postmodern, with which we are now thoroughly familiar. We encounter instances of it every day in the *lebenswelt*, where we randomly engage people and ideas that can be foreign and disturbing. Warnings of imminent brushes with chaos abound—in Cindy Sherman's photographs, Barbara Kruger's installations, in popular cinema and television entertainment. These all reiterate the idea that meaning is situational, fleeting, and arbitrary. A minor scene in Quentin Tarantino's hugely popular 1994 film *Pulp Fiction* succinctly defines the postmodern *Zeitgeist*. John Travolta plays a blissed-out thug, Vincent Vega, who has recently returned from a brief exile in Paris. He reports on his European encounter with the Big Mac to Samuel L. Jackson, his colleague killer. With a sense of surprise, he explains that in Paris the famous McDonald's hamburger is called a Royale, and fries come with mayonnaise, not tomato ketchup. The puzzle for Vincent is that the McDonald's promise—to be everywhere and always the same—has not been kept, but at the same time it has not really been broken. Tarantino's parochial thug muses on how a Big Mac can be anything other than itself and how fries can be eaten differently. Vincent is disturbed to have learnt that the world is polysemic, but at the same time, the more he contemplates it, the more pleasure he derives from the cosmopolitan edge this perspective has given him.

Vincent's elementary introduction to the postmodern world reveals the fundamental unreliability of the taken-for-granted everyday. It is a lesson apparent at every level in society and at all times, but one that needs constant reiteration. In the novel *Herzog*, by Nobel Laureate Saul Bellow (1964), the protagonist laments that the benefits of higher learning are of little value to him in moments of anguish. Aristotle and Spinoza have nothing to offer when a marriage fails and the heart is broken. What is needed instead is a quick McFix, a "five-cent synthesis" (Bradbury 2001: xv). In this realization of the failure of the Great Works, Moses Herzog, like Vincent Vega, has discovered that the taken-for-granted world is not reliable. The enduring, dependable truths that produce a sense of order can in a moment dissolve into disorder, novelty, and chaos.

The works of Thomas Kuhn (1962), Paul Feyerabend (1978), Jean-François Lyotard (1984), Fredric Jameson (1991), and others have delivered this same message into the domains of higher learning. As a result, hybrid and transdisciplinary studies have pushed the boundaries, especially of the humanities and social sciences, in an effort to be more relevant to current concerns. In the postmodern world, the idea that chaos is the next bead on the chain has migrated from the periphery to the center, and in so doing it has reinstalled the ontological crisis of knowledge as a central feature of contemporary Western culture— and not for the first time; the genealogy of this idea is diverse. It can be traced through Heraclitus, Vico, and Hegel, as well as Nietzsche, Freud, and Foucault. Yet despite the numerous reiterations, it is necessary to be reminded that the flow of events, the appearance of coherence, the taken-for-granted everyday is unstable, and the numerous eruptions and contradictions that constitute crises in meaning can be seen as sites of unexpected pleasures. This is what makes Vincent Vega's mental tussle with the Royale a cultural portal to the Western ontological crisis as well as an amusing cinematic moment. It is also what makes the McDonald's phenomenon more than a fascinating study of modern wealth creation; it too is a tool for understanding the contemporary crisis in meaning.

## A CRISIS OF CULTURAL CONFIDENCE

The disquieting crisis of knowledge in the West is frequently repudiated by invoking the successes of closed systems of thought and practice such as scientific management or Taylorism or McDonaldization. According to George Ritzer (1996: 1), McDonaldization, in particular, is becoming commonplace in all aspects of Western society such as education, work, health care, travel, leisure, dieting, politics, and the family. Across these diverse social arenas, it attempts to establish efficiency, calculability, predictability, and control as the dominating values (Ritzer 1996: 10–11). These emerge from Taylor's scientific management that developed in the American factory of the 1940s, where it revolutionized conveyor-belt manufacture by unifying the machine and its human operator into a functional whole. Now the system is applied variously and perhaps most successfully in the stand-alone minifactory of the McDonald's fast-food outlet. Every McDonald's restaurant follows rules and procedures that comply with Frederick Taylor's injunctions. The colossal wealth created by the McDonald's organization in 50 years of existence has much to do with its astute application of Taylorist principles. Clearly, the rational values of a closed system produce benefits. At the same time, there are contradictory signs. The befuddlement of Vincent Vega with the Parisian Royale, in contrast to the familiar Los Angeles Big Mac, cannot be dismissed as just an idiosyncratic cultural moment. It encapsulates too precisely an ironic feature of McDonaldization.

Vincent Vega, like Herzog, has discovered the crisis of meaning in Western culture, that there are no abiding universal truths or rules. The McDonald's promise to be always and everywhere the same, and the great works of the Western canon promising to explain the great dramas of the human condition, are two instances where the assumptions have failed to deliver. Indeed, the extent of McDonald's success in Paris, Vienna, Moscow, the subcontinent of India, Singapore, and Kuala Lumpur, in Kentucky and in South Carolina, is due in part to its situational flexibility and not an imposition of universal homogeneity. It is this practice of meeting parochial interests with the inclusion of local items into its menu that has allowed McDonald's to appear to be the universal taste of everyone. This marketing ploy contains hidden and unanticipated benefits. For example, Vincent's exile in Paris forced him to realize that McDonald's was not always the same, and in time, after the shock, the realization gave him pleasure. Vincent saw behind the official McDonald's message. He had encountered the unexpected and undesired and had come to see their value which had been previously hidden from him. It was as if Vincent had tasted of the "tree of knowledge." This brush with the polysemic instigated his training in the intellectual task, in being able to see behind received ideas, to delegitimate knowledge and question self-evident truths. Thus an unanticipated consequence of Vincent's new relationship with McDonald's is his engagement with cosmopolitanism and learning to see that the world is more than it appears.

The benefits of a critical perspective, of living in a destabilized world, of comfortably occupying the epistemological crisis on a daily basis, are not widely known, yet they are the undertakings of institutional scholarship and higher learning, especially in the humanities and pure sciences. The traditional position of the university has been as the bastion of such critical and polysemic knowledges. It is only a recent permutation, since the nineteenth century, that has seen it perform the alternative task of training professionals and experts in applied techniques. Yet even in this function the academy has not completely abandoned promulgating the view that uncertainty has attractions. The extensive influence of Max Weber, for example, and the more recent postmodern viewpoints have encouraged critiques of closed systems. Economic rationalism and scientific management are understood as the building blocks of global corporations such as McDonald's, IBM, Bayer, and Shell; they are even part of the scaffolding of the new corporatized university itself, but significantly that does not mean the flaws in the system go unrealized. The university itself is a mixture of closed and open systems. While it codifies, categorizes and commodifies knowledge, the university also deregulates modes of thinking and encourages exercises of human ingenuity. It is a site where recognitions of the irrationality of scientific management or McDonaldization are to be found as often as instantiations of it. Thus discoveries of the irrational are often integral to the very enterprise of maintaining these systems. This is precisely the mechanism by which the brand name McDonald's has been redefined into a code for McDonaldization. It is this manner of critical thinking that makes the success and ubiquity of McDonald's the impetus that succeeds in mobilizing its own critique.

## SYSTEMS OF KNOWLEDGE

Meaning is more reliable when the rules of communication are predictable, and when the next move can be accurately anticipated. A consensus of meaning comes from the stability of social forms and patterns of thought. Hence much of McDonald's success rests on its recognizable appearance, its iconic golden arches, and its promise (not necessarily realized) to deliver formulaic products. In a controlled system of knowledge, conventional meanings are reinstated and given closure. Ambiguities, differences and dilemmas are resolved, and in this way, a particular perspective is privileged, namely that of the uncluttered, simple cultural field. While this is obviously functional to the maintenance of normativity, there are contraindications: when meaning is too readily predicted, when there is overregulation, then the result is a closed system where meaning becomes a cliché and the epistemological horizon is reduced to unobtrusive banalities.

To escape from tautology, meaning must be discoverable in the juxtapositions of improbabilities—a process not unlike that of chaos theory. As we encounter differences and improbables, we are directed toward fresh ways of thinking and understanding; new ideas and forms emerge. This is what happens when McDonald's is parodied, when, for example, the golden arches are depicted as grotesque, overdrawn lips, or inverted to resemble well-nourished buttocks, or when mass-marketed television broadcasts are referred to as McNews, or under-employment as McWork, or the diet industry as McHealth, or legal obstructions as McLibel, or formulaic higher education as the McAdemy. At these times, the name McDonald's has been rewritten as a code for the delegitimation of the product in question. The "Mc" prefix indicates the overly simplified, trivialized and dangerously sanitized. In this way, the celebrated closed system of McDonald's is revealed as inferior to more open, less predictable systems. An unanticipated consequence is that McDonald's finds itself in the same territory as Kuhn, Feyerabend and Lyotard, delivering the message that highly circumscribed meanings provide only a fleeting sense of order and stability. Oddly enough, the McDonald's global industry, in its parodic mode, has become a synecdoche of all that it opposes, and in so doing, it can be argued that it inadvertently promotes the attractions of the intellectual life.

Ritzer has repeatedly described the McDonaldization of higher education as a sign of social decline (1996: 42, 64, 86, 106). As the university gets more regulated and circumscribed by mendacious measures of best practice and international standards of accreditation, then it becomes overregulated, and its practices are in effect commodified and trivialized. This is a process that endangers the traditional claims of the university to engender critical, new thought. As well it signals a generalized anxiety about the quality of the knowledge being delivered—just as did the recent inclusion into the academy of gender, postcolonial, and cultural studies. This anxiety has itself come about as the character of the university itself has changed from a bastion of the critical intellect to a storehouse of vocational training. Elements of the problem have always been apparent. Almost fifty years ago Jacques Barzun (1959: 128) asked:

Are the universities going to continue to regard themselves as existing only to turn out an elite of highly trained, urbanely specialized race of men and women, and to gear their whole approach and teaching methods to endlessly reproducing dons and higher civil servants? Or are they going to accept the logic of expanding higher education—which is also to make the mass of people now just below "university standard" more educated than they are?

Barzun goes on to complain that the new universities which are providing mass education are uninterested in the real processes of learning and do not attempt to understand the "age-old difficulties in imparting knowledge" (1959: 131). His is a dyspeptic view. He disparages the universities for reproducing generations of the same closed elite, but at the same time he is critical of universities lowering standards in order to escape the charge of elitism by giving access to those below "university standard."

## THE AUSTRALIAN EXAMPLE

Many of these features of the pedagogical dilemma have now become the ordinary concerns of modern universities. They describe, for example, the problems of higher education in Australia, thereby suggesting that the effects of

McDonaldization are already taking hold. During the last half-century, substantial changes have influenced the higher-education sector in Australia, changing it from an elite system to a more democratic system delivering mass education. In the 1950s, the university expanded to allow more students to enroll, but there were still considerable financial costs to be borne by being a student, and this kept it still a small sector. In the 1960s a dual system of tertiary education commenced, with universities maintaining traditional areas of study and professional accreditation and the new Colleges of Advanced Education providing tertiary qualifications in more vocational areas. In the 1970s, the higher-education sector expanded again, doubling its enrollments in less than ten years (Norton 2000: 4). At the same time, all fees were abolished, and the Federal Government took over from the different systems of the six states of Australia to centralize education finances and policies. In the 1980s, a tortuous process began of unifying the education sector by drawing together the parallel systems of the universities and colleges of advanced education into a single system, with a complex fee system applicable to all students. In the 1990s, the distribution of Federal funds to universities was thoroughly revised, student enrollments continued to increase, and the funding, held static at first, then began plummeting downwards. Only 50% of total university revenue now derives from Federal Government sources. This signals a sharp decrease in spending on higher education, from 3.1% of total government spending to 2.2%. The acquisition of maintenance funds by universities requires complex applications to the Federal Government, detailing all the research, teaching, and administrative activities of all segments of each university. In effect, these institutions have entered into competition with one another for central funding, and the consequence has been a turn toward industry sources for substantial private funds as well as a displacement of costs onto student users.

Despite being an economically stressed sector of society, higher education still attracts strong interest. While there are evident trends away from generalist education enrollments in humanities and science subjects at university, nonetheless these enrollments are still growing, even if it is at half the rate of other more vocationally oriented programs in law, business, engineering, and medicine. Almost 20% of all university students are in humanities programs (ABS 1998). The attractions of a liberal education are easily enumerated (Hart 1990): they are that reading literature and philosophy, political theory and history enables students to find ways of explaining human behavior; that learning about the great accomplishments of humanity and the cultural ingenuity evident in all societies gives a sense of the civilizing and humanizing function of ideas. Furthermore, the humanities and social sciences show education to be a democratizing influence and a source of civil liberty and individual freedom. Finally, reading and thinking generates a critical perspective that provides individuals with the intellectual tools to challenge received doctrines. These are widely accepted as admirable and largely uncontested values that continue to provide status and prestige to those who succeed in gaining a higher education. Yet it is these values and ideals that are seen to be in danger of trivialization and commodification as the effects of McDonaldization and economic rationalism encroach into the education sector of society.

This minihistory of higher education in Australia demonstrates the rapid emergence of the market as a driving influence on the growth of certain sectors of the university. This is often interpreted as having a dumbing-down effect because the stringencies of economic rationalism can lead to substantial increases in staff–student ratios, and this too is evident in Australian universities, where the ratios have soared from an average of 13:1 in 1990 to 19:1 in 2000. The huge growth of student enrollments in some fields and the decline in others has meant an uneven distribution of academic teaching load across the university. The initial response to this situation has been for universities to cut staff numbers by natural attrition and early retirements, and in so doing attempts are made to redistribute funds to certain areas of growth. This is employing a market-driven analysis and solution to the immediate problem of student demand, which can be seen to overlook long-term national interests. Australia has slipped down the OECD comparative scale that measures government expenditure on higher education, research, and development. It is estimated that Australia would need to spend $13 billion over the next five years to catch up with average OECD spending of 2.2% in this sector as a proportion of GDP (Pockley 2001: 40).

A further complicating feature in this McDonaldization of the university is the evolving dot.com revolution and the introduction of Web-based learning systems that can make educational outcomes appear to be marketable commodities. The rate of adoption of these systematized learning programs continues to increase rapidly despite the unprecedented high costs for the new teaching–learning technologies. Integral to this growth is the international Instructional Managements System (IMS) protocol. The significance of this global teaching and learning measure is the standardization it imposes on the pedagogical process. In this way, the dot.com revolution is bringing McDonaldization to university education even more quickly and consolidating even further the previous economic rationalism of the market. The scenario of being able to enroll in leading universities such as Harvard or Oxford for a degree taken online could have the consequence of creating a competitive global marketplace in which universities with the established brand name will dominate, thereby making local institutions, where instruction is provided in a traditional face-to-face lower-cost environment, appear to be of lesser worth.

At the same time that these developments and innovations are being evaluated and debated, they are also being more widely disseminated, and it must be remembered that the circulation of information is always the precursor to the growth of knowledge. The invention of the Internet, geostationary satellites, and fiber optics have totally changed the communication infrastructure of the world, as did the previous inventions of the telephone and camera. The current technologies have created a dense communication stream along which every kind of information can travel without much interference. Institutions and governments may try to block television signals and to censor pop song lyrics, or they may try to prevent access to the digital emissions of both West and East, North and South, but the free flow of information through the various interconnected systems now operating in the global marketplace means that there can be no reliable exercise of control either by governments or by private interests.

The telco world is different from the Gutenberg Galaxy: digital information appears to be more highly elastic, more organic, and more chaotic, thereby preventing a reliable form of information control from being exercised. In contrast, access to the Gutenberg hard copy has been successfully contested throughout history—at one time the clerisy only, or men only, or men only of a certain income, could have access to the text—now it is impossible to police the flow of information and to ensure its use by authorization only. Ultimately, this means that systems of control such as McDonaldization will only work for a time, and in certain circumstances. Eventually and inevitably, because they are closed systems of knowledge, they will spawn their own critique. This is a fundamental impulse in the construction of the social world and the reason why it does not get frozen into any particular formation—even, say, with the ascendancy of such a comprehensive and totalizing system as McDonaldization. That very process of social construction enables the next generation of thought to be always and already invented. As Alberto Manguel in *A History of Reading* states:

It is the reader who grants or recognizes in an object, place or event a certain possible readability; it is the reader who must attribute meaning to a system of signs, and then decipher it. We all read ourselves and the world around us in order to glimpse what and where we are. We read to understand, or to begin to understand. We cannot do but read. Reading, almost as much as breathing, is our essential function . . . reading is at the beginning of the social contract. [1996: 7]

## CONCLUSION

The McDonaldization of higher education is a recent expression of cultural anxiety that draws attention to the dumbing-down effect that can be generated by overregulated or systematized education. Applying the same methods of production to the mass delivery of the higher-education curriculum can mean a simplification of content in order to reach the largest number of clients. At the same time, there are always unanticipated consequences of such sweeping social processes. In the case of McDonaldization, those consequences have a distinctly ironic effect. Take the example of the McDonald's training program. The service staff in McDonald's restaurants commonly enact formulaic exchanges when interacting with customers. At one level, these patterned practices are an attack on the reflexive forms of sociality that enable individuals to create and maintain a cooperative society. Yet, the formulaic greeting, "Have a Nice Day," and the predictable questions, "Can I get you something else?" "Will that be all?" have been so successfully parodied that at another level of consideration their functionality has been hijacked to serve other interests. The uniform use of these banal phrases has taught a new generation of social actors that dissemblance undergirds sociality. This is an essential lesson in the civilizing process; it is embedded in the works of Baldassare Castiglione (1974), whose dialogues of the Courtier were written in the second and third decades of the sixteenth century; it is illustrated again and again in Norbert Elias's (1978) history of manners and in Georg Simmel's (1950) essays on social formations. Unfortunately, the reader-ship for these canonical texts is small, but the reach of the McDonald's credo, in contrast, is comprehensive. Thus, the situation arises that the civilizing messages of the West's canon are reaching millions of individuals—not in their pristine form, but through the parodic existence of the McDonald's empire. This makes Vincent Vega's trip to Paris and back all the more significant because it raises the question: does it matter how he learnt that the world was polysemic or only that he learnt?

The ubiquity of McDonald's has made it into a site of parody and satire. As we have already seen, the "Mc" prefix is a code for irony: "McDoctor" means poor health care, "McJobs" means there is little valuable work to be done, "McNews" signals that it is entertainment, not reportage. By activating McDonald's as a sign of satire and impoverishment, the effect has been to bring a sharper perspective to the topic of McDonaldization. By scrutinizing higher education in the McAdemy, attention is brought to bear on the underlying episte-mological crisis that inflects western knowledge. As more people recognize the problems posed by the process of McDonaldization, greater value is being given to the legitimation crisis in knowledge that has been the signature of western thought. It is a debate that has always been central to Western thought and the ambitions of higher education; it is an idea enunciated by Plato, Rousseau, Barzun, Allan Bloom (1987), and many others (Rieff 1972). It is an idea at the heart of the university.

Throughout its history, the university has rarely been a closed system, unre-sponsive to its sociohistorical context. Over its 900 years of existence, it has constantly adapted, making its business more and more obviously the brokering of new disciplines and categories of knowledge. This successful history of relevance and viability rests with its capacity to splice together and simultane-ously to differentiate pure and applied systems of thought in ways that have increased their utility and accessibility. It is not, then, a sharp reversal or deep change of character that is now visible in universities, although it is often portrayed in such hyperbolic terms in the mass media. Rather, the changes taking place in higher education and the new categorizations of knowledges are them-selves integral to the business of learning and always have been. Being able to unpack the vested interests in these debates reveals how the manufacture of meaning itself is sustained and how fundamental the epistemological process is to all intellectuals and knowledge workers. So now even if the McAdemy ap-pears to undercut the critical urge with its closed system of knowledge, it does simultaneously deliver the tools of critique to a broader audience. In this way, the benefits of being taught to read badly are that within this process are the beginnings of being able to read better. McDonald's itself has instructed a generation in the deficiencies of McDonaldization. Perhaps it will be the same for the McAdemy, and while it may initially be frightening that the new student reads badly, if this is the worst effect of the McAdemy, is it really as bad as not reading at all?

## REFERENCES

ABS (1998). *Education and Training in Australia.* Cat: No. 4224.O. Canberra, Australia: Australian Bureau of Statistics.

Barzun, J. (1959). *The House of Intellect.* Chicago, IL: University of Chicago Press.

Bellow, S. (1964). *Herzog.* Harmondsworth, U.K.: Penguin.

Bloom, A. (1987). *The Closing of the American Mind. How Higher Education Has Failed Democracy and Impoverished the Souls of Today's Students.* New York: Simon and Schuster; Harmondsworth, U.K.: Penguin.

Bradbury, M. (2001). Introduction. In S. Bellow, *Herzog.* Harmondsworth, U.K.: Penguin (v–xxi).

Castiglione, B. (1974). *The Book of the Courtier.* London: Everyman, Dent.

Elias, N. (1978). *The Civilizing Process.* New York: Urizen.

Ellis, B. E. (1987). *The Rules of Attraction.* London: Picador.

Ellis, B. E. (1991). *American Psycho.* New York: Vintage.

Feyerabend, P. (1978). *Against Method.* London: Verso.

Hart, D. (1990). The importance of the liberal arts to education: An historian's perspective. In A. M. Gibbs (Ed.). *The Relevance of the Humanities.* Canberra: Highland Press (69–75).

Jameson, F. (1991). *Postmodernism, or The Cultural Logic of Late Capitalism.* Durham, NC: Duke University Press.

Kuhn, T. (1962). *The Structure of Scientific Revolutions.* Chicago, IL: University of Chicago Press.

Lyotard, J. F. (1984). *The Postmodern Condition: A Report on Knowledge.* Manchester, U.K.: Manchester University Press.

Manguel, A. (1996). *A History of Reading.* London: HarperCollins.

Norton, A. (2000). Degrees of difficulty: The labour market problems of arts and social science graduates. *Issue Analysis,* 19 (12 July) <http://www.cis.org.au>.

O'Brien, T. (1978). *Going After Cacciato.* London: Cape.

Pockley, P. (2001). Research stays in the poorhouse. Higher education. *The Australian,* 30 May.

Rieff, P. (1972). *Fellow Teachers.* Chicago, IL: University of Chicago Press.

Ritzer, G. (1996). *The McDonaldization of Society,* 3d ed. Thousand Oaks, CA: Pine Forge Press.

Simmel, G. (1950). *The Sociology of Georg Simmel.* New York: Free Press.

# 14

## Does Rationality Gum Up the Educational System?

*Ngure wa Mwachofi*

The primary objective of this chapter is to explain *why* and *how* "McDonaldization" or the "rationalization" of higher education happens. The Western context of higher education is examined from multicultural perspectives that involve, among other approaches, critical theory and multiple disciplines like economics, management, and philosophy. I take the United States as my focal point that represents the epitome of Western rationalization of higher education.

In the New Century Edition of *The McDonaldization of Society*, Ritzer (2000) discusses the sense in which nearly all aspects of everyday living are subjected to McDonaldized systems. Since Ritzer's coinage of the term "McDonaldization" (1993), the phenomenon has acquired an identity of its own and has fascinated many scholars (Alfino, Caputo, & Wynyard 1998). It is fair to say that Ritzer's dubbing of the phenomenon "McDonaldization" has helped to identify and anchor the discussion around "rationality" (Kellner 1998; wa Mwachofi 1998).

Because McDonaldization is a complex phenomenon, to interpret it in a binary logic of either "good" or "bad" is too simplistic. I seek to explain the complex sense in which *rationalization* functions to both undermine and enhance the choices that society makes. Such an endeavor requires articulation of the logic (the discursive authority) of McDonaldization and the role of individual ideology.

The basic argument is that rationality "gums up" the higher-education system by offering delivery systems that are *efficient* but short on *effectiveness*. This seems like a good idea, but it just does not work in practice. Efficiency is a logical product of the privileging of mathematical modeling (rationalization). In early-twentieth-century America, developing universities were modeled on successful industrial practice, thus exhibiting high degrees of rationality in the production of material products like automobiles. This represented a triumph of business rationalization, and self-made men from the world of industry turned their attention to shaping university education (Cetron, 1985). The process was mistaken from the start, mainly because of the simple fact that the total rationalization of industrial production is indifferent to qualitative differences. As long as one automobile functions better than another does, then other considerations, like the aesthetics of design, do not have to be taken into account. With mass production techniques unique problems are not considered; such unique problems would require a relentless feedback loop. This is an expensive technical problem requiring the captains of U.S. industry continuously to evaluate the "fit" of solutions to the unique problems they were meant to solve. Second, most people uncritically believe in the "objectivity" of rationalized systems, and third, the individual motives of corporation owners did not take into account the fact that the wider American community might want to study things other than engineering problems, which befitted the already millionaire entrepreneurs.

In his book, titled *Management Fads in Higher Education: Where They Come from, What They Do, Why They Fail,* Birnbaum (2000) offers a historical evaluation of the trend pursued by most universities. He makes the point that business metaphors still dominate American higher education in ways that undermine the process. The desire to be efficient is the result of the dominant logic of this early industrial rationality, which assumes that one solution fits all problems. In the same vein, Schon observes that the birth of "professionalism" occurred in 1918, at a time when engineering and business programs were being introduced in higher education. They were meant primarily to teach "technique" (how to do things). The idea did not go unchallenged. He points out that in accepting technical rationality as the driving paradigm, the practice of higher education is "instrumental, consisting in adjusting technical means to ends that are clear, fixed, and internally consistent. Instrumental practice becomes professional when it is based on the science or systematic knowledge produced by the schools of higher education" (1995: 29). The tension here is between two visions of the ideal university: (1) the university as the place for technocracy (doing, practice, e.g., engineering and business), and (2) the university as a place for philosophy (thinking, theory, e.g., philosophy and sociology).

Who it is that makes these decisions about what is taught in the university is the key issue in this chapter? This is a political question that requires a broad societal context in which to locate it. We need to clarify the dynamic nature of society: how "cultural privilege" of rationality is invented, "symbolized," and "embodied" (Scott, 2000: 10). Although in theory the *role* of decision-making in U.S. higher education is intended to be democratic, in actuality, decision-making falls in the hands of a few members of an elite class. Ordinary citizens figure very little in this decision-making process. This lack of a democratic process is complicated further by unresolved issues, such as how to go about analyzing higher education. Should we take the *individual* or *society* as our starting point?

Conceptualizing a model of society composed of individual members can help us to understand the paradoxes and dilemmas entailed in the analysis of McDonaldization. As "rhetoricians," members of society are in relentless decision-making mode on many aspects of life beyond higher education (see wa Mwachofi 1993: 142–143). Some members, especially those comprising the American elites, are more involved in social issues than others. For instance, depending on their starting point, members of society come to dramatically different conclusions on whether the famous (infamous) U.S. billionaire Bill Gates (Microsoft owner) is a hero or a villain. We could ask "Dave": Dave's conclusion would depend on many variables. For example, does Dave take Bill Gates to be dedicated to society or dedicated to making a lot of money? Does Dave belong to the elite class? Does he believe in "an ethics of allegiance to society" or in "an ethics of allegiance to rugged individualism"? The possibilities can be endless. The issue is that while it may seem okay to treat Dave's views as views of an "individual" with personal beliefs, from a critical theory standpoint we need to recognize that Dave is not strictly an individual, and therefore, it is misleading to assume Dave to be "objective," as if he could be free of ideology. In actuality, he got his views from his culture (the overarching discourse of capitalism) that emphasizes "individualism." That we are products of our environment is a view neatly summarized by Billig (1991) as follows:

the very process of thinking can be processes of ideology . . . The very contents of everyday thinking—the maxims, values and opinions which are commonly held, etc.—are themselves cultural products. In ordinary thinking, people use "common sense," which *they do not themselves invent but which has a history* [my emphasis]. As critical theorists from Marx onwards have stressed, common sense is a form of ideology . . . [As people speak or offer opinions] they will be repeating assumptions which confirm existing arrangements of power. [Billig 1991: 1]

While I like Billig's perspective, I would like to point out that aside from "confirm existing arrangements of power," individuals can, and do, *negate* existing arrangements of power. This makes problematic the relationship of individuals to society and places them in some kind of conflict.

Clearly, some individuals, like Bill Gates or John Dewey, represent a role model that individuals, *as* members of society, can both *borrow from* and *contribute to* the culture they live in. This duality is important. It clarifies the sense in which Gates and Dewey have revolutionized, respectively, the way people work with computers and the way they conceptualize education. They came up with those ideas and inventions from observing the very society they live in. They offered their rhetoric of the way things ought to be, a rhetoric that involves complex "negation" and "confirmation" of the existing arrangements of power.

To the extent that some people accepted their rhetoric, it became "reality": many people use Microsoft software for their computers, and some educators have implemented Dewey's philosophy in teaching and learning. In comparison to Gates and Dewey, Dave may appear to be an "onlooker." In actuality, he is not an onlooker, because whatever decision he takes, however passive or personal, will signal *affirmation* or *negation* of the existing power structure.

Recognizing that all people are rhetoricians with the potential of creating, buying, and selling their ideas helps us to understand the *dynamic process* of choice-making. Society, then, can be defined as a conglomeration of relentless *production* and *re-production* of rhetorical positions. In that dynamic process new ideas arise from the *reorganization, affirmation*, and *negation* of old ones, and also from the *introduction* of novel ideas never considered before. In this sense, rhetoric does not exist as an objective fact; it is made alive in the transactions between the sellers and the buyers of the ideas: for example, the case of Dave pondering the value of Bill Gates' contribution to society. We can conceptualize "objective reality" as the experience of pausing a videotape of scenery taken from the window of a speeding train. In viewing those paused "moments" of the still pictures we know full well that the scenery is only momentary and never stays the same.

The critical difference is that when we talk about a phenomenon, we "freeze" it *to allow references* to specific elements of the phenomenon. Often this "frozen glimpse" is erroneously taken to be the whole reality. I speculate that people find it easier and convenient to do so because using a "moment" helps them to select those elements that support their ideologies. In everyday parlance in the United States, it is said: "People see what they want to see." Since life is not still, in considering the effectiveness of dynamic models in favor of efficient static ones, we as critical theorists ought to be guided by our awareness of the ephemeral nature of "reality."

The popularity of the McDonaldization of society represents the extent to which the rhetoric of rationality as a philosophy has gained acceptance in society. The paradox here is that humans create systems that, in turn, compel humans to conform to the systems' logic, once accepted. At the same time systems have alarmed some and led to the questioning of the social and cultural process such systems bring about. This is why McDonaldization fascinates so many, for it can be read in the light of the reconfiguration of both social and cultural change, not only in America but in the whole world. Those who question the system are either desiring to replace the prevailing system with one that may favor their interests or perhaps because they see the flaw in the prevailing system—for example, when, "after the Civil War, ... American scholars who had gone abroad to study in Germany brought back with them the German idea of the university as a place in which to do research that contributes to the fundamental knowledge, preferably through science" (Schon 1995: 28). Commenting on this, Schon goes on to observe: "This was a very strange idea in 1870, very much at odds with the then-prevailing conception of higher education in the United

States, which was based on the British notion of the university as a sanctuary for the liberal arts or as a finishing school for gentlemen" (Schon 1995: 28).

The challenging question to be asking is: "*What* education structure is good, and for *whom*?" One way of dealing with this unresolved issue is to conceptualize institutions as products of ideology (desire, intent, or motive). So we can ask: "*Who* proposed the ideal?" "For *whose* benefit?" In doing so, we can account for competing rhetorical visions among individuals in a society and the inherent U.S. cultural ideology, as well as individual ideologies within that culture. I propose that we must conceptualize members of society as rhetoricians caught up in a relentless contestation of what worldview should set the imperative in making institutional choices. And this "unannounced but relentless contest" leaves plenty of room for individual rhetoricians to propose their viewpoint as "the standard" for higher education. Any proposal can be persuasive on its own account (see wa Mwachofi 1993: 142–143). Obviously, in a mass-mediated culture those who can afford the expense of the mass media for persuasion are likely to be the winners (Bagdikian 1990).

Businesses enter the education arena and invent rhetorical positions. "Business partnerships with schools have existed from at least as far as 1860s when, for example, the New York City Chamber of Commerce had representatives on the school board of the Merchant Marine Technical School, a public school in the New York City system" (Cetron 1985: 85). More recent examples of competing rhetorical visions in the United States are Bill Gates (the world of computing of Microsoft), Henry Ford (the world of automobile, *Ford*), Richard Warren Sears (the world of catalogue retailing of *Sears & Roebuck*). These rhetoricians are among the myriad "unknown" rhetoricians. These individuals are generally regarded as "leaders" in innovations because their proposed ideas have been institutionalized into the cultural milieu. In brief, they proposed a style of living that, once accepted by a majority of society members, became the standard. The proposals are "naturalized" as *the way things are supposed to be*. Culture is simply proposed by influential individuals, and becomes dominant once accepted by most members of society (see wa Mwachofi 1998: 147–148). As a component of culture, rhetoric is a product of selectively highlighting positive attributes of an idea and playing down or ignoring altogether any negative attributes.

With the examples of Bill Gates, Henry Ford, and Richard Warren Sears, if we take a critical look and identify the underside of these innovators, we can experience a labyrinth of interconnections. Aside from recognizing these three individuals' colossal financial contributions to educational institutions, we would also appreciate the equally colossal benefits that their organizations have received from educational institutions in form of research and trained manpower. But because such acts are often dubbed "philanthropic," the "philanthropy" metaphor *obfuscates* the owners and *highlights* their generosity. Consequently, some members of society believe strongly that we need corporations to save our schools (Cetron 1985: 85–92).

Whether computers are useful or not is a matter of context; it is not a matter of "good" or "bad." Taking just one issue, for example: Hendley, reflecting on 30 years of higher education, comments on a survey regarding technology and distance education. Among those professors surveyed, one cites a positive attribute of the electronic education, stating, "It has aided me in my research and made it much easier to find and access information, both in terms of people and of recorded and visual information" (Hendley 2000: 4).

The issue is not whether technologies change the way we do things; the issue is how the changes in turn change other unintended or anticipated aspects of the large picture. This is what I refer to as the "imperative of technology." If we focus on the imperative, we will be able to see beyond the immediate and appreciate the ambivalence resulting from technology. For example, even though posting handouts on the course webpage is a great time saver, notice the imperative brought about by this "new way" of doing things: because "posting" replaces "handing out," not only is the direct teacher–student contact eliminated, but posting will not confirm that students actually *receive* the handout, look at it, and ask questions for clarity. While professors are pleased with posting, the trade-off is a much more *efficient* system in delivering the handouts but a less *effective* one in confirming the use of the handout. While that is true, the cost of the paper used is still borne by someone. So this is not really a saving but a shifting of responsibility from the department to the students.

Likewise, we can decide to highlight the downside of the three American individuals mentioned earlier. In doing so, we will be inventing an alternative rhetorical position. In the same vein, we can analyze the legitimacy of the three earlier-mentioned institutions. First, regarding Bill Gates, we will appreciate the sense in which computer software for word-processing threatens writing-skill abilities: for example, taking the responsibility for spelling away from individuals; there is also a social cost, where the jobs of a lot of people have been taken over by computers (Greenbaum 1995). Second, regarding Henry Ford, who introduced the assembly-line car-production format, we can talk of the decline of the environment, death tolls from road accidents, and the rise as a result of catalogue retailing, in numbers of overweight people who do not walk enough. Third, in the case of Richard Sears, where we can talk of the increase in "consumerism" and the deforestation that is due to the overuse of trees to make paper for the catalogues. The analysis can go further to illuminate more and more interconnections.

This is not to claim that these three individuals have not contributed positively to society. But for each positive attribute that can be identified in any innovation, negative attributes can equally be identified. What is identified as positive or negative does not depend on common-sense perceptions—it depends on ideology: who is doing the analysis, and for whose benefit is the analysis (see wa Mwachofi 1993: 142–143)?

Obviously, if higher-education policy is a product of people in power and if corporate influence is substantial, the tendency for the university to take up corporate style management should not surprise us (the National Center for Postsecondary Improvement, May/June 2000: 53–55; see also Birnbaum 2000). Many universities are paying their president colossal amounts of money. Many have a vice-president of marketing who claims a salary the equivalent of three professors. Cetron observes: "While business cooperation with schools is not new, partnerships between businesses and schools will be a pervasive part of the daily operations in most school districts by the 21st century" (1985: 85). The question of why rational systems continue to dominate all institutions, including higher education, needs to be addressed. An analysis of rationality, as in McDonaldization, should attempt to explain the paradox of the rhetoric of rationality's prevalence. That is why rationality is attractive and, at the same time, a matter of concern.

With specific reference to higher education as a system, Ritzer illustrates the sense in which the system is subjected to "efficiency" (2000: 49–50), "calculability" (2000: 66–70), "control" through nonhuman technology (2000: 108, 114–115), and the "irrationality of rationality" (2000: 143). Offering perspectives on the struggle to deal with the McDonaldization of higher education, he observed the following: "As nonrationalized institutions [of higher education] become successful, pressure mounts to McDonaldize them" (2000: 203). He goes on to elaborate that "as creatures of a capitalist society, they [the entrepreneurs in higher-education institutions] might well succumb to greater profitability and allow their business to expand or to be franchised" (2000: 203).

Although in a democracy like that of the United States public policy is supposedly a product of much exchange of ideas among rhetoricians (e.g., between policymakers and their constituencies), in practice the role that money has continued to play in influencing public policy is significant. The market often drives education policy. Consequently, the quality of education may not reflect the interests of the majority of the people, because the shapers of the philosophy, the structure, and the processes of education have ideologies. Not only may their personal desires create a "conflict of interest," ordinary citizens who contribute little to the structure of the higher-education system may have little choice than to follow unreflectively. In summary, there is no broad consensus about higher education and who should structure it, because in most institutions in actuality decision-making fails in the hands of a few members of the elite class.

McDonaldization is a prevalent American ideology with complex implications for society and individuals. It offers primary benefits to the owners of capital and secondary benefits to the consumers and workers. But once society accepts those benefits unreflectively, it inevitably accepts the discursive authority of rationality. Like any other discourse, rationality is problematic: it appears to solve problems and, at the same time, it creates new ones. This flip-side accounts for the controversy of rationality, where some individuals find it indispensable while others find themselves closed out and seek other alternatives.

This is why Americans feel as if the goal-posts are being moved. They now need a college degree for a job that, in the past, required only a high-school diploma. *Re-training* has become the dominant mantra because each time a new technology is declared as the answer, it takes only a few days before it is declared obsolete. This relentless "upgrading" means that profits go to the owners of the "product." Thus primary benefits go to the billionaire owners of companies like Microsoft.

Higher education in America, as a logical extension of the rationalist logic, is relentlessly reconsidered and, consequently, repackaged in accord with the logic of "market conditions" (see National Center for Postsecondary Improvement— 2001: 53–56). In this sense, education is an entity, a product, which can be owned and exchanged for a price. Since education is treated as a commodity that is for sale, it follows that the market conditions dictate what programs a university may offer.

In a rationality-privileging worldview, humans are defined by their roles as "consumers" and "producers" of products. "Products" are the goods and services that are fully accounted for in a rational political economy. This is a near-perfect world of efficiency, calculability, predictability, and control (Ritzer, 2000).

My view is that the rationalist logic, being the dominant discourse in the United States, sets the imperative for how *everything else* will function. Consequently, it is imperative that all societal institutions conform to the logic of the *market economy* that requires high volumes of production and consumption. These are the cause for the current trend of e-universities that hope to offer diplomas globally, without the students ever seeing the campus. It is the *efficient delivery* (volume) that counts. In rationalist terms, higher education is "a tool" that aids individuals to be a competent "producers" and "consumers." The business phrase "cost < benefit"—that is to say, "costs" must be less than the "benefit"—is the key arbiter of production, distribution, and consumption decisions. (Business students must learn the C<B technique in order to be considered good decision-makers.)

But undue emphasis on cost–benefit techniques, in the absence of a morality or ethics, results in absurdities that predominate in the rationalized systems. For example, an employee may be rewarded with a three-day holiday, all expenses paid by the corporation, for saving the corporation money. It matters not whether the saving was due to recommending the firing of the workforce. In quantitative terms, the language of "labor costs" replaces the language of "laying people off." Again, through alternative symbols, it becomes entirely possible to hurt many people who are depended upon for their livelihoods by their families (see Schor 1991; Reich 1992) without acknowledging it.

Consumerism as a component of rationality views "education" simply as a tool for a singular purpose—to enhance the consumption possibilities of the individual—and no communal ethics is entailed. Again this is because, in a rationalized world, individual worth is defined by what one does. "What do you do, and how much money do you make?" is the key question. Quantification is logically handy for summarizing what one is worth. In the United States, for example, the billionaire clubs illustrate the "quantifiable" evaluation of worth. A car bumper sticker provides a lucid summary of this. It states: "Those with the most toys win." The amount of money people make determines how much they are capable of consuming in terms of goods and how much respect they command. Hence the famous twist on Descartes: "I consume, therefore, I am."

While taking into account the perspective of "individual" versus "society," it is a challenge to analyze McDonaldization as part of an American ideology. Equally, the various approaches to education are part of the U.S. ideology. While American society *may* seem to share the idea that education is useful to humans, different value interpretations of what education *ought to* offer and how it ought to be structured if it is to achieve the desired goals remain a challenge not yet grasped in the United States.

Depending on their starting point, members of society come to different conclusions on whether higher education should be free and accessible to every citizen. For instance, if citizens decide that education, like defense, is a national priority that should be financed by the taxpayer, it would be entirely possible to offer free education, as some European countries do. Hendley's survey goes on to point out another *underside* of technology—*the digital divide*—where people who live in places lacking the technology infrastructure will not access information. The reason for the "digital divide" is not technology; rather, it is the overarching culture that has characterized education as an individual not as a communal good.

In fact, the "digital divide" metaphor functions to create the impression that this is an isolated situation related to computing only. In actuality, capitalism as a system that emphasizes the individual rather than the community ends up with these large disparities ("divides") in every sphere of life, such as housing, education, health, and so forth.

The fact that the rich will access technology and the poor will not needs to be seen as a logical conclusion of the rational system. This metaphor of "education as a commodity for sale" sets the imperative of how the commodity is to be produced, distributed, and consumed. Moreover, as with any other commodity, it is the market conditions that dictate the flow of products.

I prefer to summarize the problems of U.S. higher education in terms of what rationality cannot achieve. Fundamentally, if human needs vary, a one-fits-all solution will fall short. The desire for efficiency inevitably requires the universal application of rational systems. It will always "normalize" the experience to conform to its logic, while the objective that it aimed to help gets lost on the way.

## REFERENCES

Alfino, M., Caputo, J. S., & Wynyard, R. (Eds.) (1998). *McDonaldization Revisited: Critical Essays on Consumer Culture.* Westport, CT, & London: Praeger.

Bagdikian, B. (1990). *The Media Monopoly.* Boston, MA: Beacon.

Billig, M. (1991). *Ideology and Opinions.* Newbury Park, CA: Sage.

Birnbaum, R. (2000). *Management Fads in Higher Education: Where they come from, what they do, why they fail.* San Francisco, CA: Jossey-Bass.

Cetron, M. (1985). *Schools of the Future: How American Business and Education Can Cooperate to Save Our Schools.* New York: McGraw-Hill.

Greenbaum, J. (1995). *Windows on the Workplace: Computers, Jobs, and the Organization of Office Work in the Late Twentieth Century.* New York: Monthly Review.

Hendley, V. (2000). 30 years of higher education: Members reflect on how far higher education has come and how far it still must go to provide every student with the best learning experience possible. *AAHE Bulletin*, 30 (No. 7, March): 1–8. (A publication of the American Association of Higher Education.)

Kellner, D. (1998). Foreword: McDonaldization and its discontents: Ritzer and his critics. In M. Alfino, J. S. Caputo, & R. Wynyard (Eds.), *McDonaldization Revisited: Critical Essays on Consumer Culture.* Westport, CT, & London: Praeger.

National Center for Postsecondary Improvement (2001). Resurveying the terrain: Refining the taxonomy for the postsecondary market. *Change* (March/April): 53–56.

Reich, R. B. (1992). *The Work of Nations.* New York: Vintage.

Ritzer, G. (1993). *The McDonaldization of Society*, 1st ed. Thousand Oaks, CA: Pine Forge Press.

Ritzer, G. (2000). *The McDonaldization of Society: New Century Edition.* Thousand Oaks, CA: Pine Forge Press.

Schon, D. (1995). Knowing-in-action: The new scholarship requires a new epistemology. *Change* (November/December): 27–34.

Schor, J. B. (1991). *The Overworked American: The Unexpected Decline of Leisure.* New York: Basic Books.

Scott, N. (2000). Review of *White Reign: Deploying Whiteness in America. AAHE Bulletin*, 53 (No. 4, December): 10. (A publication of the American Association of Higher Education).

wa Mwachofi, N. (1993). On blurring the distinction between capitalism and socialism: A critique of "scientificism" via a rhetorical approach. In R. L. Ensign & L. M. Patsouras (Eds.), *Challenging Social Injustice: Essays on Socialism and the Devaluation of the Human Spirit.* Lewiston, NY: Edwin Mellen (137–155).

wa Mwachofi, N. (1998). Missing the cultural basis of irrationality in McDonaldization of society. In M. Alfino, J. S. Caputo, & R. Wynyard (Eds.), *McDonaldization Revisited: Critical Essays on Consumer Culture.* Westport, CT, & London: Praeger.

# 15

# Hamburgerology by Degrees

*Robin Wynyard*

In this chapter I critically examine Ritzer's comments on what he terms McUniversities and go on to look at the parallels made between these and McDonald's Corporation Hamburger University (Ritzer 1998, 2000). I argue that in the United Kingdom we might be at Ritzer's McUniversity stage, but we have not progressed to the full-blown American Hamburger University. My thought equates with a relative optimism, *not* the pessimism Ritzer seems to be suggesting concerning the future of global higher education.

Likening the American Hamburger University (and its international satellites) to what Baudrillard calls a *black hole,* which attracts everything, Ritzer (1998: 159) says that the relationship of Hamburger University to the nascent McUniversity "Will be a simulated world of education very similar to such obvious simulations as Hamburger University" (Ritzer 1998: 160). Conceptually we are presented with the real Hamburger University (HU), Hamburger University (simulated), and McUniversity (already existing in whole or in part). Here there are some very important ideas on the future role of higher education, but a conceptual tangle might confuse Ritzer's readers. Ritzer seems to be saying that the real Hamburger University is no different in kind—that is, physical presence and the consumer commodities produced—from the McDonald's fast-food restaurant. His concern lies at the level of form rather than that of content. You cannot literally eat with any enjoyment a degree certificate in *hamburgerology* from the HU. Similarly, it is the actual receipt of a Big Mac that is important; the eating of it is quite incidental. The philosopher Doug Kellner expresses this when he says: "We do not just go into McDonald's for mere food that has a calculable use and exchange value. Rather we purchase a whole new identity and way of life. The product itself is not of primary interest, it must be sold by grafting onto it a set of meanings that have no inherent connection with the product" (Kellner 1994: 77).

To talk about HU is easy, existing as it does in both space and time. The difficulty lies with what Ritzer calls the McUniversity, which is named by him, from a simulated form of Hamburger University. Hamburger University Ritzer sees as only feigning to be a university in the business of awarding degrees for academic achievement. In reality it is no different in kind from the process involved in buying eatables from McDonald's fast-food outlets. When we actually buy our Big Mac and fries, we go through a commodity purchase, but consciously or unconsciously we are buying into something else. Once you start with this simulation exercise, it has to continue into the fast-food restaurants as well. Take a young person in a country like Greece that prides itself on the freshness and uniqueness of its food. This person buying a burger in Athens is buying something that looks like food and *could* be eaten, but is really something else, as well as food that equates with the United States as a foreign country. Likewise, the new graduates from HU, on receiving their degree certificates, are not shaking the hands of the *real* HU Dean, but they might perceive themselves to be stepping into the shoes of the manager of the biggest McDonald's restaurant wherever! If the so-called *Ambassador's Course* (McDonald's *National Training Prospectus* 1999) is part of the award, the graduate might be seeing his- or herself as a McDonald's executive, jetting around the 120 or so countries where the Corporation sells burgers. If the HU/McDonald's way of production is so profitable and efficient in producing an end-result of identical burgers, might it not be that cash-strapped U.K. universities would seize upon the whole Corporation business, using it as a model of effective and appropriate practice?

If the McUniversity is with us, we will have moved from university education for education's sake to university education for something entirely different. I am tempted here by the American word *infotainment*, which is defined as "the practice of presenting serious or instructive subjects in a style designed primarily to be entertaining" (Collins *English Dictionary* 1991). The McUniversity will still be in a real building, with real people holding real university qualifications. The difference is that the pedagogical process conveys a product that is much richer and more varied than the original view of the graduate degree as showing excellence in an academic subject. Once, reaching this standard of educational excellence was deemed to be reward in itself. Being further rewarded for this by an impressed employer was an added bonus, but not the main reason for spending three years or more in near-poverty. What might be "richer and more varied than the original view?" In the context of the U.K. McUniversity this *could* mean an education that is *loosely* allied to the acquisition of a job, but it is more likely to be about consumer entertainment, choice, and interest. An example of this could be the burgeoning university degrees in *cultural studies*. Criticism of these is that they are not academic, as they are seemingly cobbled together from many clear-cut academic fields. Neither are they vocational, as they do not equip you to write and edit a TV script, nor do they enable the recipient to do practical things like work a camera. Lastly, it is argued that they are for "substandard" students who cannot get into *bona fide* university subjects, but need to be accounted for in the increased take-up of higher education. As McGuigan aptly puts it: "I would argue that the turn to a postmodern cultural studies is a response to a new era of global capitalism. . . . During the current stage of cultural studies there is a widespread tendency to decentre, or even ignore completely, economics, history and politics in favour of emphasis on local pleasures, consumption and the construction of hybrid identities from the material of the popular" (1997: 20).

Getting back to Ritzer, if we were to posit a continuum running from existing university institutions to McUniversities (employing at least some of the practices of the real or simulated Hamburger University), to the actual Hamburger University in its totality, I argue that along this continuum there are always tendencies to move toward HU. This lies in the fact that in a cost-conscious world most U.K. universities aspire to Ritzer's universal process of *McDonaldization*—that is, *efficiency, calculability, predictability* and *control* (Ritzer 2000: 11–15).

However, what stops the McUniversity from going down the road to the full-blown Hamburger University lies in the nature of U.K. society, which is both fragmented and inconsistent. I would not necessarily term this postmodernist, but I would see it as a society that embodies a wide-ranging and skeptical attitude to many of the principles and assumptions underpinning Western thought and social life. As Lyotard says: "these [different] languages are not employed haphazardly however. Their use is subject to a condition that I could call pragmatic: each must formulate its own rules and petition the addressee to accept them" (Lyotard 1986: 42). Cutting Lyotard's thought down to basic principles in modern society, universities do not validate a unified and hierarchical knowledge. This quite simply is because they do not know what *is* unified and hierarchical knowledge! There might no longer be knowledge at all, only the form of eclecticism preferred by Lyotard (1986: 76). It does not seem much, saying that the only form of resistance we can expect in modern U.K. society lies by virtue of multiplicity of choice in societal form.

In reality, though, the American McDonald's alma mater, and other such *universities* founded by global corporations, exist as a result of specific societal conditions fostering large business training institutes. For whatever reason, these institutions quite incidentally attract the title *university*.

The societal and cultural worlds we inhabit become increasingly ambiguous. Far from providing stability, the new millennium will still exhibit ambiguity and will continue to shock, confound, and amuse, in varying proportions. Continuing ambiguity supremely exemplifies the fickleness of discourse change, but what change is now based upon is very difficult to predict. Once television advertisements were judged on how successfully they sold products by their witty and informative content; now it is simply too difficult to predict the criteria of success. In a competition, run by a Sunday newspaper to discover the hundred best television advertisements of all time, the eventual winner, a *Guinness* ad of surfing white horses, seems to have been chosen for *both* aesthetic appeal *and* paucity of content. Likewise, today, in British higher education, there seems to be a mixture of change and flux allied with elements of certainty and tradition, cultural appeal and paucity of content, all of which are difficult to separate. Such a society, it is argued by Delanty, is about reflexivity: "Reflexivity is a cultural feature of contemporary society and is very much related to the capacity of individuals to learn to cope with cultural choices and uncertainty. The problem of choice cannot be solved by reference to a set of stable cultural norms or by recourse to a permanently constructed identity" (2000: 160).

At this point it is appropriate to say something about the McDonald's Corporation Hamburger University (HU). This I designate, along with other corporate institutions organized on entirely new and different premises, as *not-universities*. Many people would not accept them as universities, so they are and they are not, if you see what I mean? However, we must be very careful not to misjudge their global importance; as the *Economist* says: "There are now some 1,600 corporate universities in the United States, four times as many as a decade ago. That the practice is also increasingly popular in Europe and that Anglian Water has a University of Water; Unipart, a British car-parts company, has a place that likes to be known as the 'u'" (*Economist* 1999: 78).

With Hamburger-type universities the curriculum aims not just to train in vocational skills, but also to transmit a spirit of self-defined education onto the shop floor. Of course, this does not make the job you do any more secure. All we can say about such institutions is that if the pedagogical process is successfully imbibed, it removes, for a time at least, the guilt of failure. As a graduate of such a *non-university*, if you keep your job when other nongraduates on the shop-floor have been made redundant, then you can rejoice that you have been cleverer than the rest! So McDonald's becomes your life—a life where the nearest tuition coming to the general public is through the antics of Ronald McDonald on television. Going to university was at one time thought to instill a certain maturity into the school-leaver; McDonald's at whatever level seems to reverse the process, making adults into children.

McDonald's is in the same game as Disneyland, about which Baudrillard has said, "It is meant to be an infantile world, in order to make us believe that the adults are elsewhere, in the 'real world', and to conceal the fact that real childishness is everywhere, particularly among those adults who go there to act the child in order to foster illusions of their real childishness" (Baudrillard 1988: 172).

In building the above childhood regression into its training programs, Hamburger University not only aids and abets, but also actively propagates Baudrillardian simulation. In HU the relationship between education and vocational worlds and the discursive context relating to it is changed. The teaching technique employed in doing this is to some extent where HU and the nascent McUniversity might show some overlap. In the former, solely, and increasingly in the latter, the catalyst lies in the use of educational initiatives like the assessment of competencies and modularized courses. My personal view is that both of these initiatives exhibit a kind of childishness in the way students have to be led through them, incidentally increasing the need for support staff like counselors and others trained to help the student to know what he or she wants in educational terms. But such expansion comes at a cost; in education it means a cutting back in more expensive academic staff.

Modularized courses have recently been fair game in the re-engineering of U.K. further and higher education. What seemed fantastically straightforward to many politicians and educationalists is in reality nothing of the sort. This sleight-of-hand psychologism (Usher & Edwards 1994: 110) lies in the fact that the surface structure of such initiatives changes behavior in a clear-cut way (behaviorist), but the underlying discourse does not (humanist). With surface behaviorism there is a notion of competence, which can be clearly tested in terms of success. There is no sense of failure as such, only the need to repeat the exercise until it comes right. However, the real work goes on at a deeper humanist level, where there lies a powerful psychological sense of incompetence and failure. Competence-based qualifications can only be done on the shop floor and can only be organized in a modular form. Hamburger University has recognized this and implemented such programs brilliantly. Those British institutions of higher education pushing for the title of McUniversity may not have got into assessment of competencies in the way that further education institutions have. But they have flirted with modularization, which they have totally misunderstood. The McUniversity, for all its modular innovation, cost-cutting, and fast processing of students, is neither financially, technologically, ideologically, nor vocationally as astute as Hamburger University, which allies technology and psychology in its pedagogy: "To test how well people are getting it on the fly, an instructor need simply offer a quick multiple-choice question, look at the computer readout of the students' answers, and make adjustments accordingly . . . an infrared audio-projection system offers ten different channels for international students who rely on the lightweight, wireless headsets that carry running translations from the interpreters" (Schaaf 1994: 18).

The investment McDonald's have made in their university is purely and simply for calculated material purposes, and it is not about philanthropic academic advancement of the masses. It is about mass education all right, but one that increases and confirms the necessity of large numbers of people eating McDonald's products on a daily basis.

The McDonald's Corporation University is situated on a 130,000 $m^2$ state-of-the-art facility on a campus in Oak Brook, Illinois. It occupies a $40 million facility, offering 36 hours of courses accredited by the bona fide *American Council of Education*. It takes two weeks to gain a *bachelor of hamburgerology* degree, and 65,000 have graduated with this qualification since it opened its doors for the first time. HU is part business-school and part teacher-training college, whose graduates go on to teach others and instill a mood of education on

McDonald's shop floors around the world. More than half the students at HU come from overseas, although these are starting to get directed to other international campuses. In the early days of HU the idea was purely one of instruction, but the present HU dean wants to integrate training more closely with McDonald's research laboratories. The HU curriculum is offered in 26 languages with simultaneous translation and focusing on management training, human relations, interpersonal communication, leadership, and problem-solving skills.

On the one hand, Hamburger University fits with high-modernity—that is, it exhibits a high degree of rationality that is brought to bear on everything, from the conveyor-belt techniques of burger production to staff behavior and customer manipulation on the shop floor. On the other hand, the concept of *hamburgerology* fits with postmodern society, being constituted in, and through, complex interrelating relationships, with older ideas rubbing shoulders with new-generation technologies. There might be an ambiguity between the modern and the postmodern, but this does not mean that they are incompatible, as both can be accommodated in society: "For Baudrillard, modern societies are organized around the production and consumption of commodities, while postmodern societies are organized around simulation and the play of images and signs, denoting a situation in which codes, models and signs are the organizing principles of a new social order" (Kellner, quoted in Wynyard 1998: 170). Given that the object of McDonald's lies in creating as much possible profit worldwide, seating education, as part of the "simulation and the play of images and signs," alongside the production process seems totally reasonable and justifiable to the Corporation. Today's global world means that the use of attendant technology alongside higher education does not seem strange at all and is just an extension of the process.

This book has been produced by modern technology and written by scholars from three different countries who in the main have never met each other. Its publication will have brought together business, production, a steep learning curve, and a lot of fun. McDonald's Hamburger University works in the same way, bringing together business, education, infotainment, eating, and plain fun. Best and Kellner express this well in saying: "Moreover transnational corporations are growing in power and wealth, with a global market economy disseminating throughout the world fantasies of happiness through consumption and products that allow entry into the phantasmagoria of consumer capitalism" (Best & Kellner 1997: 14).

Today, with globalization and the rapid spread of ideas, such *non-university* ideas can spread to other cultural establishments. Without too much thought, such ideas, wholeheartedly supported by the financial and political sectors with their attendant technologies, become easily adopted as the cultural standard. One sees U.K. examples in the new Tate Modern gallery, which was opened by the Queen in 1962 as a power station, and opened by her again in 2000 as the biggest gallery of modern art in the world. Whatever else it may be, it certainly gave Britain something to cheer about in the new millennium.

As Baudrillard argues, culture in any guise and purporting to be about education for the masses *has* to be good. What he shows is that significant discontinuities have taken place in the configuration of Western culture. If Baudrillard wrote on HU, he would see it as a model through which a world could be created. This world appears *real* enough, constituted as it is on a value-exchange relationship. Although the title remains, the images, codes, and subjects of the academic universities have been fundamentally transformed. The main differences between *non-universities* like HU and *real* academic institutions lies not just in the fact that the technology employed in the former is state-of-the-art, and the training highly rational. More importantly, the cultural transmission conveyed back to the shop floor is one of a wonderful learning experience. It is an experience where things seem to happen, not technologically, but symbolically, irrationally, and magically. (Not even the most optimistic would claim this about the average U.K. University course). A manifestation of magical process of adults getting turned into children lies in the observation of adults keeping the *McCollectable* and rejecting the *happy meal* that goes with it. Whether the toy is for their children or for them as part of the *McCollectors' Club* is all part of the magic. So, in Baudrillard's terms, there is no longer the ability to appeal to a *real* referent mediating between representation and object. The production of food, in the shape of burgers or whatever, is simply a simulation—that is, something standing in for something else! This something is certainly not unique, but whatever it is, it signifies more value than the actual burger itself, which can be thrown away with no adverse consequences to the purchaser, almost as if it "is not real food after all!"

As Ritzer develops his McDonaldization thesis, he seems to be moving theoretically from a straightforwardly Weberian model of ever-increasing systematic and universalistic rationality to a more postmodernist Baudrillardian outlook. If this is correct, then we generally are not entering a world of the *non-university hamburgerology degree*. This is a world with identical burgers and graduates all mass-produced to the same standard, not a world of unlimited choice, constant fluxes, and changes. This constant flux and change hinders rather than helps the ever-increasing nature of McDonaldization. Ritzer's shift from Weber to Baudrillard weakens the McDonaldization thesis: "In developing his McDonaldization thesis, Ritzer now concedes the value of the Baudrillardian perspective on the consumption of signs, postmodern reflexivity and so forth. This may undermine his own argument about rationalization and standardisation" (McGuigan 1999: 28).

There is a correspondence between notions of high modernity, where temples of rationality like HU, with their attendant *iron cages*, are at the pinnacle. Compare this with postmodernity, where aspirant McUniversities, although adopting some of HU's overt features in their public persona, show much more divergence than similarity. An obvious comparison would be between Oxbridge-type universities and new inner city universities formed from earlier polytechnics. This is not about better or worse; it simply exemplifies the point that U.K.

universities are part of postmodern society, where vast differences and non-standardization are allowed to flourish alongside each other. The more we see postmodernity as a feature of our society, the more we will see differences between our university institutions. Ritzer does in fact seem to acknowledge this in saying: "Of course, all of us will come to know the 'code' that allows us to 'read' the differences between degrees from McUniversity main campus, a McUniversity satellite, and Hamburger University" (Ritzer 1998: 157). Ritzer in fact draws a direct parallel with the early Baudrillard when he says in the preface to Baudrillard's book, *The Consumer Society*: "However, in Baudrillard's view, it is the code, or the system of difference, that causes individuals to be similar to, as well as different from, one another" (Baudrillard 1998: 8).

In HU, where vocational education supports consumerism in the maintenance of capitalism, the mass-produced objects (hamburgers) undergo a process transmitted to all those involved, thus enabling mere burgers in buns to emerge as universal signs. Nothing could be more universal than McDonald's *Golden Arches* signs around the world. The unstoppable replicability of McDonald's is an indication that all those involved have received internalized and transmitted something very special indeed. This transmission is related neither to the food nor to its exchange value in passing from producer to consumer. As Alfino argues: "McDonald's has become adept at inserting itself into dozens of cultures that share no culinary tradition with it or its original culture, the United States. . . . McDonald's exports a cultural message that is clearly appealing to billions of human beings" (Alfino 1998: 184).

It depends on individual preference how we see or judge Hamburger University. It can be seen as the shining example of high modernity, or as a new type of postmodern educational establishment existing alongside other educational establishments, the difference being in both of these senses is that it is a true *non-university* as opposed to a true university. Hedging one's bets, it is possible to see HU on the cusp of the modern and postmodern. High technology and singularity of purpose in the HU pedagogy are certainly there—trademarks of modernity. Quite incidentally, though, it has also got caught up in a technological revolution that presages a new society, one that goes beyond technology and has in turn impacted on (by aiding and abetting) postmodernity. "Perhaps the most significant aspect of the conflation of culture and society today is the effect of the technological mediations of reality which have loosened our grip on a sense of the real. At the heart of the reactionary search for a golden national age is the very sense of a loss of reality brought about by the blurring of the frontiers between representation and the real (Silverman 1999: 108).

If the McUniversity is not to turn into the Hamburger University, then continued societal ambiguity is needed, and this seems the likely scenario for the new millennium. With constant societal ambiguity, particularly concerning the nature and role of U.K. higher education, there will never be enough stable conditions to permit Ritzer's McDonaldization to make inroads. This will prevent the hundred or so U.K. universities, from turning out millions of identical hamburgerology-type graduates. To be fair, Ritzer never actually says that the McUniversity is inevitable: "fast food restaurants, for example, have been heavily McDonaldized, universities moderately McDonaldized" (2000: 19). He only says that "Immediately relevant models for tomorrow's university, are today's McDonald's Hamburger University" (1998: 154). But without empirically examining the ideas embodied in both concepts, such a position is one of all or nothing!

There will always be differences *and* similarities in comparing the aspirant McUniversity with Hamburger University. "To start with, McUniversity will continue to have a central campus, but it is likely to be more compact and run by a meaner, leaner organization. (McDonald's is famous for running its far flung operations with minuscule staff)" (Ritzer 1998: 155). Nor are such movements toward HU by the McUniversity seen as awful ones. The goal of the (Mc) university will also be able to make it far easier for students to obtain the various services it offers. There is always this danger of making things easy with the introduction of the modularized degree program. These in their totality would seem to be the quintessential McUniversity outlined by Ritzer. The university modular movement seems to have come and gone—that is, some universities have adopted modularization more than others, while others have not embraced it at all. Unlike the American norm, to my knowledge no totally modularized university exists in the United Kingdom. If the McUniversity is not to turn into the Hamburger University, there has to be a continued emphasis on the unity of subject knowledge rather than seeing students as recipients of what Persell calls "packets" of knowledge (chapter 5, this volume). That this still exists to some degree gives us some hope that university teachers will continue to make students think critically.

Although the degree of resistance in the U.K. university is debatable (see Smart 1999; Hayes, chapter 10, and Wynyard, chapter 15, this volume), my argument sees a rough equation—that is, resistance existing more where less emphasis is placed on modularization within the university. Embedded in this is also a question as to how far U.K. universities go in dumping content in favor of form. This involves the way the student gets degree credits when accumulating appropriate (not necessarily related) modules every ten weeks or so. Once students are allowed to forget any content and just concentrate on accumulating module credits, and then we really are in *hamburgerology land.*

McDonald's Hamburger University, in seeing education as form not content, means that detailed treatment of subject content gets squeezed out. "All training that managers receive supports the three Company goals of achieving 100% customer satisfaction, increased market share and increased profitability, through the leadership and development of people" (McDonald's *Narional Training Prospectus* 1999: 1)

Still, it is easy to be complacent by arguing that as long as postmodern conditions exist, the McUniversity will not become the Hamburger University. All is not one-way traffic, for Hamburger University is not totally rigid and can adapt to market conditions if it has to. In this version of postmodernity there is an alliance of capitalism with democracy: for example, "In the UK (back in 1997) a decision was made to rename our Hamburger University in London the Management Training Centre (MTC). This has been the name used in the UK ever since, and is regarded as being more appropriate to the UK culture."[1] There is some flexibility to adjust and adapt suiting societal perspectives, and giving an impression of less rather than increasing rigidity.

Still by far the greatest danger comes from the other side, with movements toward the Hamburger University from the McUniversity. Often shifts in this direction are not consciously perceived, and there does seem an element of naiveté in such moves; for example, the recent acceptance by two universities of vast sums of monies to set up *Centres for Ethical Business,* donated from private corporations deemed the "most unethical on earth" (Jon Snow *Radio 4,* 5 December 2000). Such practice is more common in the United States, where the McUniversity move to HU status has progressed much more quickly. Here the marriage of corporations to universities is a common sight. Wherever and whenever public coffers do not provide funding for research, then the private sector will. This entails all the consequences that go with acceptance, and acceptance, albeit reluctant, becomes ever more true of the U.K. higher-education sector.

U.K. academics may not like the changes taking place in our universities occasioning the prefix *Mc.* Without being complacent, the main thing to put into context is that the university is still taken seriously, even when *Mc* changes take a hold. Contemporary societal discourse of the university sits on the cusp of arguments concerning modernity/postmodernity. In spite of the many moves toward the McUniversity, there are still plenty of people who believe in a university education, such as the parents of prospective students and, not least, students themselves. The university is now popular in the sense that going into a McDonald's restaurant is popular, passing through the hallowed portals of academe might be likened to passing through the Golden Arches. The argument of this chapter is that continued societal ambiguity leaves it unresolved whether university education will be about gaining knowledge or the experience of a simulated fantasy world.

## NOTE

1. Source: McDonald's U.K. Corporate Training Department (May 2000, personal correspondence).

## REFERENCES

Alfino, M. (1998). Postmodern hamburgers: Taking a postmodern attitude toward McDonald's. In M. Alfino, J. S. Caputo, & R. Wynyard (Eds.), *McDonaldization Revisited: Critical Essays on Consumer Culture.* Westport, CT, & London: Praeger (179–189).

Baudrillard. J. (1988). *Jean Baudrillard: Selected Writings* (edited by M. Poster). Cambridge, U.K.: Polity.

Baudrillard, J. (1998). *The Consumer Society*. London & Thousand Oaks, CA: Sage.

Best, M., & Kellner, D. (1997). *The Postmodern Turn*. New York & London: Guilford Press.

Delanty, G. (2000). *Modernity and Postmodernity*. Thousand Oaks, CA, & London: Sage.

*Economist* (1999). Face value. The burger king. *Economist*, 23 October: 78.

Kellner, D. (Ed.) (1994). *Baudrillard: A Critical Reader*. Oxford, U.K., & Cambridge, MA: Blackwell.

Lyotard, J. F. (1986). *The Postmodern Condition. A Report on Knowledge*. Manchester, U.K.: Manchester University Press.

McDonald's (1999). *National Training Prospectus*. London: McDonald's Restaurants Ltd.

McGuigan, J. (1997). *Cultural Methodologies*. London & Thousand Oaks, CA: Sage.

McGuigan, J. (1999). *Modernity and Postmodern Culture*. Buckingham, U.K.: Open University Press.

Ritzer, G. (1998). *The McDonaldization Thesis: Explorations and Extensions*. London & Thousand Oaks, CA: Sage.

Ritzer, G. (2000). *The McDonaldization of Society: New Century Edition*. Thousand Oaks, CA: Pine Forge Press.

Schaaf, D. (1994). Inside Hamburger University. *Training Minneapolis* (December): 18–25.

Silverman, H. (1999). *Facing Postmodernity*. London & New York: Routledge.

Smart, B. (Ed.) (1999). *Resisting McDonaldization*. London & Thousand Oaks, CA: Sage.

Usher, R., & Edwards, R. (1994). *Postmodernism and Education*. London & New York: Routledge.

Wynyard, R. (1998). The bunless burger. In M. Alfino, J. S. Caputo, & R. Wynyard (Eds.), *McDonaldization Revisited: Critical Essays on Consumer Culture*. Westport, CT, & London: Praeger (159–174).

# Index

# About the Editors and Contributors

**Mary Evans** is Professor of Women's Studies at the University of Kent in Canterbury. Her research interests are feminism, sociology of gender and the study of family, literature, and culture. Her numerous publications include *Jane Austen and the State, A Good School, The Woman Question, An Introduction to Contemporary Feminist Thought*, and (with D. Morgan) *The Battle for Britain*. Her most recent publication is *Missing Persons: The Impossibility of Auto/biography*.

**Joanne Finkelstein** is Associate Dean in the Faculty of Arts at the University of Sydney, Australia. She teaches sociology and cultural studies in the School of Society and Culture and is the author of *Dining Out: A Sociology of Modern Manners, The Fashioned Self, Slaves of Chic*, and *After a Fashion*.

**Claire Fox,** who is regularly invited to comment on developments in culture, education, and the media, has been a regular guest on the *Today Programme*, the *Moral Maze* and *Any Questions*. She is also an experienced television commentator, and her program appearances include *Newsnight* and *Edinburgh Nights*. She writes regularly on educational issues for the national press. Her essays and articles have appeared in many books and journals. She is currently the Director of the Institute of Ideas—a rolling program of conferences, salons, seminars, exhibitions, and publications, committed to forging a public space for debate and the robust exchange of views.

**Frank Furedi** is a Professor of Sociology at the University of Kent in Canter-

bury. His main intellectual interest is the institutionalization of risk consciousness in Western societies. He wrote *Culture of Fear*, which dealt with the
ascendancy of risk aversion and the tendency for society to panic. More recently,
his best-selling *Paranoid Parenting* examined the way in which risk aversion
shapes contemporary parenting. In numerous publications he has explored the
question of why apprehensions about science, technology, and health have assumed such significance in contemporary society. Furedi is also preparing a
study: "The Emptying out of Academic Life." He regularly writes on issues
associated with higher education. His articles have been published in *The Guardian, The Independent on Sunday, The Independent, Wall Street Journal, The
Times, The Daily Mail, Punch, New Statesman, New Scientist, Spectator, Toronto Globe and Mail,* and *Die Zeit,* among others.

**Dennis Hayes** is the Head of the Department of Post-compulsory Education at
Canterbury Christ Church University College. His major research interest is the
impact of vocationalism on all aspects of education and the response of employees to the changing nexus between education and work. With his colleagues, he
published a very successful textbook, *Teaching and Training in Post Compulsory Education,* and other volumes are underway. He is the coordinator of the
Education and Work Research Group that researches aspect of the changed
world of work, the creation and adoption of new identities among workers, and
new forms of training and vocationalism, and he is the editor of a series of
critical monographs that the E&WRG publishes on these themes. His latest book
(with Alan Hudson) is *Basildon: The Mood of the Nation.*

**Alan Hudson** is the Director of Social and Political Science in the Department
for Continuing Education in the University of Oxford. He is the coauthor of the
Demos publication *Basildon: The Mood of the Nation.* His current research is on
qualifications in the retail sector: "Human Capital, Cultural Capital and Aesthetic Labour: Educational Qualifications and Hiring Decisions in the Retail
Industry." He is also the coauthor of *Attitudes to Work,* and he has edited and
written an introduction to Frederick Engels' *Socialism: Utopian and Scientific.*

**Martin Parker** is Reader in Social and Organisation Theory, Department of
Management, University of Keele. His research and writing is mostly in the area
of social and organizational theory, ethics, and culture. He has written articles on
the McUniversity and has coedited a book, *The New Higher Education: Issues
and Directions for the Post-Dearing University* (with David Jary).

**Caroline Hodges Persell** is the author or coauthor of nine books, including
*Preparing for Power: America's Elite Boarding Schools* (with Peter W.
Cookson, Jr.), *Understanding Society,* and *Education and Inequality,* as well as
scores of scholarly articles and book chapters. Professor of Sociology at New
York University since 1986 and department chair for six of those years, Profes-

sor Persell is currently conducting research on digital technologies and teaching and learning, the effects of for-profit postsecondary education on the political involvement of students, and the implications of privatization for education. Named a Carnegie Fellow for 2000–01 by the Carnegie Foundation for the Advancement of Teaching.

**Gavin Poynter** is Head of Department of Innovation Studies, University of East London. He has recently published a book *Restructuring in the Service Industries* and has written many articles and reports on employment, technology and the transformation of work. He previously worked for the TUC.

**Jane A. Rinehart** received a doctorate in sociology from New York University in 1981, and is a professor of sociology and women's studies at Gonzaga University. She is one of the founders of Gonzaga's Women's Studies Program (established in 1991) and served as an administrator in the program for six years. Her publications include a chapter in *McDonaldization Revisited*, chapters in two books on women's studies, articles in *Teaching Sociology, Women and Politics, Feminist Teacher*, and *Frontiers*, and a coedited anthology, *Taking Parts: Ingredients for Leadership, Participation, and Empowerment.*

**George Ritzer** is Distinguished University Professor of Sociology at the University of Maryland. He has served as Chair of the American Sociological Association's Sections on Theoretical Sociology and Organizations and Occupations. He won the ASA's Distinguished Contributions to Teaching Award in 2000. His seminal book *The McDonaldization of Society* has been described as one of the most noteworthy sociology books of all time, with more than 100,000 copies in print and a dozen translations. A new century edition has just appeared. Among his many other books are *The McDonaldization Thesis* (1998) and *Enchanting a Disenchanted World.*

**Barry Smart** has worked at Universities in England, Australia, New Zealand, and Japan. He is currently Professor of Sociology in the School of Social, Historical and Literary Studies, University of Portsmouth. He has recently published *Facing Modernity: Ambivalence, Reflexivity and Morality*, and he has coedited with George Ritzer *Resisting McDonaldization* and *Handbook of Social Theory*. He has published numerous articles in books and journals on various aspects of social theory, the transformation of modernity, the postmodern condition, morality and ethics, and the work of Michel Foucault. He is currently completing a research project on culture and economy.

**Ngure wa Mwachofi** is Director of Ideas Unlimited. He was an Associate Professor of Communication & Interdisciplinary Studies at Florida Gulf Coast University, Fort Myers, Florida, USA. He has a Ph.D. in Communication (College of Communication, Ohio University, Athens, Ohio, USA). His articles have appeared in *The Howard Journal of Communication, Journal of Communication Inquiry,* and *Human Communication Studies.* He has also contributed book chapters in *Organization & Communication Emerging Perspectives, Challenging Social Injustices,* and *McDonaldization Revisited.*

**James Woudhuysen** is Professor of Innovation, De Montfort University, Leicester, and a regular contributor to *IT Week.* In 1988, at Fitch, he codirected Britain's first major study of e-commerce; in 1992, at the Henley Centre for Forecasting, he proposed that the Internet be delivered over television; over 1995–97, he managed worldwide market intelligence for Philips consumer electronics in the Netherlands; over 1997–2001, he was a director of the international product designers Seymour Powell.

**Robin Wynyard** is a sociologist. Before taking very early retirement, he worked for several British universities and was visiting professor at universities abroad, particularly in Pakistan and the United States. Still very much involved in writing and journalism, his interests include cultural transmission theory and its relationship to popular culture, and the sociology of art and literature. His publications include (along with M. Alfino & J. Caputo) *McDonaldization Revisited: Critical Essays on Consumer Culture.* Just recently he has been coaxed out of retirement, accepting the post of Visiting Lecturer at Canterbury Christ Church University College, Kent, U.K.